"*Teenagers Matter* is a benchmark book for the field of youth ministry, a book that will be widely read and referenced for years. Mark Cannister champions youth ministry's value and mission in a book that will make readers feel like they're getting the 'inside word' on what's happening in youth ministry from one of the leading thinkers in the field. And they are. This book will renew concern for teenagers and provide direction for youth ministry to move beyond 'good enough' as a standard for excellence. I thoroughly enjoyed reading *Teenagers Matter* and know that it will become one of youth ministry's significant books."

—**Terry Linhart**, Bethel College–Indiana

"Mark Cannister is a fresh voice, reminding the church of the reasons for and the ways to do authentic youth ministry. I love his tone: both helpful and hopeful. This is a must-read book for pastors, church leaders, parents, and youth workers."

—**Len Kageler**, Nyack College

"Mark Cannister has made a significant contribution to the field of student ministry. His thoughtful, comprehensive approach shows concern for those within the congregation, while also reaching out to the young people of the community. He has provided an abundance of academic research in a way that is accessible for students and practitioners alike. I encourage every youth ministry leader to get at least two copies of this book—one for yourself and one for a church leader who has influence on the student ministry of your entire congregation."

—**Wes Black**, author of *An Introduction to Youth Ministry*;
coauthor of *Four Views of Youth Ministry and the Church*

TEENAGERS
MATTER

Youth, Family, and Culture Series

Chap Clark, series editor

The Youth, Family, and Culture series examines the broad categories involved in studying and caring for the needs of the young and is dedicated to the preparation and vocational strengthening of those who are committed to the spiritual development of adolescents.

TEENAGERS
MATTER

*Making **Student Ministry** a Priority in the Church*

MARK CANNISTER

Baker Academic
a division of Baker Publishing Group
Grand Rapids, Michigan

© 2013 by Mark Cannister

Published by Baker Academic
a division of Baker Publishing Group
P.O. Box 6287, Grand Rapids, MI 49516-6287
www.bakeracademic.com

Printed in the United States of America

Library of Congress Cataloging-in-Publication Data is on file at the Library of Congress, Washington, DC.

ISBN 978-0-8010-4852-4 (pbk.)

13 14 15 16 17 18 19   7 6 5 4 3 2 1

In keeping with biblical principles of creation stewardship, Baker Publishing Group advocates the responsible use of our natural resources. As a member of the Green Press Initiative, our company uses recycled paper when possible. The text paper of this book is composed in part of post-consumer waste.

To Kasey and Ryan:
these teenagers matter most

CONTENTS

SERIES PREFACE

In many ways, youth ministry has come of age. No longer seen as "a stepping-stone to real ministry in the church," especially in North America, youth ministry is now seen as a viable career option. Over the last few decades a wide range of professional resources, conferences, periodicals, and books have been developed on this topic. Most Christian colleges and seminaries now offer a variety of courses—if not degree programs—in youth ministry. Youth ministry has all it needs to continue to push the church to care about and serve the needs of the young in God's name, except for one thing: we have a long way to go to develop a rich, broad, and diverse conversation that frames, defines, and grounds our missional call.

There is good news, of course. There is a professional organization, Association of Youth Ministry Educators, that sponsors an annual conference and publishes a solid emerging journal. Several thoughtful books have helped to shape the discipline's future. There are also now two major publishers who have academic lines dedicated to furthering the field of youth ministry. We have made great progress, but we must all work together to continue deepening our understanding of what youth ministry should be.

The purpose of Baker Academic's Youth, Family, and Culture series is to raise the level of dialogue concerning how we think about, teach, and live out youth ministry. As a branch of practical theology, academic youth ministry must move beyond a primarily skills-based focus to a theologically driven expression of a contextualized commitment of the local church to a targeted population. James Fowler defines practical theology as "theological reflection and construction arising out of and giving guidance to a community of faith in the *praxis* of its mission. Practical theology is critical and constructive reflection leading to ongoing modification and development of the ways the church shapes its life to be in partnership with God's work in the world."[1] And as Scott Cormode reminds us, we must not shirk our calling, but "must strive to nurture leaders that are faithful. . . . Schools must prepare leaders to translate this faithfulness into effective action."[2] This is precisely what those of us who are called to engage the church in theological reflection of contemporary youth and family issues must do—develop a practical theology that takes seriously the reality of the context we are in, regardless of how and where it takes us. This is the future of youth and family ministry in the church.

Chap Clark
Fuller Theological Seminary
September 2013

PREFACE

Teenagers matter! When teenagers matter, the church comes alive! Teenagers bring life and vitality to nearly every sector of society when they are valued. Have you ever been in a nursing home when a group of teenagers arrive to sing Christmas carols to the residents? The place comes alive. Have you ever witnessed teenagers playing with children in an orphanage? The place comes alive. Have you participated in a Youth Sunday when teenagers lead the whole congregation in worship? The church comes alive! When they feel valued, young people bring an innate vitality to every setting.

Schools that value teenagers are filled with energy and enthusiasm. Schools that don't are boring and underachieving. Sports teams coached by people who value teenagers are vibrant and exciting communities for the participants. Coaches who care more about winning than about the players create teams filled with hostility and animosity that spectators often find hard to watch. Music and drama groups in which teenagers matter are filled with joy. When the performance becomes more important than the performers, the joy turns to fear and the audience can feel the difference. When teenagers matter, they bring life and vitality to the very fabric of a community.

Student ministry in the church has come a long way in the last century. In 1881, Francis Clark sensed a need to pay special attention to the young people in his church in Portland, Maine, and created the Society for Christian Endeavor. Soon thereafter, nearly every denomination created a youth society to ensure that their young people would stay connected to the local church. Despite the leaders' best intentions, these efforts proved unsustainable, and churches in the twentieth century found it difficult to maintain strong connections to their young people.

Parachurch organizations such as Young Life and Youth for Christ arose to reach students who had left the church or had never been a part of the church. Although they are successful by almost any measure, the Achilles' heel of most parachurch efforts is integrating young people into the local church. This is not due to a lack of effort on the part of parachurch organizations. Often, parachurch organizations have made heroic efforts to integrate their young people into local churches—only to find churches less than receptive to their efforts.

Why such a lack of partnership between church and parachurch? Why are most churches failing to reach out to young people beyond their own walls and failing to partner with organizations that are faithfully doing this work? While most churches today have some sort of ministry for their teenagers, few have made student ministry a high priority. Few have developed a comprehensive view of student ministry, and those that do are often unable to attain the resources necessary to fully implement the depth and breadth of their vision. The inability of most churches to develop a comprehensive student ministry that both nurtures teenagers growing up in the church and reaches out to teenagers beyond the walls of the church seems to be, first and foremost, a matter of priority in the church.

Any given church contains numerous influential stakeholders: elders and deacons, pastoral staff, parents of teenagers, and financial supporters. As influencers of church vision, we stakeholders have a couple of significant decisions to make. We can choose to value teenagers and applaud the life-giving breath they bring to every aspect of the church, or we can choose to lock our teenagers away in a youth program for seven years so that they don't mess up anything. Too often we have chosen the latter approach: we develop wonderful age-appropriate programs for teenagers while isolating them from the greater community of the church. In addition, we can choose to simply provide a safe place for *our* teenagers to grow in the faith, or we can choose to also reach out to the vast teenage population in our local community who have no church connections. When we engage teenagers in the whole life of the church and reach out to those in our communities, we must provide the resources necessary to achieve such a bold vision.

When teenagers matter, everything changes! But it takes boldness to make teenagers a priority in the church. Bill Hybels describes the necessity of making such bold moves in the church: "As the years went by, my teammates and I began to notice that the primary reason we were making significant progress as a church was that we had enough people making 'bold moves.' They were thinking fresh thoughts, pioneering new programs, and trusting God to accomplish significant kingdom-building activity in their midst."[1] Does this have a familiar feel to it? Have you ever been engaged in a church that made a bold move in the direction of teenagers? Has God called you to lead such a bold move in the years to come? I hope this book brings you to the point of answering that last question with a resounding yes!

ACKNOWLEDGMENTS

The genesis of this book dates back to my own teenage years, when I crossed paths with some faithful people who believed that teenagers mattered and that I mattered to them and to God. When I was a teenager, Mike Henning taught me what it means to have a relationship with Christ and contribute to the community of the church. As an emerging adult, I learned what it meant to be a leader working alongside Jim Welch in every aspect of ministry imaginable. Throughout my years in ministry, my friend Chuck Rosemeyer was a constant reminder of the importance of leadership development and networking. Interestingly enough, these three men were each involved in both local church and parachurch ministries. These dual involvements brought a comprehensive view to every aspect of their work in student ministry, which no doubt has influenced my own thinking about student ministry and the church over the past thirty-some years.

The student ministry leaders with whom I have served shoulder to shoulder over the years have all contributed to the formation of my thinking about adolescents and ministry. Kip Crumrine, Mike Dunlap, Rob Melgard, Gary Wieder, Ted Melnyk, Patrick Dominguez, Beth Ruzanic, Todd Szymczak, and Andrew Breton, to name a few, have thus contributed to many of the thoughts expressed in this book. Likewise, the robust conversations among those with whom I have served on the board of elders at Grace Chapel over the years have helped me clarify many of my perspectives on ministry.

This book certainly would not have been possible without the support, encouragement, and assistance of my colleagues at Gordon College. I am thankful to Mark Sargent, former provost of Gordon College, for his encouragement and for the college's generous sabbatical program, which afforded me the concentrated time to research and write this book. This uninterrupted time would not have been nearly as productive without the support of my wonderful friends and colleagues whose offices flank my own. Bob Whittet protected me from countless distractions by absorbing my departmental responsibilities while I was on sabbatical, and Sharon Galgay Ketcham sharpens my thinking every week with gracious, insightful, and challenging conversations. Lastly, my administrative assistant, Elisabeth Whittet, spent countless hours proofreading and editing the manuscript, bringing clarity and consistency to many of my sometimes incoherent thoughts.

I called upon a variety of former Gordon College students to deliver some wisdom from the trenches. These youth ministers crafted discussion questions for each chapter and contributed sidebars throughout the book. I am indebted to the thought-provoking contributions of these Gordon College alumni: Andrew Beach, Andrew Breton, Niki Brodeur, Sarah Dickinson, Chad Fransen, Kirsten Gillette, Alan Inacio, Leah Knight, Mike McGarry, Kori North, Seth Philbrick, Adam Rowe, Morgan Schmidt, Aaron Stetson, Todd Szymczak, Ryan Ventura, Garrett Walston, and Kendra and Nathaniel Williams.

I especially want to thank my wife, Nancy, my daughter, Kasey, and my son, Ryan, for giving me the space to work at home in peace and tranquility. I am grateful for the role model that Nancy is as a loving mother of two teenagers, and I am constantly in awe of Kasey and Ryan, who make great contributions to our home, our church, their high school, and our community on a regular basis. They demonstrate that teenagers are truly treasures to behold.

Finally, to Chap Clark, Bob Hosack, and the entire team at Baker Academic, without whom this project would never have seen the light of day: thank you for your personal encouragement, wisdom throughout the process, and excellence in publishing.

INTRODUCTION

*S*tudent ministry is a moving target.[1] You have to keep pace with the culture. Teenagers today are not the same as teenagers ten, twenty, or thirty years ago. Sound familiar? As a group, youth leaders are not big on tradition—at least that's what they say. But if you scratch the surface, you will quickly find a different story. The fact is that youth ministers are fastidious followers of tradition, doing things in student ministry today that worked for earlier generations of youth leaders. And as I can attest, that can be very healthy indeed.

I came of age as a teenager with bell-bottom jeans, leisure suits, and the classic music of the 1970s. Bruce Springsteen declared that we were "Born to Run," Led Zeppelin was building a "Stairway to Heaven," the Eagles moved into "Hotel California," John Lennon could only "Imagine," and Stevie Wonder was filled with "Superstition." We were the coolest generation, radically different from our parents and more sophisticated than the rebels of the 1960s. We had it all figured out, and student ministry in that era was much different than it is today. Or was it?

One of the most memorable things from my teenage years is the weekly breakfast my youth leader had with my friends and me. He drove around town early in the mornings, picking us up before school to have breakfast and talk about God. Nothing heavy—just breakfast and a conversation—but I wouldn't have missed it for anything, not even sleep. A decade later, I was a youth minister doing the same thing with kids: breakfast at Wendy's every Wednesday morning before school for a time of sharing, perhaps a devotional, and prayer. If I canceled a week, I heard about it. "You can cancel youth club, cancel church, and cancel the retreat, but *never* cancel breakfast," kids warned.

Fast-forward to 2013. My daughter is in high school and loves to sleep in. Getting her out of bed requires a nuclear weapon—except on Wednesday mornings! What happens on Wednesday mornings? Breakfast with youth leaders, of course! She's up and out to breakfast by 6:00 a.m., ninety minutes before school begins.

Some things in ministry transcend cultural changes. Most often they are timeless principles of ministry, but occasionally programs that are deeply rooted in core principles have also transcended shifts in culture. Before we get ahead of ourselves, let's consider four core principles that student ministry has embraced in one form or another over the last century: clarity of purpose, authentic leadership, the transformation of lives, and genuine relationships.

Clarity of Purpose

Where there is no vision, the people perish. (Prov. 29:18 KJV)

From the very beginning, ministry to teenagers was marked by a clear sense of purpose.[2] Men and women of integrity sought to help young people. The YMCA movement in America (1851) aimed to help young people maintain their faith after they moved to the city. Francis Clark's Society for Christian Endeavor (1881) in Portland, Maine, strove to strengthen the faith journey of his young people. The chief goal of Evelyn McClusky's Miracle Book Clubs and Torrey Johnson's Youth for Christ was to reach out to youth with the gospel of Christ. These early ministries helped set the stage for contemporary student ministry, and each subscribed to a bold sense of purpose. Perhaps Mike Yaconelli said it best when he declared: "Youth ministry is about bringing kids into the presence of Jesus Christ."[3]

This sense of clear purpose has marked student ministry from the beginning, and each time student ministry has veered off course, it has been, in part, because of confusion of purpose—not unlike the church in general. In the late 1990s, Doug Fields operationalized this concept for youth leaders in the best-selling student ministry book of all time: *Purpose Driven Youth Ministry*.[4] Fields was able to articulate for the student ministry world what most youth workers intuitively knew to be essential but struggled to implement. Merton Strommen's exhaustive research confirmed the importance of this principle, as 2,416 youth workers declared that a "clearly stated mission" was one of the most critical aspects of a successful student ministry; without it, they would be lost in a fog.[5]

Mark DeVries has recently confirmed the importance of this principle, based on consultations with over one hundred churches striving to reengineer their student ministries.[6] Simply put, if you have not discovered the purpose of your ministry or if you are unable to communicate that purpose to students, volunteers, parents, supervisors, and colleagues with absolute clarity, then your ministry will eventually run out of steam. I strongly suspect that every person you consider a hero in student ministry has developed his or her ministry on this timeless principle: clarity of purpose.

Authentic Leadership

Not that I have already obtained all this, or have already arrived at my goal, but I press on to take hold of that for which Christ Jesus took hold of me. (Phil. 3:12)

By the 1920s, high schools had emerged in most communities, and young people were developing a sense of pride and spirit in their local schools. While churches were running "youth societies" modeled after Francis Clark's Christian Endeavor ministry, people like Lloyd Bryant, Percy Crawford, and Oscar Gillian were reaching out to young people through radio shows and youth rallies. The youth rallies of the 1930s and 1940s were wildly successful, as thousands of young people came to faith through the bold preaching of youth evangelists like Billy Graham, who began preaching at Youth for Christ rallies in 1944.

In the youth rally era, we find leaders marked by an incredibly high level of authenticity. The Apostles' Creed reminds us of the trinitarian nature of God and the triune community we are called to foster. In keeping with this calling, leaders networked with one another and shared ideas freely. This spirit of cooperation and united purpose caused speakers at rallies to declare, "It's much easier to preach in Youth for Christ meetings than any other place, as the power of the Holy Spirit is felt so much."[7] Faithful youth workers have always embraced one another with humility, caring little about who received credit for the movement's successes. David Chow opens his book *No More Lone Rangers* by recounting the movie *Remember the Titans*, in which Denzel Washington plays a football coach who, amid racial conflict, galvanizes his team to win the state championship.[8] Teamwork and unity win the day in football and in ministry.

Yaconelli proclaims, "To be effective youth workers, we have to be real—not perfect, whole, together, complete, or competent—but real.

We do not need to be afraid to show others we are imperfect. We should not fear exposing our messiness."[9] Authenticity requires us to teach the whole counsel of God, even the messy passages of Scripture. Authentic youth workers are great listeners and care more about entering into a student's story than "fixing" her problem. To be authentic, we must also be humble—willing to admit that we don't know all the answers but willing to work through issues.

Sixty some years ago, student ministry pioneers had the audacity to be creative and experiment with new ideas while remaining teachable and righteous before God. Trusting the Holy Spirit to guide them in ministry, these leaders found that this principle of authenticity served them well. With the same spirit, Youth Specialties (1969) and Group Publishing (1971) were created to provide resources for youth leaders in churches. Youth Specialties founders Mike Yaconelli and Wayne Rice, who also founded *YouthWorker Journal*, used the resources they had developed with Youth for Christ to bring relationally driven, Christ-centered, biblically based student ministry to their churches, and immediately began sharing their ideas with other youth workers through their *Ideas* books. Similarly, Thom Schultz started a student ministry resource exchange through his *Group* newsletter. Over the next decade, student ministry grew exponentially through the resources, seminars, and conventions offered by Youth Specialties and Group.[10] For nearly half a century, these organizations have trumpeted the *High School Musical* theme song: "We're All in This Together!"

Transformation of Lives

> Therefore, if anyone is in Christ, the new creation has come: The old has gone, the new is here! (2 Cor. 5:17)

While Francis Clark's Christian Endeavor movement was established on a firm foundation of biblical teaching and an unwavering commitment to Jesus Christ, most denominational youth societies of the early 1900s drifted from those principles and began to emphasize leadership training and the uniqueness of their denominational positions. Training up the next generation of Presbyterians or Methodists or Lutherans or Baptists became more important than raising up the next generation of Christ-followers. Later, the nondenominational youth rallies and radio ministries of the 1930s and 1940s reclaimed the christocentric biblical foundation of student ministry, emphasizing life-changing transformation as central to its mission.

Transformation has always been at the heart of student ministry. Strommen's research found this to be as true today as it was in the past.[11] Call it what you will—evangelism, discipleship, spiritual formation, or Christian education: the bottom line is transforming lives with the message of God's grace. Transformation always begins with compassion for teenagers and a passion to introduce them to the life-giving message of the gospel. For decades, faithful youth leaders have worked tirelessly to clearly communicate the Word of God and engage students in formative experiences.

If our aim is to bring students into the presence of Jesus Christ, then reaching students who are currently outside the presence of Jesus Christ is imperative. These teenagers can be found both inside and outside of the church. We don't need to look far to find them—they are everywhere. And the desire to reach them has been a source of the most creative and effective programs in student ministry history. Of course, we are not simply in the salvation business, and we cannot assume our work is done following the recitation of a prayer accepting Jesus as Lord and Savior. On the contrary, the work has just begun. Conversion is merely the starting point of the long and costly journey of sanctification that, as shepherds, we must nurture through the community of believers. This dichotomy between evangelism and discipleship has plagued student ministry for ages. Perhaps in the twenty-first century we will overcome this debate and emerge with a more holistic view of ministry that acknowledges the interdependence of the two. The truth is that, as Lee Vukich and Steve Vandegriff suggest, "the aims of youth ministry are no different than the aims of the local church."[12] If God is not transforming lives through our ministry, then perhaps we are not doing ministry at all.

Genuine Relationships

The Word became flesh and blood, and moved into the neighborhood. (John 1:14 Message)

Even as the youth rallies were in full swing, another style of student ministry was emerging in the 1930s. In Portland, Oregon, Evelyn McClusky began teaching the Bible conversationally by using storytelling. For McClusky, the Bible was a storybook filled with the great dramas of God and God's people. She assumed that her students had yet to encounter these dramas in any meaningful way, and she mesmerized young people by recounting the grand narrative of the Scriptures. Instead of mounting the stage of a youth rally, she gathered young people in the intimate atmosphere of her living room for what became the Miracle Book Club movement. This conversational style of teaching and relational style of ministry stood in stark contrast to the youth rallies, which were often marked by brazen preaching to massive crowds.

McClusky's clubs spread across the country like wildfire and attracted the attention of Jim Rayburn, who became a Miracle Book Club leader in Dallas, Texas, before launching Young Life in 1940. Rayburn mastered the art of conversational preaching and quickly abandoned youth rally programs in favor of a community-centered youth club, which was larger than a Miracle Book Club but smaller than a youth rally. The clubs were, and continue to be, large enough to establish a critical mass that provides energy and enthusiasm but small enough to ensure the development of personal relationships. Even Youth for Christ, the king of the youth rally movement, established clubs to teach students the importance of personal evangelism and discipleship. As the large rallies gave way to the club movement in Youth for Christ, numerous additional club-type organizations sprang up.

Relying on the incarnational model of Christ and a trinitarian view of God, youth leaders for nearly a century have valued community as the primary context of transformation. To this day, the Young Life leadership manual declares the importance of genuine relationships: "Ideally, we go to young people for the same reason Christ came to humanity: to reveal God to them with no strings attached. To love them in order to get the opportunity to preach to them is a string. We should love them because God loves them and wants to love them through us."[13] Developing avenues of relational connection has been a timeless principle of student ministry.

Doug Fields observes that we are surrounded by relationships and should strive to foster community through ministry.[14] Fields writes, "Relationships are the backbone of all our values."[15] Teenagers have a deep desire for community and a strong appetite for relationships. Their faith formation is, according to Chap Clark, a "complex journey, and adolescents need someone who will walk alongside them as long as it takes."[16] At times in our history, youth ministry workers have abused relationships, even out of seemingly good intentions. Thankfully, Andy Root, in his *Revisiting Relational Youth Ministry* and *Relationships Unfiltered*, has offered an essential course correction regarding relational student ministry that will assist twenty-first-century youth leaders in relating to students and families with the highest level of integrity.[17]

Why have the student breakfasts mentioned earlier transcended time? Because they are highly relational, and relational ministry has been the hallmark of student ministries since the mid-1930s. When all else fails in ministry—take some students to breakfast.

Our Beacons of Light

I live just a few miles from the Atlantic Ocean, and lighthouses mark our rocky coastline. The lights have been there for decades, serving as beacons to sailors on ships whose vision is, at times, diminished by the fog. Likewise, these foundational principles—*purpose, authenticity, transformation,* and *relationships*—have stood the test of time. When it seems as if the fog has settled on our ministries, these principles continue to serve as beacons of light.

1

When Teenagers Matter:
STUDENT MINISTRY THRIVES

ack in 2001, 181 million disposable cameras were sold in the United States, while only 7 million digital cameras were sold. Jonathan Kaplan and Ariel Braunstein recognized this gap in the market as an opportunity for a new type of camera. They formed Pure Digital Technologies and created an inexpensive, single-use digital camera. The idea was flawed from the start, as it required the customer to return the camera to the retailer, usually a pharmacy, for processing. While the company sold over three million cameras, few people returned them for processing. Some people were delighted to keep the camera and simply view the pictures on the 1.4-inch LCD screen, while others figured out how to open the camera and download the pictures to a computer themselves. The lack of returns ruined the company's business model, but Kaplan and Braunstein learned a valuable lesson: customers will sacrifice quality for an inexpensive device. Even today, the majority of cameras sold are inexpensive point-and-shoots, while single-lens reflex (SLR) cameras attract only serious amateurs and professional photographers. For the majority of the world, point-and-shoot cameras are good enough.[1]

The "Good Enough" Principle

The principle of "good enough" is well understood in business, especially the technology business. A product needs to be just good enough to meet the consumers' needs. This "good enough" concept relies on the Pareto Principle, named after the Italian economist Vilfredo Pareto. This principle is also known as the 80/20 rule. It suggests that 20 percent of the features of a product will satisfy 80 percent of the customers, making the product good enough. If you have an SLR camera and are not a professional photographer, think of all the features you never use. The reality is that 80 percent of the population tends to be satisfied with 20 percent of the features of high-end products. This produces a massive market for "good enough" products like point-and-shoot cameras.

In the church, we often settle for "good enough" student ministries. The vast majority (80 percent) of stakeholders in most churches, including pastors, elders, deacons, parents, and students, tend to be satisfied with the small slice (20 percent) of a comprehensive student ministry that is typically known as discipleship. This kind of student ministry is good enough because it is economical and it delivers the slice of ministry desired by most Christian parents with teenagers: safety.

Many Christian parents are filled with an exorbitant level of fear concerning the influence of secular culture. In an effort to protect their children, some become "helicopter parents," hovering over their children from an early age through young adulthood in an attempt to let no decision or activity go unchecked. Some parents strive to protect their children from the influences of secular education by opting for Christian schools or homeschooling. While not all shun public schools or become helicopter parents, responsible Christian parents do strive to socialize their children with a particular set of normative values that reflect the faith and practice of their particular theological tradition. This desire of Christian parents to infuse their teenagers with the values of their faith, coupled with their fear of the influences of secular culture, produces a view of the church as a place where their teenager is safely protected from the culture while soaking in the core values of the faith. Pete Ward describes this effect on student ministry: "Parents are concerned that their children should be protected and kept safe from what they regard as the disturbing and dangerous world, which threatens to engulf them during adolescence. In this context youthwork becomes the means by which Christian parents seek to extend their influence on teenagers who are seeking more independence and freedom from the home."[2] Most

Beyond the Trap of "Good Enough"

As a youth pastor, I too fall into the trap of running a "good enough" ministry. If the parents are happy, the pastor is happy and my job is safe. But this is not what I was called to do, as a Christian or as a youth pastor. Since day one, my senior pastor's wife has challenged me to "Be bold!" I realize the "good enough" mentality I wrestle with comes from a spirit of fear. It is only when I start spending more time with Jesus on a consistent basis that I see the vision God has for the student ministry of our church. It is not about having greater numbers of students every year. It is about having an obedient student ministry that follows the example of Jesus Christ. Doing so will potentially bring push-back and confusion, but I am learning to keep my eyes on Jesus. Jesus hasn't called me to live a "good enough" life or lead a "good enough" ministry—and for that I am grateful.

Ryan Ventura, Walnut Hill Community Church,
Bethel, Connecticut

student ministries respond to these parental desires, offering a safe haven of encouragement and support.

While teaching a class for parents of teenagers, I assembled a panel of exemplary parents to share their wisdom. Responding to a question from the audience about keeping teenagers out of trouble, one of the panelists replied, "Keep them busy!" Her point was that if teenagers are involved in enough activities, they won't have idle time to get into trouble. She went on to say that this is what she really appreciates about the church youth group. It was a safe alternative to the other possibilities on any given Friday night. I know she appreciated the student ministries of the church for more than just being a safe place, but every parent in that room resonated with her response. It wasn't long before parents were asking questions and making suggestions for how the student ministries could provide more activities that would, ostensibly, protect their teenagers. Christian parents tend to desire a student ministry that will protect their teenagers and instill their faith values. For them, that is good enough.

The Problems of "Good Enough"

When we produce a student ministry that is only good enough to service the desires of Christian parents, we fail to develop a thriving, comprehensive student ministry. When *all* teenagers matter to ministry leaders, problems begin to emerge from the "good enough" model of a service-driven student ministry.

Indifference to God's Redemptive Activity

There is no question that our fallen world is a dangerous place. As the apostle Paul suggests, we continue to live in a "crooked and perverse generation"—but not only does he exhort us to lives that are blameless and innocent, he also exhorts us to "shine as lights in the world" (Phil. 2:15 RSV). To shelter student ministry in a strategy of safety and protection is to fall short of God's intended purpose of redemption. The fallen world in which we live is the very object of God's love, and, as theologian William Dyrness writes, "God's commitment is a continuing personal activity that supports the created order."[3] God has never abandoned creation and remains committed to its redemption. As human beings created in God's image, we are partners with God in this mission of redemption.

The world is not absent of God's presence, and our investment in the worldly culture is theologically meaningful. Dyrness puts it this way: "Because of God's presence and action, our involvement in culture has real theological significance. We are called to reflect God's own commitment to the world."[4] Our reflection of God's commitment calls us to a ministry that touches the world beyond the safety of our faith community. "God's hands are already upon everything that our hands touch. His mind already sustains everything that our minds address. The world is not a place from which he is absent, however much it may grieve him. The work of God in Christ brings redemption into his creation-sustaining activity."[5]

If student ministry solely protects adolescents from the secular world, then we are in danger of becoming theologically indifferent to God's redemptive purpose.[6] Such indifference results in a hollow ministry marked by inward self-satisfaction, a ministry that is not fully immersed in God's story of redemption. We connect with God's story fully "by working alongside God in bringing people and the earth to the place where they reflect the divine glory."[7] When we find ourselves in God's story, we find ourselves fully engrossed in the world God created, filled with a passion to redeem that which is not yet reflecting God's glory.

Creation of an Alternative World

The culture of our world, thanks in part to technology, is so pervasive that the alternative world comprising Christian schools, churches, and student ministries actually offers little, if any, protection from the dominant culture. Quiz any homeschooled teenagers on their knowledge of pop culture, and they will ace your test. No Christian environment automatically guarantees safety. Even separatists like the Amish struggle with the influences of the dominant culture that surrounds them. The Corinthians employed this strategy after Paul instructed them not to associate with sexually sinful people. Believing that Paul wanted them to disassociate from all sinful unbelievers, they abandoned their pagan neighbors. Paul corrects their actions concerning this earlier advice by explaining: "I wrote to you in my letter not to associate with sexually immoral people—not at all meaning the people of this world who are immoral, or the greedy and swindlers, or idolaters. In that case you would have to leave this world" (1 Cor. 5:9–10).

We are enmeshed in a fallen world, yet called to be in the world, but not of it. Before Paul admonished the Corinthians, Jesus taught this lesson through his intercessory prayer: "My prayer is not that you take them out of the world but that you protect them from the evil one. They are not of the world, even as I am not of it. Sanctify them by the truth; your word is truth. As you sent me into the world, I have sent them into the world" (John 17:15–18).

Parents are often highly selective when it comes to the particular features of the world from which they want their children protected. They may desire to protect their children from drugs, sex, movies, or violent video games but have little concern for protecting them from consumerism or individualism, which may be equally detrimental to spiritual health.[8]

Short of becoming a cloistered nun or monk, everyone must eventually learn to navigate the world in which we live. Creating an alternative world for students throughout their teenage years only prolongs the inevitable; we offer parents and students a much greater gift when we teach adolescents to make wise decisions when they encounter all that the world has to offer them. When Esau sold his birthright to his brother Jacob for a bowl of stew, he was consumed with his immediate desire and ignored the long-term consequences of his actions (Gen. 25:19–34). Teaching students to invest in something that will last, even at the expense of instant gratification, is a gift that lasts a lifetime.

Walt Mueller has created a simple, robust process for analyzing the worldly culture in which we live. Mueller's *3(D) Guide to Making Responsible Media Choices* includes a three-step process for making wise decisions: (1) Discover what the culture is saying about an issue; (2) Discern how the message of the culture compares with God's truth concerning the issue; and (3) Decide how to respond to the message of the culture in a manner that is honoring to God.[9] Too often we view the world as black and white, resorting to the extremes of either fleeing the culture or embracing it. Student ministry leaders must *engage* the culture with wisdom and strength, teaching students to do the same, so that we all might become creators of culture.

Belief That "Those People" Threaten Us

When singer Susan Boyle stepped onto the stage of *Britain's Got Talent*, the judges did not expect much.[10] They knew "her type," and they had seen it time and time again. Based on her appearance and mannerisms, the judges and the audience thought that this woman's audition was going to be a waste of time. Then she began to sing, and the beauty of her voice amazed everyone in the auditorium. Rather than seeing her for what she could be, the audience had prejudged her according to preconceived stereotypes of how good singers look and act. Likewise, most adults prejudge teenagers they do not know based solely on an ingrained stereotype of adolescents. Because of this stereotype adults often feel threatened by and fearful of teenagers they do not know.

Nigerian novelist Chimamanda Adichie speaks about the dangers of the "single story." She grew up in a middle-class Nigerian family; her father was a professor and her mother was an administrator. At the age of nineteen, she left Nigeria to attend an American university. Her roommate was shocked that Adichie spoke English so well and was surprised to learn that English is the official language of Nigeria. When she asked to listen to some of Adichie's tribal music, she was stunned when Adichie produced a tape of Mariah Carey. Adichie's roommate possessed only a single story of the African continent and applied this singular mind-set to all Africans. Adichie reflects, "The single story creates stereotypes, and the problem with stereotypes is not that they are untrue, but that they are incomplete. They make one story become the only story."[11]

Single stories of people are created when the same story is repeated over and over again. Eventually we come to believe that this single story is true of all the people we associate with the story. "The consequence of the single story is this: It robs people of dignity," Adichie writes. "It makes our recognition of our equal humanity difficult. It emphasizes how we are different rather than how we are similar."[12] The story of the American teenager is often a single story. For most adults it is a story of confusion, bad behavior, poor decision making, and raging hormones.

Chap Clark argues that "most adults fear and in many cases are basically repulsed by what they see in the adolescent world."[13] One study revealed that seven in ten adults describe teenagers as rude, irresponsible, and wild.[14] Adults have a single story of teenagers outside of their homes and outside of their churches. Their teenagers are the exception to the rule, and teenagers they do not know fall into the single story that frightens them.

Pete Ward writes, "The problem with church-based youth fellowship is that 'unchurched' young people can easily be seen as a significant threat."[15] We may fear that these teenagers will corrupt the lives of Christian teenagers, and yet they have the greatest need of hearing the transforming message of God's grace. If the church takes on a model of student ministry that caters to the service of Christian parents who desire a safe place for their teenagers, then where will teenagers outside the church encounter the living God? In parachurch ministries, of course! Young Life, Youth for Christ, and countless parachurch student ministries continue to thrive in part because many churches have determined that a student ministry focused on discipleship is good enough for their congregation. The 20 percent of a student ministry known as discipleship will typically satisfy at least 80 percent of the student ministry stakeholders in a typical church.

Who will rise up and speak on behalf of those students who are far from God? Most often the parents of those students are not in the church. Student ministries that understand faith formation and create a context in which students are able to grow in their faith need not fear engaging unchurched students. As students share their faith with others, they grow in their walk with Christ. As a community of believers reaches out to those far from God, the community becomes a more faithful expression of the triune God.

When we understand our identity in Christ and the mission of the church, we no longer fear the messiness that accompanies our engagement with people outside the fellowship. In fact, we come to understand that without such messiness, our faithfulness to the gospel is hollow. Embracing others requires us to move, in faith, from a position of concern about how others might affect our Christian students to a position of embracing others as we view them as God created them to be.

Tony Campolo recounts an experience that makes this point quite sharply. While teaching sociology at the University of Pennsylvania, Campolo stirred a class discussion by asking students to consider how leaders of various world religions viewed the dehumanizing practice of prostitution. As the discussion became intense, Campolo asked, "What do you suppose Jesus would have said to a prostitute?" One student responded, "Jesus never met a prostitute." "Yes, he did," Campolo responded. "I'll show you in my Bible where—" The confident student interrupted the professor. "You didn't hear me, Doctor. I said Jesus never met a prostitute." Not backing down, Campolo began searching his Bible for appropriate passages to bolster his point. Once again, the student insisted. "You're not listening to me, Doctor. Do you think that when he looked at Mary Magdalene he saw a prostitute? Do you think he saw whores when he looked at women like her? Doctor, listen to me! Jesus never met a prostitute!" Campolo fell silent. His theology had come under attack by a student who perhaps understood Jesus better than he did—a student who understood that "to be a Christian is to learn to see people as Christ sees them."[16] We, too, must see adolescents who are far from God as Christ sees them and not allow ourselves to be threatened by their morality or behavior. We must have compassion on them in a way that honors the God we serve.

Conviction in "Passing" the Faith

Another problem with "good enough" student ministries is the belief that the essential role of parents and youth ministers is to pass on their experiences and knowledge to young people. There are numerous theological and sociological problems with this reasoning. Sociologically speaking, we know that the world is constantly changing. The experiences that adults had as teenagers are no longer the experiences of contemporary adolescents. I have experienced this with my own teenagers. Through studying adolescents generally and raising two of my own teenagers specifically, I am amazed at how different my adolescence was from that of teenagers today. One is not necessarily better than the other; they are simply different. We must recognize the social structures that teenagers inhabit today, and we must guide them in discovering their own identities rather than imposing our solutions from yesteryear. While knowledge can certainly be passed along, faith must be discovered.

We also must understand the theological constraints of passing on the faith. While the desire to pass faith from one generation to the next is good and right, such "passing" language can create the idea of a static God as a commodity to be consumed. This places the teenager in the position of a consumer of the faith, and parents and youth ministers in the position of distribution managers. Sharon Galgay Ketcham described the issue this way:

If a youth's role is only to receive faith, they are not being welcomed into a faith in which they are expected to participate and contribute. People are not empty vessels into which we pour knowledge about the faith and certainly not faith itself. Passing language ignores the agency of the receiver. Might the expectations of an adult who seeks to "pass faith" underestimate the need to engage with youth in conversation, dialogue, and exchange that will further shape mutual understanding and experience of God? At worst, passing language can degenerate to adults controlling a youth's knowledge and experience of faith, neglecting to invite youth to join with the community's faith.[17]

If we serve a living God and read God's living Word, then our lives and the lives of teenagers will encounter the living presence of God. How much better this is than a static faith in a stagnant God, passed down from one generation to the next.

We can find such a living faith only when we trust that God has not abandoned this world and that Christ is active in the world through the Holy Spirit. We must believe that God has equipped the church with the gifts of the Spirit to transform all manner of persons near and far from their Creator. We are not simply passing on the faith to teenagers; we are cultivating the faith of teenagers as we seek to merge their story with God's story. We are helping them embark on a lifelong journey of discovery through contribution to and participation in the faith community.[18]

The Philosophical Decision

One of the most important philosophical decisions that a church makes is whether their student ministry will be a service ministry to the families of the church with teenagers or a comprehensive ministry that moves beyond the church walls and into the community, reaching out to unchurched students. Failure to intentionally make this decision results in the default position of "good enough" ministries that serve the desires of parents with teenagers in the church.

I regularly receive calls from pastors searching to fill open student ministry positions with our students from Gordon College. Most often they are looking for graduating seniors or recent graduates to fill full-time positions, but occasionally a pastor will call looking to fill a part-time position. I am always curious about part-time positions and often ask the caller, "How many teenagers are there in your community?"

The response is always the same: "We only have about ten or twelve teenagers right now."

"Really! There are only a dozen teenagers in your local school district?" I'll reply.

"Oh no, there are only about a dozen teenagers in our church."

"Well, how many teenagers are in the town where your church is located?"

"I don't know," the person will say. "Hundreds, I suppose."

"Then why don't you hire a full-time youth minister?"

"Oh, we can't afford to do that."

I have never pushed the conversation into the budgeting arena, but I suspect that most churches willing to hire a half-time person *could* afford to hire a full-time person if creating a comprehensive student ministry were a real priority. Many churches never take the time to truly consider the importance of student ministry. They simply respond to the felt needs of families with teenagers in their church and, by default, create a service ministry.

Service Ministries

A service view of student ministry, deemed good enough for the stakeholders of the church, is not created in isolation. Rather, it evolves from a systemic model of the church, either by design or by default. Ask any church staff member to describe the typical member of his or her congregation, and the person will likely produce an image with great clarity. Without fail, the image will be of an adult of a certain age and will include a variety of metrics. Perhaps your church is predominantly made up of young, urban professionals, or with middle-income couples without children, or with middle-aged professionals with families, or with retired persons. No matter how the typical member of a church is described, it will always be the description of an adult.

Often church planters go to great lengths to describe their "target audience" in the hope that they can create a church ethos that will be attractive to the defined target.[19] Once again, this is always an adult. It may be a young adult, a professional adult, or an urban adult, but it is always an adult. Churches are created and designed by adults and for adults! Once members of a local church establish—often subconsciously—a normative understanding of the typical church member, they design ministries to serve the typical church member. Some congregations go to great lengths to become "full-service" churches that meet every need of their membership profile. If this profile includes families with young children, there will surely be a children's ministry. This is not because the church is passionate about ministering to children; children are not the profile of a typical member. Rather, care for children is an expressed need of the typical adult member of the church.

This view sits in stark contrast to an organization such as Child Evangelism Fellowship, whose target audience is children. The same is true for organizations such as Young Life or Youth for Christ, which center on ministry with teenagers. For these organizations, ministry with children or teenagers is not a byproduct of ministry with adults. Ministry with children or teenagers is the essential mission of the organization.

When families with teenagers populate the church, congregations will always put forth some effort to meet the needs of these parents by providing programs for teenagers. The concern here is not for teenagers as much as it is for the parents of teenagers. It is not uncommon to hear church-growth gurus suggest that if you want your church to grow, you need to have excellent ministries for children and teenagers, because that is what attracts families. The emphasis is primarily to meet the felt needs of adults, by providing programs for children and teenagers. This is very different than making the genuine needs of children and teenagers primary. You can test this theory by attending a new members' class at your church. Typically at the first meeting, the class leader will ask participants to share what attracted them to the church. Some will declare the preaching, or the denomination, or the location. But if you listen to the reasons given by those who have children, you will hear that their number-one reason is often the reputation of, or their experience with, the ministries for children or teenagers.

Once this becomes the mindset of a church, a student ministry that serves the desires of parents quickly becomes good enough. As long as most parents are happy with the student ministry, the ministry is declared excellent, and a trickle of growth (often transfer growth) may occur through parents telling other parents how great the student ministry is at their church.

If something goes awry and parents are no longer satisfied with the student ministry, the ministry is declared a failure. Most often parents become dissatisfied for one of three reasons. First, if their children don't like the ministry for some reason, they will either begin refusing to attend, or they will attend the programs begrudgingly and only at their parents' insistence. This does not make for happy parents. Second, while their children might enjoy participating in the student ministry programs, parents may feel that the ministry is not contributing to their children's spiritual formation. Parents often frame this concern by requesting more "depth" of teaching in the ministry, or more formal discipleship programs, or youth leaders who establish stronger mentoring relationships with the teenagers.

Finally, parents can become dissatisfied with the student ministry when they perceive that it is no longer a safe place for their children. Safety may be construed either physically or spiritually. Parents might decide that the chaos they observe at a middle school meeting is out of control and that kids are not physically safe. If too many students return from a retreat with physical injuries from playing football, ultimate Frisbee, or red rover, parents may also question the physical safety of the ministry. Spiritually, parents will declare a ministry unsafe when they feel that participating in the ministry is weakening their child's faith. This often occurs when parents notice their teenager raising doubts or hard faith questions. This may also happen when parents feel that the ministry is exposing their child to negative influences. Most often this happens when the ministry strives to reach out to students beyond the church walls. When unchurched students begin to join the ministry, bringing with them their doubts, foul language, and immoral habits, Christian parents raise concerns that their child may be influenced negatively. When a teenager comes home from a conservative church's youth meeting and tells her mother that she spent most of the night listening to a new girl talk about why she is a lesbian, there is no doubt that the youth minister will be receiving a phone call from a parent concerned about the influence the ministry is having on her daughter.

This view of student ministry is often supported by the idea that we are to pass on the faith from one generation to the next. This is understood as a primary duty of parents in the Old Testament. Deuteronomy 6, which contains the oft-quoted Shema, begins with a description of God's provision for the faith formation of children.

> These are the commands, decrees and laws the LORD your God directed me to teach you to observe in the land that you are crossing the Jordan to possess, so that you, your children and their children after them may fear the LORD your God as long as you live by keeping all his decrees and commands that I give you, and so that you may enjoy long life. Hear, Israel, and be careful to obey so that it may go well with you and that you may increase greatly in a land flowing with milk and honey, just as the LORD, the God of your ancestors, promised you.
>
> Hear, O Israel: The LORD our God, the LORD is one. Love the LORD your God with all your heart and with all your soul and with all your strength. These commandments that I give you today are to be on your hearts. Impress them on your children. Talk about them when you sit at home and when you walk along the road, when you lie down and when you get

up. Tie them as symbols on your hands and bind them on your foreheads. Write them on the doorframes of your houses and on your gates. (6:1–9)

Elders were also expected to impart the faith to children, as described in Deuteronomy: "Remember the days of old; consider the generations long past. Ask your father and he will tell you, your elders, and they will explain to you" (32:7). Fathers and elders were expected to explain the ways of the Lord to children. When these expectations were not met, the next generation would fail to embrace the faith, as described in Judges: "After that whole generation had been gathered to their ancestors, another generation grew up who knew neither the Lord nor what he had done for Israel. Then the Israelites did evil in the eyes of the Lord and served the Baals" (2:10–11). So in the church today we boldly declare the words of the wisdom of the Proverb: "Train up a child in the way he should go, and when he is old he will not depart from it" (22:6 RSV).

All of this teaching is given to those who were faithful followers of the Lord, and it is good teaching for us to continue giving Christian parents. It is without question the responsibility of Christian parents to raise their children in the faith, and they should be able to count on the community of faith to help them do so. At best, parents who take seriously the responsibility of raising their children in the faith look to the church for help in accomplishing this high calling. The church, in turn, often provides specialized ministries for children and teenagers in an effort to come alongside parents in this quest. At worst, parents view the church as responsible for raising their children in the faith and expect these ministries to accomplish the faith formation task for them.

Whether parents and student ministries work together or parents delegate the task of faith development to student ministries, the driving force of student ministries becomes the felt needs and desires of Christian parents for the faith formation of their teenagers. Coming alongside parents is *a* significant mission of student ministry, but it is only one aspect of a comprehensive student ministry. Nevertheless, many churches have determined, intentionally or by default, that providing this service to Christian families is good enough for their student ministries.

Comprehensive Ministries

Serving the teenagers of the church and their families has been the common view of church-based student ministry for many years. Relatively few churches have taken a comprehensive approach that cares for the sheep within the flock while simultaneously reaching out to the young people of the community. To embrace this approach requires a great deal of intentionality on the part of the entire church leadership. A comprehensive view of student ministry is perhaps best described by Doug Fields in *Purpose Driven Youth Ministry*.[20] Fields' book was published three years after Rick Warren, who was then Fields' senior pastor, published *The Purpose Driven Church*. By that time, many youth ministers were serving in churches that had embraced the purpose-driven values described by Warren.[21]

The values of a comprehensive ministry are most often based on the brief description of the early church in Acts 2:42–47.

> They devoted themselves to the apostles' teaching and to fellowship, to the breaking of bread and to prayer. Everyone was filled with awe at the many wonders and signs performed by the apostles. All the believers were together and had everything in common. They sold property and posses-sions to give to anyone who had need. Every day they continued to meet together in the temple courts. They broke bread in their homes and ate together with glad and sincere hearts, praising God and enjoying the favor of all the people. And the Lord added to their number daily those who were being saved.

This description of the early church is supported by a trilogy of Jesus' teachings, which are often labeled the Great Commandment, the Great Commission, and what I refer to as the Great Charge.

The Great Commandment

Jesus first commands us to love God and neighbor. "'Love the Lord your God with all your heart and with all your soul and with all your mind.' This is the first and greatest commandment. And the second is like it: 'Love your neighbor as yourself.' All the Law and the Prophets hang on these two commandments" (Matt. 22:37–40).

All of our ministry may be derived from this Great Commandment. To love God is to know God in all aspects of life. We often segregate our love for God into areas of knowledge and experience, as if one can exist without the other. Many speak of an intellectual knowing of God through the life of the mind, while others declare their love of God through their experience. In Hebrew the word *yada*, "to know," captures both knowledge and experience. For the Hebrews, to know about God was to experience God, and to experience God was to know God. It would have been unimaginable to speak of knowing God without experiencing God personally. Marvin Wilson writes,

Knowledge and wisdom are related concepts; both are rooted in God, and both share in the application of learning to life. In the Western world knowledge has often been limited in definition, confined to abstract concepts or theoretical principles. But in Hebrew thought to "know" something was to experience it, rather than merely to intellectualize it. To "know" someone was to share an intimate personal relationship with that one. Thus the Hebrew verb *yada*, "to know," means to encounter, experience, and share in an intimate way. . . . The idea of knowledge thus embraced the whole human personality. A grasp of so much information was not enough; it also implied a response in the practical domain of life, in behavior and morals. . . . Thus, social action and good character result from a right relationship with God through his revelation. To "know" God is to walk faithfully in his ways and to live out the terms of his covenant. It included both the internalizing of truth and its outworking in the affairs of life. In short, for the Hebrew, to "know" was to "do". . . . It included down-to-earth activity or personal know-how applied to various realms and experiences of life.[22]

When we reflect on the meaning of loving God with all of our hearts, souls, and minds, we dare not give in to the temptation of deconstructionism, as though we can segregate our love of God into component parts of heart, soul, and mind.

"Knowing God" has nothing to do with abstract, intellectual knowledge about God but, in Scripture, is connected to God's acts of self-revelation (Schmitz, *NIDNTT* 2:395). Knowing God's acts in history and God's promises to act in the future leads one to honor God as the one true God (Rom. 1:21) and to enter into a proper relationship with God based on trust. The problem for the "wise" is that God's acts in history are so unexpected and so enigmatic that they fail to recognize them as God's acts. It may seem as if God deliberately blinds them so that they cannot see (Isa. 29:9–10). But only those who admit that they see through a glass darkly and are open to God's revelation can truly know God and receive God's offer of salvation.[23]

When the lawyer in Luke 10 asks Jesus to define who his neighbors are, Jesus turns the man's question on its head with the story of the Good Samaritan. Rather than describing others as neighbors, Jesus describes what it means to be a neighbor to others. Of course, by showing mercy to the man who was beaten and left for dead, the outcast Samaritan turns out to be the model neighbor. We typically understand the person in need to be a neighbor that we should not ignore, but Robert McAfee Brown suggests that we come up short when we simply conclude that our neighbor is anyone we meet along life's journey who is in need.

Brown further argues that this view minimizes the drama and sacrifice of the Samaritan's encounter with the beaten man lying on the side of the road. The Samaritan does not simply give aid to a person he happens upon in his travels. Rather, he crosses over into another culture with great intentionality, engages the man's needs, and goes out of his way to ensure the man's extended care through the innkeeper's help. "The neighbor was not the wounded man, 'the neighbor was the Samaritan who *approached* the wounded man and *made him his neighbor*'. . . . Being a neighbor makes the one who is approached into a neighbor also. The neighbor is not the one whom I find in my path but rather the one in whose path I place myself, the one whom I approach and actively seek."[24] The Samaritan understands the imperative of the Great Commandment, extending himself as a neighbor to someone in need outside of his ethnic culture. Likewise, comprehensive ministry calls us to extend ourselves to students in need beyond the walls of the church.

The Great Commission

Having come to understand the meaning of loving God and neighbor, the disciples meet Jesus in Galilee, shortly after his resurrection, and he commissions them. "Therefore go and make disciples of all nations, baptizing them in the name of the Father and of the Son and of the Holy Spirit, and teaching them to obey everything I have commanded you. And surely I am with you always, to the very end of the age" (Matt. 28:19–20).

In this Great Commission, Jesus commands his disciples to make more disciples through baptizing people and teaching them all that he had taught them. Making disciples begins with evangelism. Youth Specialties co-founder Mike Yaconelli suggests that youth ministers are not social workers, or counselors, or social change agents, or family therapists, or family arbitrators, or stepparents, or activities coordinators, or recreation directors, or programmers, or educators. While youth ministers certainly help kids relate to their families, obtain social services, counsel, program, and educate, student ministry is primarily missional in nature. The purpose of student ministry, according to Yaconelli, is simply this: "Youth ministry is about bringing kids into the presence of Jesus Christ."[25] And which students are we to bring into the presence of Christ? Students who are *outside* the presence of Christ. Making disciples is about reaching lost people and ushering them into the fellowship of believers—that is, the church.[26]

The Great Charge

After appearing to the disciples for forty days and teaching them about the true meaning of the kingdom, Jesus declares his Great Charge to them in Jerusalem, prior to his ascension. "Then they gathered around him and asked him, 'Lord, are you at this time going to restore the kingdom to Israel?' He said to them: 'It is not for you to know the times or dates the Father has set by his own authority. But you will receive power when the Holy Spirit comes on you; and you will be my witnesses in Jerusalem, and in all Judea and Samaria, and to the ends of the earth'" (Acts 1:6–8).

This final charge to the disciples echoes the Great Commission while offering a distinct message.[27] In the Great Commission, Jesus empowers the disciples to go forth and make disciples using everything he has taught them. In Acts 1:8, Jesus charges the disciples to be his witnesses. This holds a twofold meaning: eyewitness and confessing witness. As eyewitnesses, the disciples bear witness to the factual events of Jesus' life. But Jesus does not merely instruct them to be faithful historians: he charges them to proclaim the significance of his life, death, and resurrection to Jerusalem, Judea, Samaria, and the ends of the earth. They are charged with bearing witness to both the events of Jesus' life and the consequence of the incarnation. While we cannot serve as eyewitnesses to the life of Christ, we are called to serve as confessing witnesses who have grasped, in faith, the significance of Jesus.[28]

From these passages, we understand the climate of the early church as described in Acts 2 and catch a vision of the church that we are to become.

- The community of faith loves God.
- The community of faith reaches out to and loves neighbors.
- The community of faith makes disciples of those far from God, baptizing and teaching.
- The community of faith bears witness to Jesus Christ, near and far.

This is the framework of a comprehensive ministry. The core values of worship, outreach, ministry, faith formation, and community are all represented in Christ's directives to his followers.

Components of a Comprehensive Ministry

Comprehensive ministry has been described as having an assortment of components, ranging from as few as three to as many as eight. Today the most popular model seems to be that of Warren and Fields,[29] who define five components of a comprehensive ministry: *worship, discipleship, evangelism, fellowship,* and *ministry.* Various authors have written about these components, and many churches have adopted them, using differing terminology. *Discipleship* may be described as *spiritual formation, Christian formation,* or *faith formation.* Each term for discipleship can be differentiated when exploring the theology of sanctification, but for our purposes they can serve synonymously. *Evangelism* is often considered tantamount to *outreach, fellowship* is often described as *community,* and *ministry* is often referred to as *service.* Some churches reduce these five to three or four, by combining evangelism and ministry into one component of *outreach* or by understanding *fellowship* as something that happens organically. One danger with this reduction is that folding evangelism and ministry into outreach typically results in the loss of an evangelistic edge to the outreach component. In the same way, when the term *outreach* is used for evangelism, it is important to maintain *ministry,* or *service,* as another distinct component. Finally, when *fellowship* is not an explicit core value, the importance of connecting and contributing to the community can be lost, and people quickly become mere consumers of the community.

Malan Nel describes the eight components of a comprehensive student ministry as: *preaching, worship, pastoral care, management and administration, teaching, fellowship, deeds of mercy,* and *witnessing.*[30] In reference to Warren's model, Nel attains eight components by making *preaching* distinct from *worship,* dividing *ministry* into *pastoral care* and *deeds of mercy,* and adding *management and administration. Teaching* is comparable to Warren's *discipleship,* and *witnessing* is Nel's term for *evangelism.*

After visiting a hundred churches and surveying nearly two thousand Christian adults, Steve Macchia concluded that healthy churches share at least ten characteristics.[31] Interestingly, these ten characteristics fall directly in line with the five components that Warren describes. Healthy churches, Macchia found, exhibit (1) God's empowering presence, and (2) God-exalting worship, both attributes of Warren's tenet of *worship.* Healthy churches are composed of people (3) learning and growing in community, with an emphasis on (4) spiritual disciplines, certainly hallmarks of *discipleship.* Healthy churches are committed to (5) loving and caring relationships, as well as (6) networking with the body of Christ, both aspects of *fellowship.* Healthy churches intentionally focus on (7) servant leadership development and (8) wise administration and accountability, two of the pillars of *ministry.* Finally, healthy churches possess (9) an outward focus and are marked by faithful (10) stewardship and generosity, both essential to *outreach.*

While Nel presents a strong theoretical argument for his eight components, and Macchia offers keen insights to the core values of a healthy church, both present significant challenges for implementation in ministry given the amount of pragmatic overlap. Reducing Warren's five components to four or three may result in a less-than-comprehensive ministry, while expanding the components of a comprehensive ministry may become overwhelming and confusing. Yet in the proper context Nel, Macchia, and others provide helpful insights into the five components described by Warren and Fields. These five components provide enough breadth to be truly considered comprehensive while maintaining a manageable strategy for implementation.[32]

Aligning Student Ministry and the Church

Even though scores of youth ministers have embraced the comprehensive approach described above, many have struggled to implement a fully functioning comprehensive ministry. I remember well the year that Fields' book was released, because my phone kept ringing with distraught youth ministers on the other end. "Have you read Fields' book?" they would ask.

"Yes, I have."

"So, what do you think of it?"

"I think it's great—wish I'd written it!"

"Me too, but I just can't get the model to work."

I would talk them through all the aspects of their ministry, as if I were working for Purpose Driven Tech Support, and then wish them well on their endeavors, all without feeling confident that I had been very helpful. After about three or four conversations, I finally asked one youth minister a question, almost by accident, that unlocked my thinking significantly. "Are you serving in a purpose-driven church?" I asked.

"Um, no, not really."

"Has your pastor read Rick Warren's book?"

"Yes, he has and frankly he didn't like it that much."

And therein lies the problem. From that point on, I began every conversation with a question about the senior pastor's view on the purpose-driven church model. Not surprisingly, there was a direct correlation between the values of the church and the values of the student ministry. For better or worse student ministry will almost always reflect the values of the church at large.

When youth ministers were not serving in purpose-driven churches, the problem areas of the student ministry were almost always areas that the church in general did not value. As Todd Erickson has said, "Student ministry needs to be aligned with the church. The church is not just a feeding trough for student ministry. We are all in the same ministry together."[33] The area of greatest contention was almost always evangelism; sometimes, to a lesser degree, worship; and occasionally ministry. The discipleship and fellowship components of a comprehensive ministry were never a problem. In fact, churches always wanted more discipleship and fellowship in the student ministry. Why? Because Christian parents desperately wanted *their* teenagers to be connected and "discipled." Majoring in two of the five components described in Fields' model was good enough for many churches, but youth ministers wanted more. They wanted a God-honoring ministry that nurtured students within the broad community of the church, reached out to students beyond the walls of the church, and engaged students in meaningful acts of service.

When youth ministers serve in purpose-driven churches, it is relatively easy to troubleshoot the issues in their purpose-driven student ministries. Even some youth ministers serving in churches that embrace a comprehensive model, however, struggle to develop a comprehensive student ministry. While the church may value outreach and strive to reach people beyond the walls of the church, adults often remain the target audience. In terms of commitment and resources, outreach in student ministry is not always supported by the church leadership. Even in a seeker-driven church, it is the Christian parents of teenagers who are making their needs known, not the unchurched parents of unchurched teenagers—they are simply not present. Hence, in a church that is highly committed to evangelism, an important strategic question must be raised. Will the church be content to simply receive new teenagers into the student ministry as a byproduct of reaching out to adults? Or will the church also strive to reach out directly to teenagers in the local community through the student ministry (and perhaps draw in new parents as a result of reaching teenagers)? In the first scenario, student ministries become rather passive in the area of outreach and are once again meeting the needs of parents. In the second scenario, student ministries are actively striving to connect directly with students outside the church.

Making a conscious, prayerful, thoughtful decision about the approach of a student ministry is one of the most important decisions a church leadership team can make. Neither the youth minister nor the student ministry leadership team should ever make this decision alone. This decision must be owned, embraced, and supported by the entire leadership of the church, because it holds significant implications for the kind of person needed to serve as youth minister, the type of volunteers to be recruited, the kind of volunteer training that is necessary, and the kinds of programs needed to achieve the goals of the student ministry. Everything in student ministry rides on this decision. When a church chooses the service mode of student ministry, the charge is to maintain a ministry that meets the needs of the parents of teenagers. When a church chooses a comprehensive mode, student ministry thrives and the church is filled with life and vitality. Students become engaged in the whole life of the church, students far from God are attracted to a community of people who are passionate about their faith, and the entire congregation is blessed with the contributions of adolescents. Student ministry is not simply an arm of Christian education. Student ministry is ministry and embraces all aspects of ministry. Kenda Creasy Dean describes student ministry in this manner:

> What makes youth ministry distinctive is not its form, but its flock. Ministry with young people is, after all, *ministry*—not so different from ministry with anybody else. Yet because young people demand that the church address them in their particularity (in other words, from the perspective of their specific cultural and developmental experiences as adolescents), youth ministry serves as a laboratory where we can learn to contextualize ministry. When we walk alongside young people as Christ's representatives, we become incarnational witnesses, people who must use our own lives to "put wheels on the gospel" for the flock at hand.[34]

When we choose to view student ministry as simply an arm of Christian education—that is, the nurturing of students growing up in the church—then we fail to fully engage in the ministry of the gospel within the particular context to which we have been called.

Robert Frost's classic poem "The Road Not Taken" provides a clear metaphor for this important philosophical decision concerning student ministry.

> Two roads diverged in a yellow wood,
> And sorry I could not travel both
> And be one traveler, long I stood
> And looked down one as far as I would
> To where it bent in the undergrowth;
>
> Then took the other, as just as fair,
> And having perhaps the better claim,
> Because it was grassy and wanted wear;

Though as for that the passing there
Had worn them really about the same,

And both that morning equally lay
In leaves no step had trodden black.
Oh, I kept the first for another day!
Yet knowing how way leads on to way,
I doubted if I should ever come back.

I shall be telling this with a sigh
Somewhere ages and ages hence:
Two roads diverged in a wood, and I—
I took the one less traveled by,
And that has made all the difference.[35]

While the two roads of student ministry may look similar at the outset, they are truly very different paths. Frost desired to travel both if he could. In student ministry, choosing a comprehensive approach actually provides the opportunity to do just that. There is nothing on the "good enough" road that is not included on the comprehensive road, but the "good enough" road is incomplete, unfinished, and left wanting. Like Frost, the comprehensive road is less traveled by church leadership and requires a greater investment, but this courageous decision will lead to such a thriving ministry that the desire to return to the first road will be short lived. Thankfully, there are switchback trails for those already on the road of "good enough" to make their way to the road of comprehensive student ministry at any moment. Choosing that road will make all the difference in the vitality of student ministry and the vibrancy of the local church.

Students Thrive in Ministries with Purpose

One of the most deplorable atrocities of World War II occurred in a prison camp where the inmates were forced to perform meaningless work. One day they would move a massive pile of garbage from one side of the camp to the other. The next day they would be ordered to move the pile of garbage back to its original location. Day after day, this meaningless work—relocating the garbage pile from one side of the camp to the other—continued. Eventually the mindless task began to take a toll on the prisoners. One day a prisoner began crying uncontrollably and had to be removed from the group. Another man began screaming until he was beaten into silence. Another man who had served in the prison for three years ran from his garbage-pile duty toward the electric fence surrounding the encampment. Ignoring the warnings to stop, he hurled himself onto the fence and was instantly electrocuted. As the guards showed callous indifference to the plight of the prisoners performing the mind-numbing shifting of the garbage, more men went insane. The inmates did not know that they were part of a Nazi experiment on mental health designed to determine the human capacity for meaningless activity. Through this experiment, the Nazis determined that a life devoid of purpose can result in insanity and suicide.[36]

Clearly, we understand that purpose is a pivotal factor in determining the quality of human life. This is no less true in student ministry. The quality of a student ministry is strongly correlated to its purpose. When we are foggy concerning the purpose of ministry, we accomplish little that honors God.

I remember one incident at Boston's Logan Airport with great clarity. I was heading to Long Island, New York, for a meeting. When I approached the ticket counter with my reservation in hand, the ticket agent informed me that I was far too early to check in for my flight. Knowing that I was running late, I asked, bewildered, "How can it be too early to check in for an 8:00 a.m. flight?" She pointed out that my flight was departing twelve hours later, at 8:00 p.m. I had mistakenly booked the wrong flight!

Now there was nothing wrong with my flight. It included a fine aircraft and was headed to the right destination, but it was leaving too late. Other flights on the airline departed at 8:00 a.m., but they were headed to the wrong destinations. I did not need a good aircraft that was heading to a random location at any old time; I needed a good airplane that was headed to New York in time for my meeting.

Likewise, our ministry vehicles must be headed in the right direction at the right time. Flying around from one ministry activity to another week after week, month after month, year after year, with no purpose in mind quickly becomes meaningless and tiresome. When we are guided by clarity of purpose, however, we are infused with energy that transcends the fatigue of the toil, and ministries thrive as lives are transformed.

Remember the wisdom that the Cheshire cat imparts to Alice when she asks which way she should go? "'That depends a good deal on where you want to get to,' said the cat. 'I don't much care where—' said Alice. 'Then it doesn't matter which way you go,' said the cat."[37] When we ignore the purposes set forth for ministry, we are apt to become disobedient to God by omission. We may be on a great journey, but if it is not a journey aligned with God's purposes, the journey is worthless.

Start with the End in Mind

When we have the opportunity to disciple teenagers, we start with the end in mind. What do we hope this student's faith will look like fifty years from now? We also train students to be a winsome witness on their school campus. When this happens, they are no longer bored by church or student ministry activities. They are in training . . . knowing they might be held accountable for this training tomorrow at school. This changes everything.

Kendra and Nathaniel Williams, Youth for Christ,
Auburn, California

The purpose of life, in God's view, is not differentiated by age. Men and women, young and old, are all called to fulfill the Great Commission. Sometimes we act as if Matthew 28 begins: "When you become an adult, go and make disciples," or "When you become a deacon, or elder, or pastor, go and make disciples." Yet there is no age distinction when it comes to loving God, loving neighbor, or making disciples. The purposes of student ministry are the same as the purposes of the church. "Christian young people cannot choose what aspect of the Great Commission they will or will not obey," write Lee Vukich and Steve Vandegriff. "Hence we must structure our ministry in such a way so that the opportunity to obey each aspect of the Great Commission is given."[38] The same can certainly be said for the Great Commandment.

The construction industry is held accountable for following strict building codes, and for good reason. If a builder decides to cut corners on the materials necessary to support the structure, disaster can occur. So it happened once with a simple home that was constructed with half the number of wall studs necessary. Rather than building walls with vertical studs every sixteen inches, the builder constructed walls with studs every thirty-two inches or so in order to save money. The home looked great when it was finished, but once winter rolled around and the snow piled up on the roof, the walls began to buckle. Eventually the house simply collapsed, as the walls could not support the weight of the snow-packed roof.

When we design a ministry solely around the two studs of nurturing and fellowship, we fail to provide students with the opportunity to engage in ministry, outreach, and worship, which are essential to God's purpose for all Christians—not just adults—and we fail to be faithful to that which God has called us. While the students may look great for a time, eventually the pressures of the world pile up. Students who have not learned to engage in ministry, outreach, and worship collapse under the pressure, and their student ministry comes under fire for not preparing them for a life of meaningful purpose.

Clarity of purpose brings vitality to student ministry and provides a structural support upon which student ministries thrive. Only through a comprehensive approach to student ministry will we fulfill our God-given mandate and provide contexts filled with joy, purpose, meaning, and adventure in which teenagers can discover and engage God's story. When that happens, all teenagers matter, lives are transformed, the whole church is engaged, and student ministry thrives.

Embracing Outreach

In February 1812, Adoniram Judson and a small group of passionate believers set sail from Salem, Massachusetts, to India, becoming the first group of American Christian missionaries. For over two hundred years, American Christians have been traveling overseas to proclaim the good news of Jesus Christ. More missionaries have traveled the globe from the United States than any other country. In 2010 there were an estimated 400,000 global missionaries, and 127,000 of them were sent from the United States. Brazil sent the second-most missionaries that year, with 32,400.[39]

Ironically, the country that has sent the greatest number of missionaries around the world has failed to spread the gospel among its own people. In the American Religious Identification Survey, the number of people who identified themselves as having no religious affiliation nearly doubled from 1990 (8 percent) to 2008 (15 percent).[40] This increase was found in every single state across the country, making it a national trend. It may be difficult to imagine America, a historic exporter of missionaries, as a mission field, but we are truly in need of a missionary-type effort, especially among teenagers. In his blog *Church and Culture*, James Emery White explores three essentials of being a missionary: *learn the language, become sensitized to the culture*, and *translate the gospel*.[41]

Learn the Language

Every missionary understands the importance of communication. A language barrier is a foundational obstacle that must be overcome, and missionaries strive to learn the language of the people they are trying to reach. Learning the language of a people group is more than simply learning words; it is learning how to converse with people in a manner that can engage thoughts, feelings, hopes, and dreams. While most U.S. teenagers speak English, they have their own tribal dialects of words, sounds, and symbols, all of which are constantly changing.

I recently attended an awards ceremony of the state high school theater guild, where teenagers were being honored for their skill and creativity as actors, musicians, writers, and designers. At one point, a prominent adult began to describe an award that required contestants to submit a collection of works. Without considering the language of his adolescent audience, he said, "This award is based upon the actor's entire package." The young audience erupted with laughter at what they heard as a sexual innuendo. (If you don't get it, ask a teenager.) If adults desire to engage teenagers in meaningful ways, they must learn the language of adolescents.

Become Sensitized to the Culture

Missionaries understand that to function well in a foreign land, they must become such good students of the culture that they are sensitized to every nuance they encounter. Culture exists both externally and internally. We can describe the culture of the world in which we live while being sensitive to the culture that lives in our own being. Everything is cultural: we are affected by culture, and we affect culture. "Culture is the comprehensive, penetrating context that encompasses our life and thought, art and speech, entertainment and sensibility, values and faith," writes White.[42] Outreach occurs in this context, and while we would never want to "cave to the culture," we must be willing to make accommodations for the context in which we are ministering.

When visiting baseball teams come to Boston for a game with the Red Sox, they find themselves in historic Fenway Park, which is more than one hundred years old. Even with modern renovations, the park still has many quirky aspects, most notable among them the left field wall known as the Green Monster. A visiting left fielder who does not make accommodation to the rather short 310-foot left-field line and the rather tall 37-foot left-field wall will be in for a very long day of baseball. Major league outfielders rarely have to field balls ricocheting off the outfield wall—but if you play left field at Fenway, it becomes routine.

Adjusting to the context of one's surroundings in ministry is no less important. Ministry always occurs in a specific context, and becoming sensitive to the adolescent context is essential for reaching out to teenagers.

Translate the Gospel

Missionaries translate the gospel to provide people with a clear understanding of God's message. This is not about transforming the gospel into something that was never intended by the biblical authors. Those committed to outreach must "translate the gospel so that it can be heard, understood, and appropriated."[43] While the gospel must always be translated for a unique context, it should never be transformed. Every generation creates a unique cultural context, and reaching out to teenagers requires that adults faithfully and effectively translate the gospel for an emerging culture. This is a delicate and sensitive task that requires a keen understanding of the author's words in the original context, and the wisdom to translate that meaning into the modern context of adolescent life.

Over the last two hundred years, American missionaries have influenced the world with the message of the gospel by traveling great distances to engage people in distant lands. Today many young people live in a foreign culture. Understanding local adolescents as a mission field and engaging them with the three essential tasks of missionaries are foundational to student ministry outreach.

Comprehensive Congregations

Second Presbyterian Church

The Second Presbyterian Church in Memphis, Tennessee, has embraced a comprehensive approach to student ministry. Todd Erickson and his ministry team have received extraordinary support from the church leadership at Second Presbyterian Church to create a comprehensive ministry through which God is transforming adolescents throughout the city of Memphis. Their emphasis is leading students in growing relationships with Christ. When Erickson speaks of "students," he is not simply referring to the teenagers in the church. He is talking about teenagers throughout the community in which his church is located. When he speaks of "growth," he refers to a journey that begins when students encounter Christ for the first time. "We want to meet students where they are. We didn't have to clean ourselves up before Jesus accepted us. He accepted us where he found us, but he also didn't leave us there."[44]

The student ministries of Second Presbyterian Church are finding students all across the city of Memphis, accepting them as they are, and walking with them on the journey of faith. Relationships are critical to their ministry, as the faith journey is personal, communal, and intimate. While programs are part of the ministry, they primarily serve as environments to stimulate authentic relationships marked by love, compassion, and perseverance. Erickson and his team see themselves as both coming alongside parents in their God-given role of raising their children in the faith *and* reaching out to the teenagers beyond the confines of the church. This church is no one-eared Mickey Mouse, in which the small "ear" of student ministry sits off to the side of the "head" of the congregation, tangential and unrelated to the rest of the church.[45] Growing in a relationship with Christ includes growing in relationship with the community of Christ—that is, the church. To this end, teenagers are highly valued as contributing members of Second Presbyterian Church.

The Falls Church (Anglican)

Another example of comprehensive student ministry can be found just outside the nation's capital in Falls Church, Virginia. Jim Byrne has consistently built comprehensive student ministries in each church he has served, and The Falls Church (Anglican) community has a long history of making student ministry a priority in their church. Like Second Presbyterian in Memphis, Byrne and his team at The Falls Church have been highly supported by the leadership of the church. His senior pastor communicates, with clarity and conviction, a biblical view of ministry centered on the Great Commission. This provides a platform for the student ministries to do the same, with the full support of a senior pastor who truly believes the gospel message is for all people—including teenagers! Byrne has felt this support not only from his pastors but also from the elders and other senior leadership in the churches he has served.

This unwavering support has allowed Byrne to create what he believes is the key to a faithful and effective student ministry: a committed team of adult leaders that he calls the "youth family." This is a group of paid and volunteer leaders who truly act as a family, gathering weekly for food, fellowship, worship, teaching, and planning. Each year, the youth family takes a retreat just for themselves, without the teenagers. The youth family is not just a group of leaders. It is an authentic community of people who love and care for one another, genuinely feel ownership of the ministry, and invest in authentic relationships with the teenagers of the church and teenagers outside the church from all over the

Falls Church community. Byrne's high level of investment in leaders and leadership development translates into a group of people through whom God works in the lives of teenagers. The ministry of this group is truly greater than the sum of their talents, because they are a family supported and energized by one another.

Both Erickson and Byrne serve in communities that believe the gospel is to be proclaimed to all people—including teenagers outside the church walls who are far from God. Having the resources necessary to be comprehensive ministries, they are able to approach the adolescent population of their communities as a fertile mission field. Arming their adult and student leaders with a missiological theology of engaging people in their own context, they joyfully get to know students in their adolescent environments. Some of the adult leaders connect with students at their schools by volunteering to serve as coaches for varsity, junior varsity, or intramural activities. Others serve in the schools by helping with annual musical or drama productions. Students are taught the importance of peer-to-peer ministry as a commitment to the world around them. In this manner, it becomes natural for students to invite students to ministry events, share their testimony with friends, and care about those students they encounter every day with a high level of authenticity. As leaders are in direct contact with new students, and committed students invite friends to youth meetings, breakfast gatherings, or retreats, new students are constantly entering their ministries. In the final analysis, Byrne says that it is about creating a culture in which "leaders care more about students than programs and are committed to the genuine sharing of life stories."[46]

Discussion Questions for Student Ministry Leaders

1. What do you believe is the purpose of student ministry? If you were to make an honest assessment of the current student ministry of your church, would you say it reflects the "good enough" principle? Why or why not? If so, what is the driving force behind the "good enough" principle? How do you think church leaders, parents, and volunteers would answer this question?

2. After reading this chapter, what inspires you in your pursuit of a comprehensive student ministry? What would be challenging about such a pursuit?

3. Which of the five components of a comprehensive student ministry—outreach, discipleship, community, worship, and ministry—are

areas of strength in student ministry at your church? Which components are areas of growth? Why?

4. What would be different about the student ministry if you were to either begin or strengthen a comprehensive student ministry?

5. Do you know the demographics in your area? How many teenagers? How many teenagers go to church? How many teenagers are in foster care? How many teenagers are in group homes or transitional housing?

6. To what student populations do you feel called to reach out, and how will you do that?

7. How can you train your students to be missionaries on their school campuses? (Youth for Christ's "3 Story Evangelism" is a great resource for such training: see www.3story.org.)

Discussion Questions for Church Leaders

1. What does the church believe is the purpose of student ministry? If you were to make an honest assessment of the current student ministry of your church, would you say it reflects the "good enough" principle? Why or why not? If so, what is the driving force behind the "good enough" principle? How would the youth leader, volunteers, and former parents and students of the student ministry answer this question?

2. Does the church leadership embrace a vision for a service ministry to the existing teenagers of the church, or do you desire a more comprehensive approach to student ministry? What are the barriers to becoming more comprehensive (e.g., resources, desire of parents, bandwidth of the student ministry leader, vision of the pastor)? What is the effect of remaining simply a service ministry to the existing youth of the church?

3. Which of the five components of a comprehensive student ministry—outreach, discipleship, community, worship, and ministry—are areas of strength in the overall church? Which ones are areas of growth? How do these answers compare to the strength and growth areas of the student ministry?

4. What might be different about the church if you were to develop or strengthen a comprehensive model of student ministry? What would be different about student ministry? What type of support would be needed for the youth minister?

5. The Institute of Educational Sciences reports that 80 percent of public school students participate in some type of extracurricular activity, and the majority of parents are transporting and participating in these activities at some level.[47] How can we train parents to be "missionaries" on their students' campuses?

6. If student ministry understands the teenage population as a mission field, where it is necessary to learn a language and culture and to translate the gospel to that culture, what does it look like for the church to support and develop a missional approach to student ministry?

7. How might the student ministries of the church partner with parachurch student ministries in the community?

2

When Teenagers Matter:
TRANSFORMATION HAPPENS

A classic tale by C. S. Lewis, *The Lion, the Witch and the Wardrobe* is a story in which the White Witch demands the life of Aslan in exchange for the life of Edmund. The laws of the deep magic of Narnia are clear: to save the life of a traitor, another must die in his place. Edmund and Aslan cannot both survive; someone must die for the treachery.[1] You can't have it both ways.

This reflects the battle that has plagued student ministry (and the church) for far too long. The dichotomies between evangelism and discipleship, outreach and education, witness and faith formation have stifled ministries. If you reach out to people far from God, then you sacrifice faith formation. If you are committed to strong discipleship, then you must forgo evangelism. You cannot have both. When one side of the teeter-totter is up in the air, the other side must be on the ground, and no one is satisfied with balancing a teeter-totter in a level position. This is the myth we have come to believe as truth because we have not read closely enough the marching orders of God's purposes for ministry.

The White Witch was ignorant of Narnia's deepest magic, which avowed that the sacrifice of an innocent person in the place of a traitor shall bring new life to the willing victim. For Aslan, the choice was not actually between death and life, for his death brought new life. Much to the dismay of the White Witch, Aslan's death on the stone table was the beginning of his new life, as well as the beginning of Edmund's new life. In the same way, evangelism is the beginning of faith formation, not its opposite. Rather than choosing between outreach and nurture, we must constantly hold the two in tension, coming to understand outreach as the beginning of discipleship, transformation, new life in Christ, and spiritual growth.

Our Historical Dichotomy

The dichotomy between mission and discipleship is deeply embedded in the history of student ministry and Christian education. Our Christian education programs typically serve students who are already in the church, and youth ministries that do the same are more properly considered youth education ministries or the Christian education of youth. Comprehensive student ministry requires that we become missionaries to a world that is increasingly unchurched.

Those who are skeptical of this dichotomy would do well to take up this simple exercise. Gather a stack of theological dictionaries and books on the history and theology of Christian education. Search for student ministry in these books. It will not likely be a major heading; rather, student ministry organizations, events, and leaders will be located under other major headings. But where have the writers located them? If you look under the "education" heading in the dictionaries, you will not find much on student ministry. You will find the Sunday school movement, Christian school movement, Vacation Bible School, and likely the Society for Christian Endeavor and its denominational clones. These movements compose the history of the Christian education of youth in the Protestant church, but they are not comprehensive youth ministries. The Sunday school movement existed prior to the advent of our understanding of adolescence. And even though the Society for Christian Endeavor and its descendants may have ministered to adolescents, they were predominantly educational programs designed to nurture Christian students of the church rather than to reach out to students beyond the church walls.

Looking further into a theological dictionary under missions/evangelism, you will find all of the great student ministry movements of the twentieth century, including the Wood brothers' Young Life Campaign in Great Britain, Jim Rayburn's Young Life, Lloyd Bryant's Christian Youth Campaign in New York City, Evelyn McClusky's Miracle Book Club, the Youth for Christ movement that launched Youth for Christ International, and a host of evangelistic radio ministries. In the Christian education history books, these student ministry movements are usually relegated to the last chapter, under parachurch ministries. Judging from the written record, they seemingly have no place in the history of Christian education.

This dichotomy has plagued ministry to and with adolescents for nearly a century, as the theology of nurture alone has been promoted in Christian education. This dates back to Horace Bushnell's theory that a "child is to grow up Christian and never know himself as being otherwise."[2] It is only in the history of missional revivals that we find the evangelistic student ministry movements of the twentieth century recorded. Student ministry is a missional ministry, the objective of which is to go and make disciples of a nation named *adolescence*.

Pete Ward has described two approaches to student ministry.[3] The first is the Outside-In approach, which focuses on reaching young people who are especially distant from the church through radically penetrating the postmodern culture with committed youth leaders. This effort works far outside the church in hopes that teenagers might be brought inside the church. The second, the Inside-Out approach, is equally committed to evangelism but aims to reach students who are less distant from the church—those who sit on the fringe of the church and can be reached through peer evangelism with a core group of Christian students. The objective of each approach is the same: go and make disciples of a nation named adolescence. These approaches reach out to students who are either far from God or very, very far from God and guide them into growing relationships with Jesus Christ and the people of God.

Far too often we settle for "good enough" ministries that only nurture the students in the church and fail to reach out even to students on the fringes. Christian teenagers inside the church walls are being nurtured, but they are not reaching outside. When the Inside-Out approach loses its outward focus, it is no longer a comprehensive student ministry but has become youth education. Christian education that is based upon a theology of nurture, and its component part, youth education, is vital to the discipleship process of young people within the church. Student ministry, however, should act in keeping with its historical purpose: to make disciples out of students who are far from God, not simply to nurture those who are already in the fold.

A Theological Understanding of Discipleship

Frederick Buechner contends that every culture creates fairy tales.[4] We believe, or at least want to believe, that there is something more to this world than meets the eye. We long for the reformation of reality, hoping that death is not the end and that the universe is something more than an enclosed terrarium. In our search for meaning, generation after generation tells tales of hope for another world.

The most common feature of fairy tales is that the enchanted world is not very far away. Step into a wardrobe and you are in Narnia. Walk through a forest and you find a cottage with seven dwarfs. Fall down a rabbit hole and you arrive in Wonderland. In every story, these other worlds always seem to be closer than anyone thought. For many people, it turns out that God is also closer than they thought. Fairy tales are not simply concerned with the transformation of the world around us; they are often concerned with the transformation of the central characters. A frog becomes a prince. An ugly duckling becomes a swan. A wooden marionette becomes a real boy.

Buechner suggests that the gospel contains these same features, with one distinct difference: the gospel is absolutely true. When real people encounter the real truth of God, who is closer than they ever imagined possible, they are transformed—not, however, from anything as mundane as frogs, ducks, or marionettes into princes, swans, or boys. They are transformed into the image of Christ. Relationships and families are transformed. Businesses and communities are transformed. Schools and churches are transformed. The lid is off the proverbial terrarium, and the story of humanity is transformed forever.

Until we come to a theological understanding of the cohesion of evangelism and discipleship, we will continue this debilitating dichotomy that impedes the image of transformation Buechner so beautifully paints. The ability to move beyond this dichotomy hinges upon our understanding of what it means to be a disciple and to go and make disciples. The term *disciple* is often defined, insufficiently, as "learner." Disciples are viewed as those who place themselves in a position where they can learn from a great teacher. In Scripture we find numerous people with varying levels of commitment to the teaching and person of Christ. Early in Jesus' ministry, people became disciples of Jesus (often those who had previously been disciples of John the Baptist), but eventually we come to understand that they were not believers at all. They were learners, but they were not disciples, in Jesus' view. Michael Wilkins explains the dilemma of viewing disciples as simply learners:

> This model has two basic difficulties. First, the Greek term for "disciple" (*mathetes*) is used in Scripture in a manner different than simply to designate a "learner." For example, the followers of John the Baptist are more like adherents to the prophet and movement surrounding him than students of a teacher. The second difficulty appears when we note the normal use

of the term *disciple* in the book of Acts. In Acts the term is generally used without any qualifiers simply to designate "Christians." For example, Acts 11:26 says, "The disciples were called Christians first at Antioch." The disciples appear to be more than simply learners.[5]

Clearly, Jesus calls his disciples to be more than learners; he calls them to a radical commitment to himself and to the kingdom.

Another view of what it means to be a disciple that has furthered the dichotomy between evangelism and discipleship is the understanding that a disciple is a highly committed Christian. This view can be found in many books on discipleship and is summarized clearly by Dwight Pentecost when he suggests that "there is a vast difference between being saved and being a disciple. Not all men who are saved are disciples although all who are disciples are saved."[6]

This view has become pervasive within American evangelicalism, and you can easily discover whether people have accepted this view. Have you bought into this understanding? Let's find out. Picture the people in your church worship service as if you are standing on the platform. Scan the congregation in your mind's eye. Now answer this question: What percentage of the group you are picturing would you consider to be Christians? There is no correct answer, so don't feel that you are being judgmental. Now, picturing the same group of people, answer this question: What percentage of the group would you say are disciples?

If you end up with different percentages for each question, you have bought into this view of discipleship. Typically, most people will say that there are more Christians in their group than there are disciples, demonstrating that they believe a person can be a Christian without being a disciple. This understanding suggests that discipleship is optional and perpetuates a view of two classes of Christians in the church: believers and disciples. Most importantly for our discussion, this view suggests that evangelism makes believers and discipleship make disciples out of believers.

Once again, Wilkins provides noteworthy insights into the problems associated with this dualistic view of faith:

> One difficulty lies in the interpretation of Jesus' discipleship messages and the spiritual nature of the audiences to whom he is directing his message. For example, when Jesus gives a message directed to the "crowds" which calls them to count the cost before they become his "disciples" (Lk 14:25–33), or when he tells the rich young ruler to give all his riches to the poor before he can enter into eternal life (Mt 19:16–22), what is the spiritual nature of the crowds? Of the ruler? Are they already believers or not?

What is the meaning of the message? Is it a call to deeper commitment or a call to salvation? An additional difficulty appears when we notice that in its various forms this model relies upon a two-class system of Christians, a problematic concept in biblical discipleship.[7]

This view allows us to differentiate and choose between ministry missions of evangelism and discipleship. It makes room for bringing people to salvation without any need for further growth—discipleship is optional. Those who choose to become disciples can take on the "extra" work of growing deeper in their faith. This dichotomy is not found in Scripture. Rather, it has been a fabrication of our faith formation programs. Our theology has been shaped by our methodology.

A biblical theology of discipleship recognizes that in the Gospels and Acts, the term *disciple* most commonly describes a true follower of Christ, and that the imperative in Jesus' commission to *make disciples* is understood to mean making disciples out of nonbelievers. To become a disciple is to enter into a journey of lifelong discipleship at the moment of conversion. Discipleship is not a second, optional step in the Christian life; discipleship *is* the Christian life. At the very moment of conversion, a person becomes a disciple of Jesus, and the process of growing as a Christian is known as discipleship.[8]

For Bonhoeffer, entrance into the Christian life is nothing less than the beginning of the journey of discipleship, and anything less is considered cheap grace. "Cheap grace is the preaching of forgiveness without requiring repentance, baptism without church disciplines, Communion without confession, absolution without personal confession. Cheap grace is grace without *discipleship*, grace without the cross, grace without Jesus Christ, living and incarnate."[9]

Bonhoeffer further addresses the church's pressing problem, which he describes as the paradox of living the Christian life in the modern world. His resolution for this problem is, of course, centered on grace.

Happy are they who have reached the end of the road we seek to tread, who are astonished to discover the by no means self-evident truth that grace is costly just because it is the grace of God in Jesus Christ. Happy are the simple followers of Jesus Christ who have been overcome by his grace, and are able to sing of the all-sufficient grace of Christ with humbleness of heart. Happy are they who, knowing that grace, can live in the world without being of it, who, by following Jesus Christ, are so assured of their heavenly citizenship that they are truly free to live their lives in this world. Happy are they who know that *discipleship* means the life, which springs from grace, and that grace simply means discipleship. Happy are they who have become Christians in this sense of the word. For them the word of grace has proved a fount of mercy.[10]

Dallas Willard further argues that the Christian faith is no two-step process in which salvation comes first and discipleship follows as an optional second step. Willard suggests that the aim of the church is "twofold: the effective proclamation of the Christian gospel to all humanity, making 'disciples' from every nation or ethnic group, and the development of those disciples' character into the character of Christ himself 'teaching them to do all things whatsoever I have commanded you' (Matt. 28:20). If these are done well, all else desirable will follow."[11]

When we fail to develop the character of disciples into the character of Christ, we have failed to make disciples. When we focus solely on building the character of disciples within our community of faith, without seeking to make new disciples, we fail to fulfill the Great Commission. Of course, the character development described by Willard is not confined to the post-conversion life. Even as we proclaim the gospel, the Spirit of God is at work in the lives of those who will one day call Christ Lord and Savior. It is essential for those seeking after God to humble themselves before God in receiving the grace that is offered to them. Such humility in the midst of conversion marks a significant moment of character development.

Therefore, we can declare that transformation is the process of developing our character into the character of Christ, and that the transformation process begins prior to conversion and continues throughout the life of a genuine disciple. Wilkins summarizes well this understanding of Christ's command. "This model of discipleship emphasizes that as Jesus called men and women to him, and he sent his disciples out to make other disciples, he was calling men and women into a saving relationship with himself that would make a difference in the new disciples' lives. Therefore, Jesus' purpose in the Great Commission included both conversion and growth—that is, 'making disciples' meant that one became a disciple at the moment of conversion and that growth in discipleship was the natural result of the new disciple's life."[12]

Comprehensive student ministry understands evangelism as the starting point of discipleship, and discipleship as a lifelong journey of faith that produces growth along the way. Failure to engage in evangelism results in our inability to make disciples. Without evangelism, we can certainly mentor the disciples within our fellowship to grow in their faith—as we should, and as Christian parents desire—but we are unable to make new disciples as Jesus commanded. New disciples are found in the conversion process that results from evangelism.

Likewise, to assume that we have fulfilled the Great Commission by ushering people into the kingdom through conversion experiences, without continuing to mentor them through the discipleship process, is to our folly. Christ intended that the ministry of his church be transformational, as his earthly ministry was transformational. We are called to meet students where they are on life's journey and to walk with them through a seamless process of discovering Christ, growing in Christlikeness, and developing a lifelong relationship with Christ and his bride, the church.

The Gift of Transformation

As a child, Steve Jobs, cofounder of Apple, was an unmotivated troublemaker in school who regularly rebelled against his teachers and the curriculum, which he found less than challenging. Reflecting on those elementary school years to his biographer, Jobs said, "I was kind of bored for the first few years, so I occupied myself by getting into trouble."[13] Pranks with friends were the order of the day. "Like we made little posters announcing 'Bring Your Pet to School Day.' It was crazy, with dogs chasing cats all over, and the teachers were beside themselves."[14] About once a year his pranks pushed the limits and he would be sent home from school, as with this third-grade prank: "One time we set off an explosive under the chair of our teacher, Mrs. Thurman. We gave her a nervous twitch."[15]

In fourth grade, Jobs' life underwent a transformation that was sparked by an insightful teacher. She saw Steve Jobs for who he could become rather than for the troublemaker that he was. "After school one day, she gave me this workbook with math problems in it, and said, 'I want you to take it home and do this.' And I thought, 'are you nuts?' And then she pulled out one of these giant lollipops that seemed as big as the world. And she said, 'When you're done with it, if you get it mostly right, I will give you this and five dollars.' And I handed it back within two days."[16]

Such bribes continued for a time, but after a few months the enticements ceased, as Mrs. Hill had captured his imagination for learning, and he would do anything to please her. Mrs. Hill ventured outside the mandated curriculum for her inquisitive student. She gave him work that was challenging and bought him electrical and mechanical hobby kits that stimulated his aptitude for problem solving. Jobs attested to the transformational impact that Mrs. Hill had on his life, saying, "I learned more from her than any other teacher, and if it hadn't been for her I'm sure I would have gone to jail."[17]

Do we, like Mrs. Hill, see students as the people they could become, rather than the troublemakers they are? Transformation occurs when we move from being the person that we are to becoming the person we were created to be. This process occurs in a variety of ways, but it is most often linked in some way to another person who speaks into our lives. Who has been a Mrs. Hill in your life? Perhaps it was a person who motivated you when you were unmotivated, inspired you when you were uninspired, challenged you when you were lethargic, or supported you when you were weak. God works through others in our transformation process, and God works through us in the transformation process of others. But before we can be of any use to God in his transforming work, we have to be willing to see others as God sees them. We must see the potential in others and see them for who they can become, not simply for who they are. Teenagers are not, in the words of Richard Lerner, "problems to be fixed, but people to be developed. They are not immature or incomplete adults; they are active partners in their own positive transition to adulthood."[18]

The opening sentences of books always intrigue me. They set the stage, spark interest, and raise curiosity. One of the best opening lines ever, in my humble opinion, is crafted as a riddle in John Burke's *No Perfect People Allowed*. Burke asks, "What do a Buddhist, a biker couple, a gay-rights activist, a transient, a high-tech engineer, a Muslim, a twentysomething single mom, a Jew, a couple living together, and an atheist all have in common? They are the future of the church in America!"[19]

Burke understands the importance of transformation and the value of accepting people where they are. He has nurtured a "come as you are" culture in his congregation, which invites people who are both near to God and far from God to enter into a community of faith that is seeking understanding. This is a community of people seeking to understand themselves, seeking to understand God, and seeking to understand who God is in their lives and their faith community.

People who are far from God tend to be keenly aware of their situation. They may not be able to articulate their spiritual condition in theological terms, but they are aware of the condition of their souls through the conviction of the Holy Spirit. They do not need a rebuke that confirms their condition and reinforces the notion that turning to God will invite condemnation. They need acceptance and understanding.

Philip Yancey recounts the story of a woman in desperate need of help. She was homeless and in poor health. Without a job to purchase food for her young daughter, she turned to prostitution, and she rented her daughter to men in order to pay for her drug habit. Upon sharing her story with a friend of Yancey's, the friend fell speechless, barely able to stomach what he had heard. Finally, he broke the silence, asking the woman if she had ever considered going to a church for help. Her response was more surprising than her story: "Church! Why would I ever go there? They'd just make me feel even worse than I already do!"[20]

Burke unapologetically declares that while he wants his church to accept new people as they are, he doesn't want them to stay as they are. Transformational growth is the goal, but acceptance is the starting point. Rather than trying to instantly fix people, Burke suggests that we must accept and love people in the midst of their current situations, while always pointing to the grace of God. The apostle Paul makes clear our role in the transformation process: "If you love your neighbor, you will fulfill the requirements of God's law" (Rom. 13:8 NLT). God does the transforming, and God does the fixing. We serve as mediators of God's grace. Burke brilliantly illustrates the proper nature of our posture toward others.

> If you saw a Rembrandt covered in mud, you wouldn't focus on the mud or treat it like mud. Your primary concern would not be the mud at all—though it would need to be removed. You'd be ecstatic to have something so valuable in your care. But if you clean it up by yourself, you might damage it. So you would carefully bring the work of art to a master who could guide you and help you restore it to the condition originally intended. When people begin treating one another as God's masterpiece waiting to be revealed, God's grace grows in their lives and cleanses them.[21]

In both the church and in student ministries, we need to first and foremost see the Rembrandt that is before us. As we encounter people who are far from God, we need to thank God for bringing them to us and offer them the grace-giving acceptance that Christ offers all people regardless of the mud that shrouds them. None of us is perfect; we are all splattered with mud and constantly require God's renewing grace in our lives as we move through a lifelong process of transformation. Accepting into our ministries people who are far from God requires understanding growth as a work in process. "All people are in process, and if they are willing, God is going to be gently cleaning the mud off his Rembrandt until their final day. So we must be patient like God."[22]

Beyond Balance, Toward Synergy

Developing a student ministry that strives to create an environment of transformation for all teenagers regardless of their proximity to God requires us to move, both theologically and pragmatically, beyond the myth of balance. For too long, the discourse has focused on finding a balance between evangelism and discipleship in church-based student ministry. Some ministries have been accused of being a mile wide and an inch deep, while others are scolded for having an inward focus and being indifferent to outreach. As student ministry continues to develop in the twenty-first century, we must recognize the need for all people to be continually transformed. We must come to understand that evangelism is the starting point of genuine discipleship, not simply a method of salvation. We must recognize that discipleship begins with evangelism and cannot be relegated to nurturing the already-convinced. If we are to go and make disciples, we must begin by sharing the good news of Jesus Christ with those who are far from God.

Searching for a balance between evangelism and discipleship is an exercise in futility. Rather than striving to gain more of one and less of another to achieve balance, evangelism and discipleship must be viewed as synergistic, since together they promote lifelong transformation. Fostering genuine transformation in the lives of *all* adolescents, regardless of where they are in their spiritual journey, is the mission of student ministry. This process of transformation occurs when we meet students with *authenticity*, and with *unconditional love*, and when we offer them *genuine relationships*.

Authenticity

In previous generations, students were skeptical of the message. Today, students are equally skeptical of the messenger. Our culture has changed, and teenagers no longer grow up with an innate feeling that they can trust adults. Our certificate of authenticity is no longer a given. Perhaps adults are less trustworthy than in generations past, or perhaps the prevalence of contemporary media has exposed the depraved aspects of adulthood that have always existed. Either way, young people in our culture grow up with an implicit distrust of adults, as they witness the very people they should be looking up to behaving badly.

For many young people, growing up in a postmodern culture is about growing up alone. This is an emotional aloneness that seeps into the core of one's being. Janet Bernardi describes her encounter with a twenty-something friend who captures this sense of aloneness.

> Not long ago, I found a friend crying because her brother had failed to fulfill a promise—again. She was devastated by the realization that she had

never been able to rely on him, or on anyone. My friend . . . learned very early to rely only on herself. She felt abandoned by her father, who had left after her parents' divorce. She felt abandoned by her mother, who had pursued her career and left her with a nanny. And she felt she could never rely on her brother, who was following well the examples his parents had set. She felt alone.

Though a story like this could be told about individuals in any generation, the situation is so common [today] that it has become the norm. Many, perhaps most, of us have never experienced real reliability and responsibility. My friend cannot rely on her family for support—nor can she rely on her mechanic to be honest, her doctor to prescribe only the tests that are necessary, her friends to help bear her burdens, or strangers to be kind. She feels afraid of being shot, afraid of being held up at the cash machine, afraid to go alone on a date with a man. Like many her age, she is financially independent and lives with roommates. But no one really needs her, and she needs no one. This is aloneness.

My friend is like many of us. We've been raised to think only of ourselves—we've been raised by the "me generation." We were *told* to think only of ourselves, so we *had* to think only of ourselves. No one else thought about us. We raised ourselves. We couldn't really trust anyone.

Aloneness is being alone and not being able to trust anyone.[23]

How can young people implicitly trust ministers, teachers, and police officers when they are bombarded by countless stories of abhorrent behavior of people in these positions? Encountering these kinds of stories and experiences creates poor reputations for all adults and encourages a culture of skepticism among young people. Chap Clark describes this feeling of distrust through the eyes of high school students.

By the time children, even successful ones, reach high school and middle adolescence, they are aware of the fact that for most of their lives they have been pushed, prodded, and molded to become a person whose value rests in his or her ability to serve someone else's agenda. Whether it is a coach, a school teacher, a parent, a music teacher, or a Sunday school counselor, mid-adolescents intuitively believe that nearly every adult they have encountered has been subtly out to get something from them. When this awareness begins to take root during middle adolescence, it leads to frustration, anger, and a sense of betrayal.[24]

In order to address this adolescent skepticism, we must create a culture within student ministries and the church at large that welcomes and honors teenagers for who they are, rather than simply using them for our own agendas.

Unconditional Love

When the popular movie *Happy Feet* arrived at the local movie theater, our family could not resist indulging in a couple hours of entertainment offered by lovable penguins. Climbing to the top of the theater's stadium seating, we positioned ourselves in the last row, overlooking the entire theater. As the movie began, I realized that I was watching a different story unfold than everyone else in the theater. I was encountering a story about adolescents in North America.

More often than not, teenagers resemble the misfit penguin Mumble, who is born into a society of emperor penguins that value their young only for what they can *do*—rather than for who they *are*. And what they must be able to do is sing, but Mumble can't carry a tune to save his life. Apparently a penguin without a "heart song" isn't a penguin at all, so Mumble is quickly abandoned by his peers, parents, teachers, and the elders of the penguin nation.

In much the same way, teenagers today are forsaken when they cannot perform or live up to the contrived expectations of the adults around them. And while most of them tolerate this treatment through middle school, they begin to figure out what is happening to them early on in high school, and they either rebel against the adult world or retreat into the pain of isolation. Few are strong enough to follow the path of the heroic penguin Mumble, who diligently searches for his true identity and sets out to prove that there is intrinsic value in who he was created to be—a dancer—regardless of how much this differs from his community's expectations.

Not long after seeing the movie, I discussed these issues with some youth leaders and dared to ask an irreverent question: "How do *we* abandon kids in our ministries?" After a few seconds of awkward silence, one brave soul declared, "We abandon them when we build relationships with students who then don't *do* what we want—commit to Christ, participate in a Bible study, go to camp. Then we move on to other kids who *will* do what we want them to do, leaving the others in our wake." That opened the floodgates of a conversation that lasted over an hour as we discussed dozens of ways we abandon kids in youth ministries every week. (Give this conversation a try at your next leadership meeting.)

What I quickly came to understand is that we abandon teenagers in very subtle ways. Rarely is this abandonment as obvious as when a family goes through a divorce and the children feel abandoned by their parents, or when a youth minister leaves the church and the teenagers feel abandoned by their leader. It happens when teenagers graduate from the middle school ministry and transition into the high school ministry with none of the middle school leaders making the transition with them. We may feel that we are called to middle school ministry, and we may say that students all go through transitions, but we are actually modeling *conditional* love. Our love is based on the condition of a student's age. "As long as you are in middle school I'll love you, but now that you're in high school, our relationship is over." We do the same thing when high school students graduate and go to college. Yet with all the technology at our disposal—such as email, instant messaging, text messaging, cell phones, blogs, and Facebook—how can there be any excuse for abandoning our relationships with students when they go off to college? We have a long way to go in understanding genuine, unconditional love.

Adolescent psychologist Michael Bradley recounts a conversation with a fourteen-year-old who felt invisible among the adults in his life.

"So, you were saying," I continued, "that your dad can't remember how old you are, because . . . you don't do, well, *unusual* things?" "It's not my dad's fault," Matt explained. "My dad's great. He's a really nice guy. He works two jobs for us and never complains or gets mad or anything. He's yelled at me, like, twice in my life that I can remember, and once was when I let the refrigerator fall down the basement steps, so that hardly counts." Without pausing to explain the refrigerator catastrophe, he went on. "It's me, not my dad. I'm, like, so . . . boring, and . . . I don't know, so . . . *ordinary*, that no one really remembers me." He thought for a minute. "It's like I'm not there a lot even when I am," he summarized matter-of-factly. . . . "It's like at school. I don't get teased or bullied—much—you know, just the usual stuff, and I do OK with grades, so, no, I'm not *down* on myself. It's just that I'm not *up* on myself either. I mean, like, lots of kids, they're somebody. They're, like, football players or student council types or real smart or real popular—you know, the cool kids. I don't mind that I'm not like any of that. Only sometimes, it feels . . . funny. [You see] there's these teachers that I like a whole lot, and I don't think they can remember my name. And sometimes . . . well, this just happened again today . . . when I was trying to talk with them, you know, trying to hang out with them a little bit, one of the cool kids walks up—he's a basketball star—and, well, the teachers just started to talk over me to the cool kid—like I wasn't there anymore, like I just vanished in the middle of a sentence. But, I understand, you know, 'cause I wasn't saying anything important, and the cool kid, he's talking about the game Friday and all. I couldn't compete with that. I never can compete because there's nothing special about me that would make anybody interested in me. That's what I mean about not being there. Even my parents, I think they're bored with me sometimes." In spite of his words, Matt was not feeling sorry for himself, nor was he fishing for sympathy. He was simply narrating his ordinary life as he saw it. "Do you want to know what I'm thinking again?" he asked. When I laughed and nodded, he seemed pleased. "I was thinking about how I need to be more than I am, but I don't know how."[25]

How often do we do the exact same thing in our ministries? We're talking to one student when another teenager strolls into the room, and without so much as an "Excuse me," we abandon the conversation and engage the other teenager. Maybe the teen who walked in is someone we have not seen in a few weeks, or who is scheduled to lead the worship music that night, or who won the big game Friday evening. We abandon teenagers without even realizing it, and they feel the same kind of pain that Matt feels all the time.

It's common for potential volunteers to ask, "How much time do I have to commit if I get involved in the student ministry?" Frankly, I refuse to answer that question anymore, because teenagers' lives are too messy these days. If we are committed to promoting transformation in the lives of teenagers, we have to begin committing to relationships rather than to specific programs with predictable time commitments. In the words of Brian McLaren, "We need to start counting conversations."[26] Some students need more attention than others, and they all need genuine relationships with Christian adults outside of and beyond regularly scheduled ministry programs.

When Todd Szymczak was pastor of student ministries at Grace Chapel in Lexington, Massachusetts, he epitomized this understanding of student ministry with his commitment to the longevity of the faith formation process. Recently he posted this reflection on his blog after spending time with a student, who is now in college and making decisions about

Accepting Young People as They Are

It's easy for us to fall into the trap of pursuing relationships in order to satisfy our own needs for companionship, accomplishment, and self-worth. When someone then fails to live up to our expectations, we are tempted to either move on until we find another who does, or treat them as a "project" to be fixed. Our needs and personal agenda can easily cloud our vision of the uniqueness of the other, their innate gifts, and the blessing they can be to us. We need to pray for the grace to accept young people for who they are, not who we think they should be, and to love them for no other reason than because it's what Jesus calls us to do (Mark 12:30–31).

Sarah Dickinson, First Presbyterian Church,
Douglasville, Georgia

what area to major in, how best to use his time on summer break, and what the future holds after graduation.

> As I was listening to this person share all of these things, I was remembering back to when they were in junior high and high school, and how much they have grown and matured in their faith journey over the years. I remembered the highs and lows of their life, and the difference in them between then and now. To see and hear that their life is committed to God's leading was exciting. It reminded me of other students who I continue to keep in touch with who have gone on in ministry, or those who are active in their church, and those who are using their gifts and passions for ministry and service, either vocationally or as volunteers.[27]

This demonstrates the importance of longevity in relationships that are developed in ministry. Graduating from high school or from the student ministry does not mean graduating from the relationships, as if they are conditional upon one's membership in a club.

Student ministry is an unending conversation with students who are trying to find their intrinsic value in life and who need to be honored for who they are—not just what they can do. That kind of unconditional love knows no limits.

Genuine Relationships

The relationships that adults develop with teenagers must be authentic. Relationships in our society run the spectrum from authentic to abusive. While most adults are not abusive, few are genuinely authentic. Many relationships between adults and teens are highly conditional, and the relationship is often used to extract something out of the teenager. Much like the stereotypical image of a used-car salesman, the relationship is important only as long as the seller believes that the relationship is progressing toward a deal. Once the seller realizes that the customer is not buying what he has to sell, the relationship is over and it is on to the next patron.

Andrew Root suggests that genuine relationships develop out of a desire to know, love, and be with one another.[28] Friends do not choose other friends because they are easy to manipulate. Parents do not decide to have children so that they can have free labor around the house. When we are most authentic in our relationships, we fall in love, make friends, and have children because we want to be in community with the other persons—not because of what they can *be* or *do* for us. When teenagers encounter this type of authentic relationship, transformation becomes inevitable. If we truly believe that teenagers matter, then our "relational ministry must be built on unconditional love, with the hope that adolescents themselves would become incarnational agents who engage the world with compassion and care."[29]

When we approach teenagers with an agenda, we become—at best—marketing representatives for God rather than partners on a journey of faith. This occurs very easily when we use the joys and junk of a teenager's life to leverage control and promote our agenda. When we overspiritualize a student's story, we are promoting our agenda rather than valuing the student for who they are and what they have accomplished. We overspiritualize when a student shares the joy of receiving an award and we launch into an analogy about how our *real* reward is in heaven—before we even say congratulations. Or if a student tells us how upset she is over a low grade on a report card, we overspiritualize when we quickly chime in, "That's okay. God's report card is all that really matters."

Rather than engaging in the journey of the teenager, sometimes we commandeer the moment to promote our agenda. Yet instead of seizing the moment in an attempt to move the student along, the better part of wisdom tells us to recognize that the journey is already in motion; the story is unfolding, and the student has offered us the privilege of entering into that story. When adults and teenagers engage in authentic relationships, Root suggests, "they encounter one another in the reality of Jesus Christ. Thus they are given data which can transform them, their histories and their interactions with culture and its ideologies."[30] When we enter into the story of a teenager with authenticity, we find that our faith story becomes transformed as well. When we are honest, we recognize that teenagers have contributed to our faith story as much as we have contributed to theirs.

The purpose of relationships is to be together and care for one another in community. This is a biblical design for humanity that holds great significance in our contemporary context. The Triune God designed us for relationship. God's story and our story merge as God meets us in our humanity. Speaking to us and walking with us, God has chosen to make us covenant partners. Over and over again, God declared to the people of Israel, "You will be my people, and I will be your God" (Ezek. 36:28).[31] This relationship turns out to be a long and tumultuous journey for God's people. It is a story that includes times of great intimacy with God, as well as times of rebellion against God. There are no quick fixes and no easy decisions. This journey requires time and perspective, as God invites us to merge our whole story with God's story. In the same manner, we offer time and perspective as we invite students to share their whole lives with us, so that we both might experience God's grace together.

My son and I have developed, quite by accident, a summer ritual over the past few years. One summer my high school age daughter and her friends wanted to travel a couple hours from home to spend a day at Six Flags. Ryan was in middle school at the time and came along for the ride, but rather than going to the amusement park, he and I created our own day of adventure. Without any planning, we literally made it up as we went along. First we made a stop at the Naismith Memorial Basketball Hall of Fame, and then we had lunch and visited the Dr. Seuss National Memorial Statue Garden. We followed this by a round of miniature golf, a late afternoon movie, and dinner. Driving back to Six Flags to retrieve the girls, we encountered a thunderstorm, which Ryan documented with a quick finger and great timing, capturing photos of lightning strikes through the car window. A few days later I noticed that he had posted some pictures of our adventure on Facebook with the caption: *Best day of my life.*

That day was filled with ordinary activities—nothing special or planned. It was just a day together, and we continue to enjoy that experience annually, mixing in different activities each year. Transformation happens through life experiences. Taking students deeper in their faith is about having multilayered experiences and conversations. We often quip that you can't take anyone deeper in the faith than you have gone. By this, we typically mean that you can teach someone else only as much of the Bible as you know yourself. In reality, this means that you can't share your experiences with God if you are not having any experiences with God.

Root calls this kind of ministry "place-sharing," and it puts a premium on "doing life" together. Beyond simply gathering for youth meetings, it means truly engaging in the lives of students between the meetings. Transformation happens when real friends do real life together as they seek to understand one another and to process the joys and junk of life. As students and youth leaders begin to understand one another in personal ways, they cannot help but speak into each other's lives. When we imagine our ministries as being with students (all students, both near and far from God), we become a profound witness to their value and a significant witness to a God who values them more than we could ever imagine.

When students matter, transformation happens. Accepting students where they are and offering authentic and unconditional friendship provides a context in which students thrive and become the people they were created to be. A group of teenagers crafted this definition of genuine relationships: "A friend is someone you can rely on through thick and thin, who understands you, and who would tell you the cold hard truth. A friend is someone with similar interests who you want to spend time with. A friend understands your jokes and makes you smile."[32]

We are called to walk with teenagers in a journey of friendship regardless of their station in life or their location inside or outside of the church. We are called to relationships that transcend agendas and are filled with compassion.

Moratorium Matters

In 2012, British singer-songwriter Adele Adkins won six Grammy awards, for everything from best album to best music video. Her treasure trove included a Grammy for best pop solo performance of her much-analyzed song "Someone Like You." Social scientists have studied the ballad, and for good reason: the music makes people cry. This phenomenon became so widespread that late-night comedians seized the opportunity to parody the tearjerker of a song, much to the delight of their audiences.

Psychologists, intrigued by this sort of visceral reaction to certain types of music, have investigated a host of songs that constantly induce physical reactions such as chills, tears, and goose bumps. Participants in one such study identified the tear-triggering moments in a variety of songs. John Sloboda's careful analysis of the participants' feedback revealed that over 80 percent of the tear-triggering moments contained a musical embellishment known as an *appoggiatura*, "a type of ornamental note that clashes with the melody just enough to create a dissonant sound."[33]

When a listener encounters the dissonance created by an appoggiatura, there is a momentary visceral reaction of tension that is relieved when the music returns to the predictable melody. Physiologically, chills, goose bumps, or tears often come upon the listener when this tension is resolved. When numerous appoggiaturas are encountered in succession, they create a cycle of tension and resolution, like the ups and downs of a roller coaster ride, which provokes an even deeper response. This is when the tears begin to flow, and a song such as "Someone Like You" is declared a real tearjerker.[34]

This cycle of tension and resolution creates something new, unexpected, and creative, and it is often something greater than the sum of its components. Such a cycle is important in numerous aspects of life. When learning to ride a bicycle, a child experiences the tension between acceleration and balance that produces stability. In politics, tension between various ideologies creates a system of checks and balances. This same cycle of tension and resolution in ministry creates a fertile environment for spiritual growth.

When students matter, we value the disequilibrium in their lives. While parents, pastors, and youth leaders alike wish that the faith formation of teenagers looked like a straight line constantly moving up and to the right, such a romantic view of faith formation is neither realistic, healthy, nor biblical. Faith formation necessitates questioning, exploring, and wrestling with contradictions. A church that values the faith formation of adolescents must become a hospitable environment in which they can work out their understanding of God.[35]

We see this kind of faith formation throughout the Scriptures. Moses wrestles with God about leading the people out of Israel. David betrays God and his people. Peter is the rock upon which Jesus will build his church one minute, and moments later Jesus refers to him as Satan. Jesus' disciples seem to understand his teachings one day and then are found to have little faith the next. Thomas raises doubts about Jesus' resurrection. Jacob, Abraham, Sarah, Rahab, and others are represented in the gallery of faith in Hebrews 11, but an examination of these lives reveals that most, if not all, of these faithful men and women experienced moments of uncertainty, doubt, concern, confusion, and questioning of the God they loved. Through the authenticity of their engagement with God, they became testimonies of discipleship, approved by faith and strengthened by their perseverance through tough times (Heb. 11:39).

When David writes: "Even though I walk through the darkest valley, I will fear no evil," he gives no suggestion that this is only a possibility (Ps. 23:4). He is not saying, "*Just in case* I end up walking through a dark valley. . . ." No, the metaphor of the shepherd instructs us that we *will* walk through dark valleys, just as sheep must travel through dangerous, narrow valleys to reach new fertile pastures and fresh water. In the same way that a skilled shepherd protects vulnerable sheep from wild animals, the Lord protects his people, refreshing our souls and guiding us through dark periods of life and along the right paths. Dissonance happens, and, if we embrace instead of resist it, it offers beautiful moments of growth in the faith formation process.

Four Identity Statuses

Identity development and faith development, while not identical, are interwoven and contain similarities. This makes identity formation research helpful in understanding the importance of allowing adolescents space to wrestle with their faith in the midst of a caring community of believers. Expanding on Erik Erikson's theory of identity development, James Marcia outlines four categories of identity status: **diffusion**, **foreclosure**, **moratorium**, and **achievement**.[36] (These terms are bolded throughout this chapter to indicate use of the terms as status categories.)

DIFFUSION

People in the status of **diffusion** have not made any commitments regarding their identity or their faith, which, for our purposes, is an intrinsic aspect of identity. Having had limited exposure to any religious traditions, they may not yet understand the choices available to them. Or they may be overwhelmed and confused by the vast array of choices to which they have been exposed. Others in this status may have an embedded, self-serving religiosity, which can be described as an *extrinsic* faith. "Extrinsic religiosity is a belief system that is compartmentalized, prejudiced, exclusionary, utilitarian, and self-serving," write Brian Griffith and Julie Griggs. "Participation in religious activities is based on a cost versus benefit analysis."[37] This is the most unsophisticated status, and it is often identified in pre- and early adolescents, though even adults can find themselves in this status under certain circumstances.

FORECLOSURE

People operating in the status of **foreclosure** conform to the expectations of others (such as parents, teachers, coaches, and pastors), without exploring a range of possibilities concerning identity, faith, values, and character. Such conformity is tied to the environment in which students are living. While they may pursue their own desires in certain areas, they also learn to accommodate to the desires of parents, teachers, peers, coaches, and youth leaders. In this status of faith development, "motivation is still external and self-serving. Adherence to religious beliefs tends to be superficial and compartmentalized due to a lack of rigorous critique and evaluation. Through religious teachings, social learning, and participation in rituals, a foreclosed religious identity is uncritically adopted."[38] Students are content to accept the norms of their faith community but may often behave differently in various social contexts, depending on the values of the group from which they are seeking acceptance.

Moratorium

As critical thinking skills emerge and adolescents are showered with the values of parents, peers, teachers, coaches, and youth leaders, they eventually begin to wrestle with issues of identity and the place of faith within that identity, questioning who they are and what they believe. Marcia refers to this status as **moratorium** because it is a time of active reflection on the beliefs and values as a person decides whether or not they actually believe what they uncritically accepted during **foreclosure**. "Honest self-reflection, guided by sincere spiritual inquiry, provides the courage to admit to and move beyond self-serving or conformist religiosity," suggest Griffith and Griggs. "These spiritual seekers are in the process of reformulating and internalizing spiritual beliefs."[39] People within the **moratorium** status are not waiting for something to happen; rather they are actively exploring various commitments but have not yet made a decision. They may appear to be experiencing an identity crisis and often feel perplexed, unbalanced, or dissatisfied, but they are in a process of moving forward toward identity formation and commitments.

Achievement

People in this status have gone through an identity exploration process in **moratorium**, questioning, searching, and evaluating their options. As a result, they have made a commitment to an identity, faith, values, and character. "Religiosity is now internally motivated (intrinsic) and pursued as an end in itself. It is an attempt to live for ideals other than self-protection, need fulfillment, or approval from others."[40] Achieving such an identity provides a sense of self-acceptance and a stable self-definition. Beliefs and practices are integrated into the whole of a person's life, and the person pursues spiritual growth and maturity with intentionality. Faith has become the central lens through which thoughts and decisions are filtered, as one's individual life story is seen in the perspective of the larger story of God and the community of God's people.

Identity **achievement** should not be thought of as a final destination. Instead, we can view it as a state of confidence and satisfaction in who a person is and what he or she believes about certain issues at a particular time in life. Think of it as a point of stability that is more embedded in one's identity than is the stability found in **foreclosure**. In the best-case scenario, individuals who have reached **achievement** status have arrived, as a result of rigorous exploration in **moratorium**, at a level of commitment that includes a thorough and precise knowledge of the faith issue; an external manifestation and operational practice of the particular belief; confidence, stability, and optimism concerning the future; and a resistance to wavering from the commitment.[41]

The Four Statuses and Faith Formation

Understanding these statuses is important for student ministry. Churches often demonstrate little tolerance for people going through **moratorium**, and parents who are delighted with the identity of their teenager in **foreclosure** often panic when their child moves through the dissonance of **moratorium**. They may think their child is losing her faith when she is actually discovering her faith in new and meaningful ways. For those in ministry, **moratorium** matters. Rather than confining teenagers to the **foreclosure** status, or behaving as if parents did something wrong to cause their child to end up in **moratorium**, the church community should support students and their parents when teenagers experience this important stage.

These statuses are helpful for understanding how adolescents adopt and experience their faith. Formation may have a general developmental flow, however, there is no clear and consistent pathway. Regardless of a person's location within the four statuses, there exists the possibility of movement in a variety of directions.[42]

Figure 2.1. Status Movements in Identity Formation

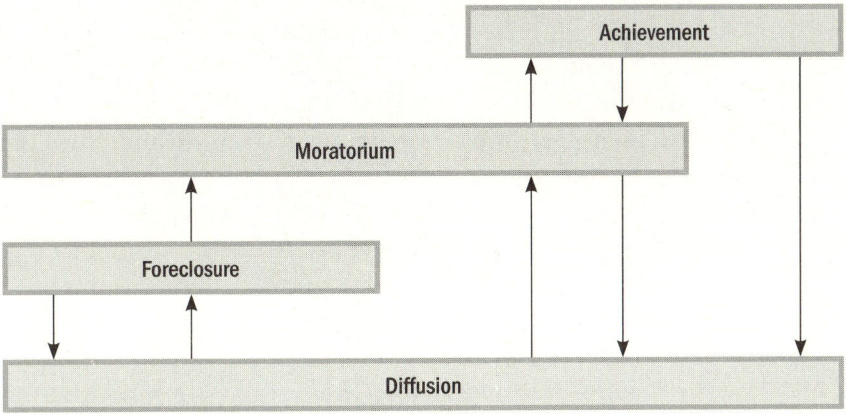

- Moving from **Diffusion**

    People who are in the status of **diffusion** may move into **foreclosure** by latching on to the faith construct presented to them by their faith community through parents, pastors, and youth leaders, without exploring other possibilities.

They may move directly into the status of **moratorium** as they begin exploring various faith constructs through theological reflection.

Or they may continue in the **diffusion** status, neither exploring issues of faith nor conforming to the faith tradition presented to them.

- Moving from **Foreclosure**

People who find themselves in the status of **foreclosure** may move into **moratorium** if certain aspects of their faith commitments are challenged and they begin to explore alternative possibilities.

Or they may continue in the **foreclosure** status, carrying into adulthood a commitment to the faith as it has been passed on to them in childhood or adolescence without questions, doubt, or exploration.

Many adolescents move into emerging adulthood in **foreclosure**, only to begin a time of exploration in an environment of freedom that is afforded them through living on their own at college or in some other context.

- Moving from **Moratorium**

People in the status of **moratorium** may move into the status of **achievement** by establishing firm, meaningful commitments to specific faith values after a time of exploration and theological reflection.

Alternatively, they may move into **diffusion** if their early faith commitments lose meaning, and they surrender their search for meaningful faith commitments.

A person in **moratorium** cannot move into **foreclosure**, since the nature of **moratorium** is exploration, not mere acceptance.

Giving up on exploration results in **diffusion**, while completing exploration results in **achievement**.

Individuals coming out of **foreclosure** into **moratorium** may wrestle with issues and recommit to the same values they were committed to in **foreclosure**.

Yet they have not returned to **foreclosure**; rather, they have moved into **achievement**, because they now own the commitments that they once accepted without question.

- Moving from **Achievement**

Finally, people in the status of **achievement** may continue in **achievement** by maintaining the battle-tested commitments they sorted out in **moratorium**.

Or they may return to the status of **moratorium** to work out a faith issue that once seemed resolved, if the resolution has been found unsatisfactory, or to deal with a newly arisen faith issue.

It is also possible for a person to move from **achievement** to **diffusion** if the established faith commitments lose their validity without triggering a return to **moratorium** for further exploration and reflection.

Cyclical Nature of the Statuses

It is extremely important to understand that neither faith nor identity formation is a linear process with a defined beginning, middle, and end. Our identities are constantly in formation, consciously or subconsciously. While we may desire to see students move from **diffusion** to either **foreclosure** or **moratorium**, from **foreclosure** to **moratorium**, and from **moratorium** to **achievement**—the process is not so clean and simple. There are many twists and turns along the journey. While a person may be **achievement**-committed in one area of faith identity, he or she may be wrestling in **moratorium** with another aspect of faith, while remaining content with a **foreclosure** commitment in another aspect of faith.

Many churches use the term *chrysalis* for their formation and discipleship programs, as it is a term that describes transformation. This biological term describes the period of time a caterpillar goes through before it becomes a butterfly. While there is little movement in this stage of butterfly development, chrysalis is the delicate process of changing the fuzzy slug of a caterpillar into a beautiful butterfly with delicate wings and vibrant colors. The butterfly emerges from the chrysalis stage as an adult, expanding its wings and bursting forth as a new creation.

This is indeed a beautiful story of God's magnificent creation, but as an analogy of faith formation, it is theologically bankrupt. The analogy suggests that faith formation is a one-time, instant transformation into Christlikeness. It maintains that our faith formation is completed in a brief and finite period of time, rather than over a lifelong journey of sanctification that requires ongoing movement and dissonance.

When an individual moves from **foreclosure**, **moratorium**, or **achievement** toward **diffusion**, this represents a setback, as the person has abandoned identity concerns, at least temporarily, without coming to any stability in either **foreclosure** or **achievement**. The movement from **achievement** to **moratorium** should not, however, be considered a regression in the formation journey. Rather, it is a natural process of reentering the exploratory exercises of identity development. These **MAMA**

(**Moratorium—Achievement—Moratorium—Achievement**) cycles reflect the continuing nature of the formation process as one strives to make wiser decisions. This understanding of identity development suggests that it is a lifelong process. A person occupies a variety of statuses at the same time, even if one is dominant. The identity and faith development in adolescence is an early creation that is subject to reformation. In this sense, identity status applies to more than just adolescent development. It represents a journey of lifelong development.[43]

Figure 2.2. MAMA Cycles from Adolescence through Late Adulthood

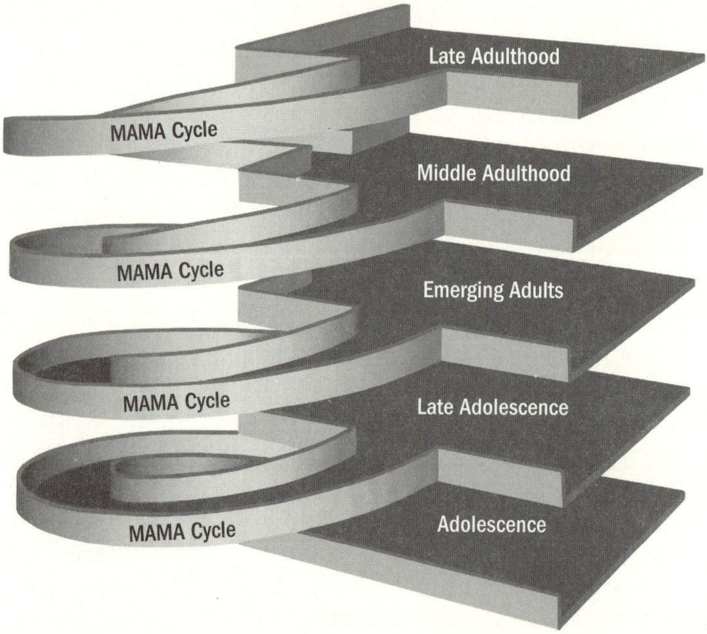

An individual might be expected to complete at least three full cycles of identity reformation following adolescence, or perhaps even more, depending on the number of identity-disrupting events the person encounters over the course of a lifetime. During each **MAMA** cycle, a person may regress into earlier identity statuses, demonstrating confused feelings, irrational thinking, and impulsive action. This is a natural response to dissonance and represents what James Marcia calls "regression with a purpose: to permit the previous structure to fall apart so that a new structure can emerge."[44]

Reformation cycles are an important process in the lifelong journey of identity development, and the time it takes to complete **MAMA** cycles differs according to the person and the surrounding social environment. These cycles may last as little as six months or as long as ten years.[45] Going through **MAMA** cycles is like ascending the spiral ramp of a parking garage, which may appear to be a road to nowhere. Yet carefully navigating the circular ramp gradually brings the car to the next level of the garage.

Traveling through **MAMA** cycles often occurs more quickly in adolescence and more slowly as we get older, because the older we become, the more strongly we tend to resist change. This reformation of identity is typically a gradual and continuous refinement process rather than a radical discarding of one identity to embrace another. Every moment of identity reconstruction represents the accommodation of a wider range of experiences as our identities become broader and more inclusive.[46]

The Mess of *Moratorium*

Generally speaking, the church doesn't like to deal with a mess, even though it is by nature in the messy business of redemption. We would prefer that teenagers embrace the status of **foreclosure** and that their commitment to the status quo be considered **achievement** of their faith identity. Identity theory and personal experience reveal that this is not the reality of faith formation. Disequilibrium in the developmental process is a necessity, but it tends to create messy spiritual formation to one degree or another. Do not underestimate the importance of this process, however: the "individual becomes more and more who she or he truly is as previously undeveloped elements of the personality become realized and new ones become added."[47]

The process by which a person wrestles with faith development is closely tied to the environment in which he or she is processing his faith. Robert Kegan describes the environmental factors necessary for one to engage in meaning making.[48] His ideas are based on the work of Donald Winnicott, who suggests that the environment determines our inclination concerning transformation.[49] Kegan suggests that an environment conducive to transformation comprises three elements: *confirmation*, *contradiction*, and *continuity*.[50] These elements are not successive but must exist at the same time, in a single environment, in order to provide the tension that fosters transformation.

CONFIRMATION

Confirmation occurs when a person is valued and affirmed for who she is without being made to feel that she is falling short of a prescribed

Facing Moratorium without Fear

As those who work with youth, we need to resist the urge to shrink away from helping young people enter into **moratorium**. We may be tempted to play it safe for fear that if we ask a question that is too tough or introduce a concept they might not like the sound of, attendance may go down, we might get an angry phone call from a parent, or we might find ourselves being asked questions we don't know how to answer. We need to pray for courage and wisdom as we lead young people to explore challenging faith issues and trust that as we do, God will do the work in us and the youth. God will help us grow and walk together as a community of disciples even when the path seems muddy and unclear.

Sarah Dickinson, First Presbyterian Church,
Douglasville, Georgia

goal. Confirmation creates an environment marked by safety and security. In the midst of stress, pressure, and others' expectations, confirmation provides a welcome dose of affirmation and acceptance. It embraces the person and her experience with no attached expectations.

CONTRADICTION

Contradiction occurs when a person is confronted with the possibility that his current understanding of faith identity may be inadequate, and he is offered the possibility of something new. Contradiction must be added to the environment because mere confirmation, though essential, is not sufficient for transformation. In fact, confirmation alone leads to stasis. When contradiction is provided, people begin to recognize the limitations of their perspectives. But recognizing the limitations of one's perspective is not enough; friends, teachers, coaches, parents, and youth leaders must offer alternative perspectives in the exploration process. Simply declaring the inadequacy of an adolescent's current perspective can be demoralizing; hence, alternative perspectives are essential for offering visionary directions that facilitate growth. While homogeneous perspectives provide confirmation, alternative perspectives provide the disequilibrium required for faith development, expose the limits of one's current perspective, and provide a vision toward new perspectives.

CONTINUITY

Continuity is essential for fostering transformation, as it provides space to move from one's current position to a new position. Authentic relationships within a community provide continuity as transformation occurs. The relationships remain constant, allowing the person to change within the supportive structure of a community. The community must provide an environment that has the capacity to represent "both old and new worlds at once."[51] This allows an adolescent to enter the environment with established perspectives (**foreclosure**) or no perspectives (**diffusion**), take the necessary time to explore new perspectives (**moratorium**), and transform some views, resulting in a more complete understanding of faith identity (**achievement**). If the environment requires that a person hold certain prescribed beliefs prior to entering, then it is a *closed* environment. Transformation cannot take place in a closed environment, as the freedom to try out new perspectives is restricted. Any exploration would have to occur prior to entering a closed environment. Continuity within a community offers the opportunity to explore possibilities, make mistakes, try on a vision, and practice a new way of understanding faith and identity.

Creating Space for *Moratorium*

Most adolescents will spend time in the status of **moratorium** as they explore their faith identity. Across the breadth of a community of adolescents, these periods of exploration will range from simple questioning that promotes deeper understanding to real crises of faith that require reconsideration of everything once held to be true. Many people fall somewhere in the middle of those extremes. Every adolescent, young adult, and adult responds differently to this exploration process. Most important to remember is that there is no right or wrong way for a person to navigate the status of **moratorium**.

A person who is experiencing **moratorium** generally demonstrates three characteristics. First, a person will pursue new information and knowledge to resolve a faith question. These additional insights should go beyond popular opinion and often involve multiple viewpoints concerning the issue at hand. Second, a person in this season of exploration will either consider a variety of alternatives, bouncing from one to another and back again and holding them all in tension, or the person will explore alternatives and dismiss implausible ones as she or he moves along. Finally, a person in **moratorium** will typically show emotional intensity and a hunger for quick resolution. Excitement and anticipation of new perspectives can easily turn to anxiety and frustration when clarity is not easily achieved. This tension makes people eager for resolution, but it is an excellent indication of healthy investigation.[52]

There are healthy and unhealthy environments for such exploration. Marcia suggests that "most **moratorium** individuals would be expected to advance to identity **achievement** given an average expectable environment. However, they might regress to either **foreclosure** or **diffusion** if their exploratory attempts are punished or discouraged."[53] When pastors, parents, and youth leaders become alarmed by a student's desire to question, explore, and challenge the status quo, they stifle the faith formation process and force the young person into **foreclosure**, at best, or even to **diffusion**. When a student ministry or a church holds exploration at arm's length, teenagers will often comply with the status quo and remain in **foreclosure** longer than they desire, only to move into **moratorium** after leaving the stifling community of their childhood and entering a new community—perhaps in college—that welcomes exploration.

The story of God is a redemptive tale, marked by God's work with humanity that offers reconciliation and continuous transformation.

> Therefore, if anyone is in Christ, the new creation has come: The old has gone, the new is here! All this is from God, who reconciled us to himself through Christ and gave us the ministry of reconciliation: that God was reconciling the world to himself in Christ, not counting people's sins against them. And he has committed to us the message of reconciliation. (2 Cor. 5:17–20)

> But whenever anyone turns to the Lord, the veil is taken away. Now the Lord is the Spirit, and where the Spirit of the Lord is, there is freedom. And we all, who with unveiled faces contemplate the Lord's glory, are being transformed into his image with ever-increasing glory, which comes from the Lord, who is the Spirit. (2 Cor. 3:16–18)

This transformational process requires an open community marked by continuity, acceptance of adolescents no matter where they are on life's journey, and encouragement to explore faith. Such a community supports and challenges them in ways that engage their curiosity and offer new possibilities. This is a messy, uneven, and at times stressful process. But it is a healthy process, not unlike the growth of our physical bodies, which can be uneven and messy.

As people grow, their skin expands and develops seamlessly, without any stress or pain. For some people, certain aspects of faith formation develop in this manner as well. The initial faith commitments made in **foreclosure** seem to be seamlessly confirmed in **moratorium** and become bedrock commitments in **achievement**. Skin is one aspect of the physical body, but muscle is quite another. For muscle to develop, it must be subjected to stress, worked hard, and even broken down, so that it can rebuild into a stronger form of itself. The bicep is still the same bicep, but it is stronger for having undergone the rigors of training. For most people, at least some aspects of faith formation develop in this manner. **Moratorium** is a time of questioning the initial commitments made in **foreclosure** or a time of exploring a variety of possibilities coming from a status of **diffusion**.

Matters for faith exploration often arise out of life events that trigger questions, inconsistencies, and even doubts. We must allow space and freedom within student ministries and churches for this exploration to occur, no matter how messy it may become. We must also help parents understand this exploration process so that they can encourage their teenagers to wrestle with important matters of faith.

Teaching adolescents to move seamlessly through the **MAMA** cycle will serve them well on a lifelong journey of faith. Our goal should never be to graduate from our ministries teenagers who have fully reached the status of **achievement**, which is tantamount to becoming fully Christlike. Rather, we strive to provide an environment in which students can wrestle with faith issues, resolving some but not all, and to model for them a healthy process of working out their commitments.

Moratorium beyond High School

Some students will not move into the wrestling status of **moratorium** until after they have exited the student ministry and entered a new environment, such as college. It is the faith community's responsibility to help them connect with a new environment that offers the same kind of support, challenge, and continuity their previous environment offered. This may come in the form of a new local church, or a college Christian fellowship group, or a combination of the two. No matter how healthy the new community is, however, for faith exploration to take place, the adolescent must develop new relationships, and this process takes time. Questions and doubts are no respecters of time, and a person may find himself in **moratorium** before he feels established and secure in a new community of faith. This is why Reggie Joiner has suggested that student ministry move the finish line and stay with students through the transition process from one faith community to another.[54] A comprehensive student ministry will make concerted efforts to stay connected with students through at least their first year of college, fostering transition into a new community of faith.

Joiner recounts the story of Kristen, a volunteer youth leader who, after four years as a high school small group leader, felt the need to extend her ministry with her group of girls after they graduated from high school.

After talking with her youth minister she decided to commit to an extra year with her group. Some of the girls were still living at home and had jobs in her area. Some of the girls had gone to local universities, and others were in private and public schools around the country. They no longer met weekly, but she stayed committed to pursuing a relationship with them. One semester she visited each of the college campuses within driving distance to spend time with the girls in their new environment. She set up a time each week to send messages on Facebook to connect with and encourage them. When the girls were home on the holidays, she planned a few coffee and dinner meetings. Over Christmas break, they had a reunion sleepover that was the group's most well-attended event in five years.

Part of her commitment to this group of girls included replacing herself. The goal of her continued commitment was not to hold on indefinitely but to love them through this crucial transition time and help them take the next step in their faith journeys. She had gone with them to a local college ministry, since there wasn't one at their home church, and she regularly checked in with them to get a feel for whether they were finding other leaders in their new locations. For those who were still at home, she looked for ways to connect them to service opportunities at their church where they could meet other youth adults and experience true community.[55]

Most of what Kristen did was organic, engaging each of the girls in her own unique transition. As she continued her relationships with them, she helped them connect with new faith communities and wrestle through challenging life situations. She also engaged in discussions with them that were more significant than any conversations of the previous four years. Kristen provided a bridge from one faith community to another—essential for students just out of high school who find themselves in the status of **moratorium** to one degree or another.

Predicting Future Faithfulness

Following the National Study of Youth and Religion's (NSYR) initial round of research into youth and religious belief published in Christian Smith and Melinda Denton's *Soul Searching*, the NSYR continued to follow teenagers into young adulthood for five years. In this phase of the study, the researchers began to identify factors in the lives of teenagers that seemed to contribute to the faith commitments of those same young people as emerging adults.[56] The research suggests that future faith commitments are highly correlated to past experiences. Strong faith commitments, as well as declining ones, can be predicted based on the combination of multiple factors.

In this study, researchers calculated young people's levels of faith commitment based on their worship service attendance, professed importance of faith, and the frequency of personal prayer. Those who attained the highest levels of these three components of faith commitment most often experienced a combination of four causal factors during their teenage years. Not all young adults experienced the same four factors, as six different paths were found to be equally effective in producing strong faith commitments among emerging adults. Christian Smith pictures these six paths in this manner.[57]

Figure 2.3. Qualitative Comparative Analysis Showing Sufficient Combinations of Teenage-Era Causal Factors Most Likely Producing Highest Emerging Adult Religious Practice

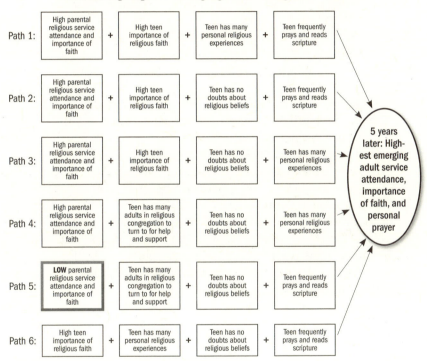

Source: National Surveys of Youth and Religion 2002–2003, 2007–2008.
Note: "Many Religious Experiences" means teen has (1) committed life to God, (2) had prayers answered, (3) has experienced a miracle, *and* (4) has had a moving spiritual experience.

Path 1 reveals that 68 percent of teenagers who had highly religious parents, a faith that was exceptionally important to them, encountered multiple religious experiences, and frequently engaged in prayer and Scripture reading were found to be highly religious as emerging adults five years later.

Path 2 displays a pattern similar to Path 1. It reveals that 70 percent of those who during their teenage years had highly religious parents, a faith that was exceptionally important to them, had no doubts about their religious beliefs, and frequently engaged in prayer and Scripture reading were found to be highly religious five years later as emerging adults. The difference between Path 1 and Path 2 is that in Path 2, "having many religious experiences" is replaced with "having no doubts about religious beliefs."

Path 3 displays a pattern similar to Path 2 and reveals that 68 percent of students were found to be highly religious as emerging adults when as teenagers they had highly religious parents, a faith that was exceptionally important to them, had no doubts about their religious beliefs, and had many personal religious experiences. In Path 3, the "frequent prayer and Scripture reading" of Path 2 is replaced with teenagers "having many personal religious experiences."

Path 4 displays a pattern similar to Path 3 and reveals that 67 percent of students were found to be highly religious as emerging adults when as teenagers they had highly religious parents, had many nonparent adults from their faith community to rely upon, had no doubts about their religious beliefs, and had many personal religious experiences. In Path 4, having a "faith that was exceptionally important to them" (a characteristic of Path 3) is replaced with "having many adults in their faith community to turn to for help and support."

Path 5 begins with what seems to be a debilitating factor: parents with a low level of religious commitment. This factor can be overcome, however, when teenagers have many nonparent adults in their faith community to turn to for help and support, have no doubts about religious beliefs, and pray and read Scripture frequently. Sixty-four percent of students on this path become highly religious as emerging adults. At this point, all five paths include strong adult support for adolescent faith formation, either through parents or other adults.

Path 6 is intriguing in that it does not include any adult support among the four factors. In this path, 77 percent of students were found to become highly religious as emerging adults when they had a faith that was exceptionally important to them, encountered multiple religious experiences, had no doubts about their faith, and frequently engaged in prayer and Scripture reading. In this path, Smith suggests that teenagers may become highly religious as emerging adults "on their own" if they are "super-religious." A closer look at the data, however, reveals that the parents of these students were actually very religious, but at a level just below the standard required in the study to be considered "highly religious." Hence, these students were not completely lacking in adult support in their faith journey.

Understanding the factors that contribute significantly to a positive faith journey into emerging adulthood is essential to the practice of student ministry. Smith reflects on these findings: "The past continues to shape the future. This is important to know, because it means that religious commitments, practices, and investments made during childhood and the teenage years, by parents and others in families and religious communities, matter—they make a difference."[58]

All youth leaders want to launch teenagers into a lifelong journey of faith, yet the amount of time a student spends in student ministries is finite. This important research helps youth ministers consider how to spend that precious time wisely. We must consider how to ensure, as much as possible, that teenagers have caring adults in their lives, that faith is becoming important to them, that students have opportunities to engage in a variety of religious experiences, that the importance of prayer and Bible reading is emphasized, and that we create an environment that allows for questions and concerns about the faith in order to guard against a downward spiral of doubts that are never addressed.

While it may seem that Smith's value of not doubting and Marcia's value of questioning in **moratorium** are at odds, there actually seems to be some synergy between the two perspectives. Smith's sociological research does not address the psychology of faith development; hence, we do not know which of Marcia's statuses of identity development the teenagers in Smith's study were experiencing. If they were in **diffusion**, **foreclosure**, or **achievement**, then it would make sense that no significant doubts were present. If they were in **moratorium**, it could be that while wrestling with faith issues, these students were in an environment in which they were finding satisfying answers to their questions and did not equate questioning with having significant doubts.

No single factor or magic bullet will guarantee future faithfulness, but Smith has revealed several combinations of factors that heighten the likelihood of teenagers moving into emerging adulthood with a strong and vibrant faith. To support students' faith formation through their teenage years so that they have the best opportunities to develop a lifelong faith, we must ensure that the church generally and student ministries specifically provide an environment in which students can engage these essential factors of faith formation.

A Sacred Environment

When **moratorium** is a valued aspect of teenagers' lives transformation happens, and transformation happens in the context of a church and student ministry environment that creates a culture of acceptance and grace. Historically student ministry has excelled in developing caring adult relationships with teenagers, championing the importance of real life faith, offering a variety of religious experiences, and promoting Bible reading. The place where student ministry, and the local church for that matter, has often failed is valuing **moratorium** and creating an environment that allows for questions, doubts, and concerns about the faith. Failure to provide this sacred space leaves many teenagers to encounter a downward spiral of religious doubts that are never addressed.

Since the process of faith formation is closely tied to the environment in which faith is being explored, many young people leave the church because they do not feel welcome to raise questions and share their doubts in the stifling environment found in many churches. Even committed Christians often find the church a difficult place to live out their faith. David Kinnaman's research concludes that too often churches either "create a toxic environment where doubts are allowed to fester. Or they never create space for questions to be raised, where pressing life issues can be openly discussed."[59] Neither situation offers people the acceptance, safety, or security necessary for authentic faith formation. As Kinnaman suggests, "We need communities where it is safe for people to talk about their deepest, darkest concerns, where expressing uncertainty is not seen as abnormal or apostate."[60]

A veteran of fifteen years in the trenches with teenagers and their parents, Todd Szymczak reflects on the importance of creating a sacred environment that affords adolescents opportunities to question, doubt, and explore their faith in the state of **moratorium**.

It's imperative that students wrestle with and explore their faith, rather than simply accepting the faith of their parents or their youth leaders. For teenagers to have a deep, meaningful faith, they need to wrestle with their faith and own it for themselves. There are two reasons why I think this is important.

The first has to do with identity. Scripture teaches that each one of us was created for a purpose and given an identity by God. Our purpose on this side of heaven is to know God and discover our identity in Christ. Each day we explore, understand, learn, and grow in our identity in Christ. During the times that teenagers question, struggle, doubt, or push back on their faith, they are not rebelling. Rather, they are figuring out their faith and their identity.

The second reason has to do with salvation. We have one mediator between God and ourselves, who is Jesus Christ. While parents and youth leaders help point teenagers to Christ, we cannot save them. That is the work of Jesus. To believe everything that their parents and youth leaders believe raises questions about what teenagers really believe themselves. Do they believe in us, or do they believe in Jesus? Do they have an adopted faith, or do they have their own refined faith? Teenagers must see our faith in action, as a community of believers who seek to trust Jesus, in order that they can take their steps toward trust in Jesus themselves.

Our job is to create a safe and intentional environment where students can wrestle with and explore their faith. We do this by not abandoning them as they go through moratorium. We can't just let teenagers "figure it out" themselves; neither can we give up on them because the process is messier than we anticipated. We also must not be fearful of "pushing them too hard" when it comes to faith. We need to walk alongside students, giving them freedom to ask questions, helping them process tough decisions by evaluating different perspectives, accepting and loving them when they don't think or believe the same way we do, and most of all praying regularly for them as they work out their faith. Walking with teenagers through the process of moratorium is one of the most authentic ways we can show students that they matter.[61]

There is without question much mystery involved in faith formation, and we should never presume to have the ability to *produce* spiritual growth—this is the work of God. Paul reminds us of our place in the process of faith formation. "I planted the seed, Apollos watered it, but God has been making it grow. So neither the one who plants nor the one who waters is anything, but only God, who makes things grow. The one who plants and the one who waters have one purpose, and they will each be rewarded according to their own labor. For we are co-workers in God's service; you are God's field, God's building" (1 Cor. 3:6–9).

We know that some environments foster the possibility of growth better than others, and it is our responsibility to create such environments for teenagers and their families. Few Christian leaders understand this concept better than John Burke, who describes our role as cultural farmers. "Church leaders, ministry leaders, and small group leaders must come to trust God who is already at work all around us, making things grow. Our responsibility is not to make people grow or change. Our task is to create the right soil, *a rich healthy environment*, in which people can grow up in faith until the invisible God is made visible through his body, the church."[62]

A rich and healthy environment that fosters faith formation offers teenagers an opportunity for self- and community reflection, calls out the gifts and talents of teenagers for the common good of the community, and values students for who they are and not just what they can do. Such a community allows space for questions, doubts, and identity reformation, and maintains authentic relationships with students, supporting them through the challenges of transitioning environments as they move from middle school into high school and from high school into college or the workplace.

Perhaps more than anything, student ministry is about creating a sacred environment of trust that provides a safe space for authentic relationships and the genuine exploration of God's story, our story, and the fruitful integration of those stories.

Discussion Questions for Student Ministry Leaders

1. Take a moment to think about the student ministry in your church. Is there a divide between your evangelism and discipleship practices? Do you focus more on one at the expense of the other? What are some practical ways you can integrate the two and embrace a more holistic view of discipleship in your ministry?

2. Do you see your students as God sees them and truly believe in who they could become? How can you be a "Mrs. Hill" to just one of your students and inspire your volunteers to do the same? In what ways might you be "abandoning" teenagers (and parents) in your student ministry when they don't do what you want or perform the way you want them to? Why does this happen? How can you show genuine, unconditional love to students and parents?

3. An environment of acceptance is necessary for faith formation. Do students in your ministry feel welcome to raise questions and share their doubts? Is there a culture of acceptance and grace at your church? If not, how can you create space in your ministry for questions to be raised and doubts to be voiced and explored?

4. What are some ways in which you can "do life" together with the teenagers in your ministry? How can you take your relationships with the youth beyond the programmed time at church?

5. How are confirmation, contradiction, and continuity at work in your student ministry? Do you find it easier to play it safe than to nudge teenagers from foreclosure into moratorium? What are some good approaches to introducing contradiction into your teaching and relationships with youth? How do you maintain continuity with youth after they graduate from high school?

6. How can you help parents understand the faith exploration process so they can encourage their teens to wrestle with important matters of faith?

7. What would it look like if your volunteers continued in their relationships with students into their first year of college? Is this something you can implement in your ministry?

Discussion Questions for Church Leaders

1. Is your church operating with a "two class" understanding of discipleship, which suggests that there is a difference between Christians and disciples, that evangelism produces converts and discipleship produces disciples? If so, how can you help your members and visitors understand that being a disciple is not just an option but is the very definition of being a Christian?

2. "Failure to engage in evangelism results in our inability to make disciples": would you say your church agrees or disagrees with this statement? Can you make disciples without reaching out to nonbelievers? Do you think the Great Commission commands us to practice evangelism? What does evangelism look like in your context?

3. Are teenagers treated differently than adults in your congregation? Are they kept at arm's length because of congregants' fear, misunderstanding, or stereotypes? How can you foster a better "come as you are" atmosphere in your church, in which youth and others feel welcomed and accepted no matter where they are on their journey of faith?

4. How does your church respond to and come alongside of young people who are in moratorium? How can you provide support and conversation partners for youth who are wrestling with questions and exploring their faith identity?

5. Reread the second-to-last paragraph of the chapter. Does this describe your church? In what areas are you excelling? In what areas is there room for improvement?

3

When Teenagers Matter:

STUDENT MINISTRY IS WELL RESOURCED

Recently I was in need of a new car and paid a visit to a local dealership. It had been years since I had looked into buying a new car, and I was a bit surprised by the grandeur of a modern dealership. At first I wasn't even sure that the salesperson wanted to sell me a car. Our time together began with a tour of the dealership. He barely acknowledged the numerous cars in the showroom and quickly escorted me to the service area, where he described in detail how they would care for my car long after the purchase. While my car was being serviced, he explained, I would be treated to a waiting room like no other. Not only could I enjoy the latest magazines, newspapers, and high-definition TV, I could also access their free high-speed internet service, high-quality reception for all cell phone carriers, and even semiprivate office space with a phone and desktop computer. After a quick stop at the parts department, where I could purchase any accessories imaginable, and a tour of the financing department, which looked like a small bank, we finally began to talk about cars.

What struck me about the contemporary dealership was that it has truly become a one-stop shop for the modern consumer who values a high level of customer service. Of course, this comprehensive service comes at a price for the dealer and ultimately the consumer. Nevertheless, you would be hard-pressed to find a dealership that no longer sells cars and only services the cars they have sold in the past decade. That would be an odd conversation indeed.

> Oh, you want to buy a car. I'm sorry, but we stopped selling cars a few years ago. When we first opened, it seemed like we had more employees than we needed. People were tripping over each other as customers trickled through the door. As we became more well known, the trickle of customers turned into a steady stream, and we were selling so many cars that we could hardly keep up with the demand. It wasn't long before customers began bringing their cars in for oil changes and minor repairs, so some of the employees began spending most of their time in the repair shop servicing the cars we had sold. As time went on, more cars needed service, and it seemed like everyone was working in the repair shop and no one was selling cars in the showroom. Potential customers were still streaming in to look at our inventory, but the wait was so long to speak with a salesperson that many left before we could make a sale. Soon the stream of buyers turned into a trickle of window shoppers. We just couldn't keep up with the demand to sell cars *and* service them. We finally decided to close the showroom so that we could commit all of our resources to servicing the cars we had sold. I suppose one day, when those cars wear out completely, some employees will come back to the showroom, and we'll start selling cars again. But for now, it's all we can do to service the cars of our valuable customers.

No dealership moves its sales force into the repair shop and closes the showroom after a fruitful decade of sales, but churches do this all the time. Recent studies suggest that new churches grow significantly faster than older churches.[1] The reason for this is rather simple: established churches are so busy serving the membership that they have little time to reach out to new people, as they once did in the early days of the church. All the outreach resources of a church quickly—usually within ten years—become absorbed in the task of nurturing new believers and serving new members.

Student ministries often follow the same pattern. Churches that have few families with teenagers often hire a youth minister whose charge is to reach out to the adolescent population of the community. Once the mission has achieved even modest success and the teenage population of the church begins to grow, there is a shift from outreach in the local community to nurturing the new crop of students. This shift is perceived as necessary because the ministry simply doesn't have the resources to continue both outreach efforts and the nurture of newfound teenagers. The ministry is trapped in the dichotomy between evangelism and discipleship, discussed in chapter 2, because of a lack of resources to holistically usher people into the faith and teach them all Christ commanded. Hence, many churches scale back or shut down the outreach while increasing efforts toward nurturing the already committed.

Shepherding Volunteers

Nurturing volunteers is key to retaining great volunteers. But how do you do that? Most of us meet with volunteers individually. This is both effective and important. But if that is all you do, there's a problem. The volunteer is only connected to you. A part of our role as leaders is to create a collective nurturing environment— facilitating friendship, encouraging sharing, and shepherding our volunteers toward spiritual growth. This creates a culture in which volunteers learn from one another, empower each other, and celebrate together. This way, our leaders are no longer dependent on any one person but rely heavily on the team for support. So the next time one of your volunteers recommends you all go out to eat after Wednesday night youth group, go! You won't regret it. Spontaneous nights like that can go a long way toward spurring a collective nurturing environment.

Andrew Breton, Grace Chapel,
Lexington, Massachusetts

Student ministry is perhaps the most under-resourced ministry in the church; children's ministry would be a close second. Few elders, senior pastors, and executive pastors understand the extent of the resources necessary to develop a faithful and fruitful ministry that values *all* the teenagers in the local community. When the local church provides just enough resources for its student ministry to meet the needs of families with teenagers in the church, the result is the zero-sum game of a ministry that is just good enough. When *all* teenagers in the local community matter, churches develop a reasonable set of metrics concerning the resources necessary to develop and sustain a comprehensive student ministry.

Rather than asking how much it will take to meet the needs of families with teenagers in the church, we must begin asking bolder questions. What would it take to make disciples of 20 percent of the teenagers in our community? What would it take to make disciples of 20 percent of the teenage girls in our community? The teenage boys? The middle school students? The freshmen, sophomores, juniors, seniors? What would it take to ensure that all the committed students in our ministries maintain their commitments after they graduate from high school? As we will discover, it is expensive to resource a student ministry at the highest level, and it will happen only if teenagers matter to the leadership of the church.

The Flaw in the Business Model of Leadership

Even when teenagers matter to the church, and leadership is passionate about reaching out to unchurched teenagers in the community, the student ministry tends to be underresourced because the church relies too heavily on a business model of leadership, which declares: recruit, train, and deploy your workforce. We certainly need to—not unlike business managers—recruit and train volunteer leaders in every church ministry. Many companies go to great lengths to recruit the best and brightest employees and then invest a significant amount of training in their new recruits. Many ministries in the church follow this pattern with great success, recruiting volunteers with the necessary gifts and talents for the ministry and then investing hours in training them to do ministry at the highest levels.

The problem with the business model as applied to the church appears in the deployment phase of the process. It is reasonable to suggest that the manager of a sales department might recruit, train, and deploy a dozen new salespeople in a year. It is further reasonable to suggest that the same manager could recruit, train, and deploy a dozen more salespeople the next year, and the following year, and so on. The beauty of this model is that the manager can rely on an additive effect of the recruit-train-deploy model that results in twelve salespeople the first year, twenty-four salespeople the second year, and thirty-six salespeople by the end of the third year. Certainly there will be some attrition, as salespeople are promoted in the company or leave for another company. So perhaps there are just thirty salespeople at the end of three years of recruiting, training, and deploying; still, the manager is averaging over 80 percent on the investment.

The difference between business and the church regarding this model is motivation. What is the motivation of the salesperson to keep selling once deployed? The salesperson has the built-in motivation of a paycheck and bills to be paid. So while some retraining and encouragement is always necessary, the manager is able to focus almost solely on the new recruits each year, as the veteran workforce is motivated to keep working.

In the church, volunteers do not have such a built-in financial reward system. Motivation to continue serving in a church ministry is a combination of intrinsic value for the work being accomplished and extrinsic support from the leader of the ministry. We often pay little attention to the tremendous amount of ongoing nurture and encouragement necessary to maintain a vital and healthy volunteer team, especially in student ministry. While the business manager can invest the majority of her energy in a new group of recruits, the youth minister must invest the majority of her energy in the existing volunteers. At some point, she will reach her capacity, at which she can no longer invest in any more people, new or old. We simply cannot approach volunteer leadership with a business model based on built-in financial incentives to keep people motivated. We must recognize the far more labor-intensive approach to recruiting, training, and nurturing volunteers in the church.

Different Ministries, Different Needs

It is important to understand that not all ministries in the church are the same. Some ministries need more resources than others, and some require greater investment in volunteers than others. May I suggest that it takes more effort to encourage and retain a middle school volunteer than a person who volunteers in the choir? While I love people who sing in the choir, several reasons validate such a statement.

First, children and student ministries are among the few that require volunteer leadership to be brought in from *outside* the ministry itself. Recruiting volunteer leaders for the men's ministry, women's ministry, or young-adult ministry means recruiting from within the ministry, but children and student ministries must draw adults volunteer leaders out of adult ministries. Hence, except for the occasional graduate who returns to become a volunteer, there is no built-in recruiting system within children and student ministries. This makes the whole recruiting, training, and nurturing process more challenging from the outset.

Second, student ministries tend to be highly relational, and it takes more effort to encourage someone who is engaged in relational ministry than a person volunteering in a programmatic ministry. The most important aspect of student ministry is the interpersonal contact made with students in between the programs, often known as *contact work*. This can be time-consuming, relational work that no one else sees. It is also the time that volunteers are most likely to feel rejected by teenagers. This is the context in which volunteers need a voluminous amount of support and encouragement. While volunteers serving on the welcome team or parking team need to be valued and thanked for their service, they rarely need the type of support required by those in relational ministry.

Third, student ministries that value authentic, unconditional relationships between leaders and students require a long-term commitment from volunteers, and it takes more effort to encourage a person who is volunteering in an ongoing weekly ministry than in a one-time special ministry. Encouraging and nurturing a volunteer who leads a small group and invests in the lives of teenagers over at least a four-year period will require far more time and energy than celebrating the volunteers who serve on the parking team for Christmas Eve services.

This is not a value judgment. Volunteer leaders are a vital aspect of every area of ministry in the church. We must recognize, however, that the time and energy required of full-time staff members to recruit, train, and nurture volunteer leaders varies greatly among ministries. Relative to other ministries in the church, student ministries require a greater investment of staff time and energy in the recruiting, training, and nurturing of volunteer leaders.

Developing Reasonable Metrics

Several years ago we put an addition on our house. I sketched out what I was looking for, and an architect drew up the plans. The builder worked from the plans, and it was amazing to see the coordinated effort of all the tradespeople and suppliers working in harmony. It seemed as if every week another delivery would arrive with just the right amount of concrete to pour the foundation, then the precise amount of lumber to frame the addition, followed by the correct amount of shingles for the roof and the exact number of doors and windows to be installed. Observing the contractor's work was like watching a conductor lead an orchestra, calling for the precise notes at just the right time.

While the builder worked with his crew on the project, two essential tools were never out of his reach: his phone and the architect's plans. Constantly checking the plans to ensure that my vision of the addition was being executed properly, he could call for the necessary resources at a moment's notice.

Student ministries are so frequently under-resourced because we often lack a strategic plan for accomplishing the vision. We are fond of reciting Proverbs 29:18 (KJV), "Where there is no vision, the people perish," and of challenging one another to dream bold dreams for the kingdom. But without plans to execute the vision, the builder or minister is helpless. Student ministries lack resources for one of two reasons: (1) The ministry does not have a new plan that clearly outlines the need for appropriate resources. Too often student ministries live from week to week, year to year, implementing the same old plan, complaining of the need for more resources but never proposing a new plan that would raise the ministry to a new level. (2) The leadership of the church that guards the resources does not value the plan. All too often ministry teams invest extraordinary amounts of time and energy in developing strategic plans, only to have those plans go unfunded and wither away in a file cabinet.

Once a vision has been cast and a plan has been established, a resource estimate can be developed. After consulting with hundreds of churches about student ministry development, Mark DeVries has established some very reasonable metrics. For as long as I can remember, the ratio of one volunteer to five students has been a staple of student ministries. Camp directors strive to have about one counselor for every five campers, and schools often require teachers to secure enough field-trip chaperones to have one adult for about every five students. Youth leaders always seem to be trying to recruit enough volunteers to have one leader for every five teenagers. When we consider the amount of time necessary to develop authentic relationships with teenagers—introducing them to the faith and teaching them all that Jesus commanded—five might even seem a bit high. Still, if we accept this long-standing ratio—confirmed by DeVries, who suggests that "realistically, most volunteers can't effectively oversee the church's Christian nurture of more than about five students on an ongoing basis"—we would expect that a ministry comprising fifty students on a regular basis would require at least ten volunteer leaders.[2]

DeVries goes on to make an important statement about a ministry's sustainability when staffed with volunteers alone. "Conventional wisdom would suggest that if enough volunteers are in place, staff will be less necessary. But our experience is just the opposite. Without sufficient staff to coordinate, inspire, and equip volunteers, the volunteers easily become stuck in competing priorities and programs that eventually erode the long-term stability of the ministry."[3]

This raises the issue of developing a reasonable metric for the number of full-time staff required to provide leadership for students and volunteers. According to DeVries's research and consulting experiences, one paid youth minister is required for every ten volunteer leaders and fifty students. This provides a 1:10:50 ratio of staff, volunteers, and students as a reasonable metric for resourcing the personnel of a student ministry (see table 3.1). If a church is in this position and seeks to grow the ministry, then additional resources will be necessary. When an under-resourced ministry expects to grow by adding new staff, they may be in for a reality check. Again, DeVries proclaims the critical importance of developing proper staffing levels. "When a church hires just enough staff to barely maintain the programs they have and then expects quantum growth from the new hire, the under-staffed youth ministry can be expected to remain mired in the climate of criticism, blaming and burnout. An over-capacity youth ministry sets up its staff and volunteers to be unable to fulfill the wide variety of expectations placed on them by the parents, the youth, the senior pastor and the church leaders."[4]

Table 3.1. Metrics for Staffing Student Ministry

	Church A	Church B	Church C	Church D	Church E	Church F
Number of Full-Time Staff	1	2	3	4	5	6
Number of Volunteers	10	20	30	40	50	60
Number of Students	50	100	150	200	250	300

Based on norms established by Mark DeVries.[5]

Church leaders who are interested in providing a ministry that is merely good enough to meet the needs of families with teenagers in the church may look at this table, match the number of students in their church with the appropriate number of students in the table, and staff their ministries accordingly. These churches will typically develop a student ministry equal to 10–20 percent of the church worship attendance. The variation is largely dependent on the commitment to the metrics above, consistency of leadership, and clarity of vision.[6]

However, when churches concerned with *all* students in the community consider creating a bold plan to reach out to a certain percentage of the adolescent population of the community, the resources increase significantly. I live in a small town in which about 1,200 students attend the local public middle and high school. If a church in my community caught a vision to go and make disciples of 20 percent of the teenagers in the community, they would be talking about ministering to 240 students. That would require five full-time staff and forty-eight volunteers, who would be divided proportionally between a middle school ministry and a high school ministry. That is a lot of resources, requiring a lot of funding, and that is why few churches choose to execute such a bold vision. Even aiming to minister to 120 students with two full-time staff, one part-time staff, and twenty-four volunteers would be a significant commitment. So how do churches develop the resources necessary to create a student ministry that is more than just good enough?

Creative Staff Building

Churches faced with the daunting task of staffing a comprehensive ministry can approach the funding question in a variety of ways. Some churches choose to redefine their *existing budgets*, others create partnerships with *parachurch organizations*, and many develop vibrant *internship programs*.

Budget Reallocations

While each church creates its financial budget differently, most use large categories to define major areas of expenditure. Each area of the budget is then further broken down into line items that compose the budget area. For example, the areas of a budget might include: personnel, worship, missions, ministry, and buildings and grounds. In this simple scenario, each area would include numerous line items. Personnel would include all the salaries, benefits, and perhaps expense accounts of the pastors and staff. Worship would include all the expenses of creating worship services, funerals, weddings, and other special services. Missions would typically include a host of missionaries and programs that the church supports locally, regionally, and globally. Ministry would include the funding for all the church's ministries for men, women, young adults, youth, children, and other groups. Buildings and grounds would cover maintenance of the church buildings, care of the landscape and parking areas, snow removal, office supplies, equipment, and utility bills for electricity, heat, air-conditioning, water, and phones.

Some churches may have many more than five budget areas, with fewer line items in each area, while others may have only a couple of budget areas that contain a long list of line items. The larger the church, the more complex the budgeting system, but one fact is always true: someone, somewhere, prioritizes how much money will be spent on each item in the budget. This may be the role of an elder board or a finance committee or a senior pastor or an executive pastor. Every year, some group decides how much will be budgeted for student ministry, and the leadership of the church agrees to that amount. In order to realistically resource a comprehensive student ministry, the church needs to strive toward allocating 10 percent of the overall budget to student ministries for staff and programs. A budget equal to 5 percent of the overall budget will typically be good enough to care for the families of teenagers in the church but not enough to minister to teenagers in the community as well. Often, churches that are committed to a comprehensive ministry resource it in creative ways. There are essentially three ways to increase the funding for student ministry through reallocating portions of the church budget.

First, the overall budget can be increased with new money as the current membership decides to give more to the church or the church grows in size and new members begin giving. Often this new money is quickly spent on salary increases, rising costs of health insurance and utilities, and maintenance of buildings. Even with these expenditures, if the increase in giving is significant, new positions could be added to the staff. This approach suggests that increasing the size of the budget pie allows each slice of the pie to increase; however, the slices are not usually equal, nor do they tend to increase proportionally.

Second, a church can reconsider its spending priorities. If student ministry is a higher priority than other ministries, some money can be moved from one line item to another. Churches don't like to do this, because it gives the impression that some ministries are more important than others. Imagine the uproar in a church that cut the women's ministry budget by 25 percent and gave that money to the student ministry. That would be a bold move that could result in a lot of hurt feelings. Holding some ministry budgets flat while increasing others that have been marked as high priorities is easier than cutting back one ministry to support another. In certain instances, though, this approach may be necessary.

A third option is to declare student ministry to be missional and fund part of the student ministry from the missions budget area. This can be a very effective strategy for a student ministry that desires to increase its outreach efforts. I have seen church missions budgets supporting Youth for Christ and Youth With A Mission ministries around the world, and rightfully so. But if a local church's mission budget can support student ministry in Sri Lanka, why can't it support youth outreach in the local community? When I was on the staff of a church many years ago, this is exactly what we did. There was a passion to reach out to students in the local community, and we needed to hire another student ministry staff person to lead that effort. The missions committee was excited about the idea and funded the new position, understanding the value of having a missionary in our own backyard.

Parachurch Partnerships

Developing strategic partnerships with parachurch organizations, such as Young Life or Youth for Christ, can help a church attain a comprehensive student ministry at a reasonable cost. Creating such a partnership typically includes working with the missions committee of the church as suggested above, though the funding could also come from the general operating budget or a source outside of the church, such as a foundation or individual benefactor. In this case, the church agrees to support a parachurch staff member at a level of at least 50 percent of their financial need, while the staffer raises the balance of support. This commitment level solidifies the relationship and provides some accountability for the parachurch staff member.

But the partnership between the student ministry and the parachurch staff member is more than simply financial. This person is treated as a full member of the church's student ministry staff and operates under the specific job description of youth outreach. The person may lead a Young Life or Youth for Christ club as the outreach arm of the student ministry or direct an existing youth outreach ministry of the church. In this partnership, the rest of the youth staff would support the outreach aspect of the ministry, and the parachurch staff member would support the other aspects of the ministry. It is critical that everyone understands the student ministry to be one entity, and that everyone is on the same team and ministering to the same population of students. When language such as "church kids" and "Young Life kids" begins to seep into the dialogue, then there is division in the partnership. It is great for a church to have a student ministry *and* support a local parachurch ministry, but that is not a partnership. A partnership happens when the student ministry of the church is seen as one ministry by parents, students, staff, and the community.

A partnership program might look something like this. On Sunday morning, there is a youth program of some sort, perhaps a traditional Sunday school program or a youth worship service. On Wednesday evening, a youth club meeting focuses on outreach. Throughout the week, small groups meet in students' homes or at the church. There might be an outreach retreat at a Young Life camp in the fall and a winter retreat somewhere else, with both retreats taking students deeper in their faith. All youth leaders would be involved in all of these programs to one extent or another. They would also take time for building personal relationships with students between the regularly scheduled meetings.

This is a view of a fully integrated partnership between a church and a parachurch ministry. When the ministries are not integrated, people tend to work against each other. The church has youth group on Sunday evening, while Youth for Christ has club on Wednesday night. The church has small groups in student homes throughout the week, while Youth for Christ has a small group Bible study on Wednesday before club. While the two ministries can certainly coexist and even support each other, they are clearly two separate ministries that are not integrated, and the age-old question of how to integrate students into the church from the parachurch typically remains unresolved. The beauty of the partnership, which creates a comprehensive student ministry, is that it provides a natural and seamless path for integrating students far from God into the bride of Christ, which is the local church.

Internship Programs

While we strive to have one full-time staff member for every fifty students, not all staff members need to be paid the same. This is where internships become a valuable part of the staffing process. Before describing various internship possibilities, I must make clear that the only way to make internships viable is for the church and the student ministries to be fully committed to leadership development. Interns are not cheap labor! Interns cost less financially because the additional expense is replaced with an investment of mentoring and leadership development.

There are *seasonal interns*, *part-time interns*, and *full-time interns*. Each of these positions offers tremendous value to student ministry for a season of time, ranging from three months to three years. While these positions are not a replacement for long-term relationships with caring volunteer leaders, interns bring a new dynamic, energy, passion, and excitement to a ministry that can support the full-time staff in numerous ways. In order to avoid feelings of abandonment by teenagers when interns leave, it is essential that students know the limits of each intern's rotation and that youth ministers carefully craft intern job descriptions as support position, rather than primary caregivers.

Seasonal interns are often college students who spend the summer serving in the ministry. Often these are alumni from the student ministry, which makes this an excellent opportunity for students to contribute to the ministry and the church. Many churches hire two, four, six, or eight summer interns, bringing a new infusion of vibrancy to the church and student ministry. Typically the interns live at home or with a host family from the congregation and are paid a modest salary, like most college students working a summer job. In addition to summer interns, occasionally a ministry might hire a person for other seasons. Some college students have long Christmas breaks and can serve for a month over the holidays. Some students take a semester off from college and can serve during that time and perhaps also the summer.

Part-time interns are usually attending college part time, attending graduate school or seminary, or are working part time in the marketplace. A part-time intern's working hours can vary from ten to thirty hours a week. The value of part-time interns is their longevity. While not working all the time, they tend to be around for several years, unlike summer interns who work full time but only for a short period. Hiring two half-time interns can cost a fraction of a full-time staff person and help achieve the 1:50 ratio.

If a church is committed to leadership development, *full-time interns* are an excellent way to achieve the 1:50 ratio without busting the budget. These staff members serve full time and have graduated from college. Often these are known as postgraduate internships and are highly sought after by the best and brightest graduating ministry majors. Students looking to enter ministry right out of college view these positions as an opportunity to grow in their ministry skills under experienced leaders before taking on the responsibility of leading a ministry themselves. Because these are very desirable positions, churches with strong post-graduate internship programs are able to be highly selective.

Postgraduate internships can last from one to three years, with two-year programs being the most popular. Interns are provided housing with a host family for the period of the internship and receive a salary (and health insurance as needed) that is typically half of what a starting salary would be for an assistant youth minister at the church. In exchange for providing high-quality leadership development, the church gains a full-time staff member for half the cost. Many churches that have developed these programs hire multiple postgraduate interns on a rotating basis, so that only a fraction of the interns are coming or going in a single year.

Exemplary Postgraduate Internships

"The Future Leaders Program isn't an ordinary internship. It is character building and will stretch you in all sorts of ways. You may be an intern, but you are in a position of leadership," declares Rachel Fabian, reflecting on her year in the Future Leaders Program at McLean Bible Church.[7] Each year, McLean accepts about a dozen young adults into its postgraduate internship program and places interns in a variety of ministry positions throughout the church, including student ministries. The year is an immersion in direct ministry experience, classroom instruction, spiritual development, and time for personal reflection and feedback. While McLean is a very large church, averaging over 11,000 people in worship every weekend, postgraduate internships can be developed at a church of almost any size when students matter and student ministry is a priority.

Chapel Hill Presbyterian Church, located just outside of Seattle, averages 1,400 people in Sunday morning worship and offers a two-year postgraduate internship program in student ministries.[8] The church offers two positions, which are staggered so that each year they hire one new intern. This model provides more time for each intern to become established in the community and develop ministry skills, while allowing for a smooth rotation of interns in and out of the church.

At The Falls Church in Virginia, a church of about 2,000 worshipers, a dozen or so recent college graduates come together each year for the Fellows Program, a leadership development program that seeks to develop Christian leaders for the marketplace, youth ministries, families, and local communities.[9] After his year as a fellow in The Falls Church youth ministries, Andrew Beach reflected on the experience: "What does it mean to invest unconditionally? What does it mean to be a part of a family? What does it mean to invest into a community? The experiences I've had are allowing me to think outside the box. I am excited to see how I can continue to grow and see where God takes me."[10] The Falls Church program is part of The Fellows Initiative, a network of fellows programs across the country.[11] In this postgraduate internship program, fellows actually raise funds to participate, thus making it very affordable for the church. Recently, The Falls Church launched another postgraduate internship program exclusively for student ministries known as the Nehemiah Venture.[12]

Second Presbyterian Church in Memphis has created a culture of leadership development throughout the congregation, and this is reflected in their student ministries.[13] They maintain a student ministry staff that includes three two-year postgraduate interns and ten summer interns. While most churches with a Sunday worship attendance of 1,800 could not afford this level of internship program, Second Presbyterian has creatively secured funding for their internships from a local foundation committed to leadership development. This internship program prepares young adults called to student ministry for vocational ministry positions following the completion of their two-year commitment.

Menlo Park Presbyterian Church is a community of 3,500 weekend worshipers that hires four one-year interns in student ministries each year.[14] Their goal is to equip interns with the leadership development that will enable them to continue in a long-term vocation in student ministries. To that end, their leadership development program is not confined to the student ministry staff. Rather, interns have the opportunity to learn from a variety of pastors across the staff, including the senior pastor. In this manner, interns receive a holistic view of the church and come to understand student ministry within the context of the whole church instead of as an isolated ministry, tangential to the church.

Not every church committed to leadership development is a megachurch. Leadership development is a value that transcends congregational size. Either it is part of the ethos of the church or it is not; either it is a priority of the church leadership or it is not. For example, Southview Community Church, whose worship attendance is a few hundred people, has made leadership development a high priority.[15] This Baptist congregation offers both summer internships and postgraduate internships through their Chrysalis Program. Interns serve eight to twelve weeks, usually in the summer; and residents serve one to two years, usually following graduation from college. They have the opportunity to serve in a variety of ministries, from student ministry to worship ministry to media ministries. Residents are also typically enrolled in seminary courses during their time at Southview Community Church.

BENEFITS OF INTERNSHIPS

This is a small sample of the numerous churches offering internship programs that can be of great benefit to everyone. Any church that values teenagers enough to create a full-time youth minister position can afford to develop an internship program. With the use of internships, a church can expand the reach of its student ministry throughout the community by increasing the student ministry staff at a fraction of the financial cost of creating new permanent positions. This approach is gaining traction across the country and is a great benefit to the interns, the students, the student ministry, the church, and the churches that eventually hire those who received such dynamic leadership development through postgraduate internships.

Often churches want a comprehensive ministry but are unwilling or unable to resource student ministry at a comprehensive level. Hence, it is critical to understand the reality of resources necessary for developing a comprehensive student ministry. When a church is unable to resource student ministry at a comprehensive level, it is essential that the youth minister, pastor, and elders all understand the level of expectations that can be fulfilled with the resources available. This alleviates the frustrations associated with trying to meet undeliverable expectations.

What Are Youth Ministers Worth?

I frequently receive calls from pastors and search committees trying to figure out how much to pay their youth ministers. Likewise, seniors graduating from Gordon College and entering the interview process with churches are curious about how much they can expect to earn as youth ministers.

National Surveys

Many national salary surveys can be consulted in this issue. Church-Staffing offers an annual *Compensation Handbook for Church Staff* that itemizes compensation by church position, church size, and general geographic region.[16] Every other year, Leadership Network publishes the *Large Church Salary and Staffing Report*, which analyzes compensation data of large churches with a minimum average worship attendance of 3,000 people.[17] Likewise, every denominational headquarters tracks compensation among its member churches and sets standards of compensation, particularly for ordained clergy. And *Group Magazine* publishes a *Youth Ministry Salary Survey* every year.[18] This survey focuses solely on compensation packages for full-time youth pastors across the country and reports average salaries by gender, church size, number of students in the ministry, level of education, experience in ministry, age, and across five regions of the country.

While these reports can be very useful for casting a broad view of the compensation picture, they have limitations. First, these surveys report on the current state of affairs. Hence, if student ministry as a profession is underpaid across the country, it is less than useful to compare one's compensation to an average number that has been generated from a pool of undercompensated staff. To do so is simply to state that I want to be underpaid at least as much as my colleagues. A slightly rotten apple in a bushel of rotten apples is still rotten. I am speaking hypothetically here and not making a judgment about the state of compensation in the student ministry profession. Perhaps everyone at this time is underpaid, perhaps everyone is overpaid, or perhaps everyone is paid just right. The point is this: we must always carefully assess the comparison group, remembering that in the land of the blind, the one-eyed man is king!

The other real concern with general salary surveys is their inability to account for the local cost-of-living index. The average salary of youth ministers for a particular region of the country is not usually specific enough to determine an appropriate salary in a precise community. For example, if the average salary for those serving in the Northeast is $36,000, and the region includes both Boston and Akron, Ohio, a cost-of-living correction must be made because Boston is one of the most expensive areas and Akron is among the most affordable areas of the Northeast. In the same way, Southern California is often in the same region as Idaho on salary surveys, and the cost of living can change dramatically from one town to the next, let alone from one state to another. So how does one account for cost of living when estimating the salary of a youth minister?

Local Teachers' Salaries

I believe it is helpful to look outside the church and into the local community for a better comparison model. Every community has professionals working in the town in which a church is located. Comparing the youth minister's salary to the average salary of those living in the town or county would be a helpful comparison. We could further compare student ministry salaries to other specific jobs in the community. How does the youth minister's salary compare to those of teachers, social workers, business owners, police officers, doctors, or lawyers in the community? The best comparison, I believe, is with the public school teachers in the community where the church is located.

Teachers' salaries make a good comparison for several reasons. First, few people believe that school teachers are overpaid, so a salary that is comparable to that of a teacher is not likely to seem exorbitant to many people. While some may not believe that a youth minister is "worth" as much as a doctor or lawyer, most would concede that youth ministers should be paid comparably to teachers. Second, most people highly value the work of school teachers and would agree that the work of a youth minister is at least as valuable as that of a teacher (and if they do not agree, I suggest you look for another church to serve!). Third, because public school teacher salaries are determined through collective bargaining agreements between the local school board and the local teachers' union, the agreed-upon salaries typically reflect the economic status of the community and represent a livable income in the local community. This is not an element that can be discerned from most national salary surveys. Finally, teacher salaries are based upon experience and education. Salary scales for public schools are readily available as a public document and may be obtained from the office of the superintendent of any public school district. These documents are typically "step scales," with four or five columns across the top representing educational levels and thirty or so rows down the left side representing years of experience.

Table 3.2. Typical Public Teacher's Salary Scale*

Year of Service	Bachelor's Degree	Bachelor's +15 credits	Master's Degree	Master's +15 credits	Master's +30 credits	Doctoral Degree
1	$39,750	$40,000	$41,750	$42,250	$42,750	$43,250
2	**$40,000**	$40,250	$42,000	$42,500	$43,000	$43,500
3	$40,250	$40,500	$42,250	$42,750	$43,250	$43,750
4	$40,500	$40,750	$42,500	$43,000	$43,500	$44,000
5	$40,750	$41,000	$42,750	$43,250	$43,750	$44,250
6	$41,000	$41,500	$43,000	$43,500	$44,000	$44,500
7	$41,800	$42,300	$43,800	$44,300	$44,800	$45,300
8	$42,620	$43,120	$44,620	$45,120	$45,620	$46,120
9	$43,461	$43,961	$45,461	$45,961	$46,461	$46,961
10	$44,323	$44,823	$46,323	$46,823	$47,323	$47,823
11	$45,207	$45,707	$47,207	$47,707	$48,207	$48,707
12	$46,113	$46,613	$48,113	$48,613	$49,113	$49,613
13	$47,041	$47,541	$49,041	$49,541	$50,041	$50,541
14	$47,993	$48,493	$49,993	$50,493	$50,993	$51,493
15	$48,968	$49,468	$50,968	$51,468	$51,968	$52,468

* This table is a generalized salary scale, based on reviews of a dozen actual salary scales.

Consulting the local teacher's salary scale in table 3.2, it is easy to observe that in this community, teachers with bachelor's degrees in their second year of service earn $40,000 annually. Likewise, one could conclude that in the same community, youth ministers with bachelor's degrees in their second year of service should be earning a similar salary.

There is, of course, one caveat when comparing youth ministers to teachers: typically, the teacher's salary scale reflects compensation for nine or ten months of work, while few youth ministers receive two or three months' vacation. Hence, it is necessary to adjust the teacher's scale for youth minister's salary proportionately. In the spirit of generosity toward teachers, let's set aside Christmas vacations and spring breaks and consider a community in which teachers work about ten months: September through June. Using our $40,000 salary, that amounts to $4,000/month. If the youth minister in the same community receives only two weeks' vacation, then the adjusted salary would be 11.5 months x $4,000, equaling an annual salary of $46,000. If the youth minister received a generous four-week vacation, then the adjusted teacher's salary would be $44,000 for eleven months of work.

It is not helpful to become too legalistic with these numbers, but a youth minister should certainly be paid at least as much as a public school teacher with comparable education and experience. Over the years I have found this advice to pastors and search committees to be well received, and youth ministers who have asked for this level of compensation have nearly always received it—or churches have at least agreed to move in that direction.

The compensation question becomes a little more complicated when a church provides housing or does not provide health insurance. In these cases, the fair market value of housing should be deducted from the established comparable teacher's salary, or the cost of health insurance should be added to the established salary. Adjustments can also be made for other benefits as necessary. Once a fair comparable salary has been established, such adjustments are easy to make.

Support and Celebrations

Everyone understands that ministry of any type is not a nine-to-five job. Life happens in very unpredictable ways, and ministry is all about doing life together in the name of Jesus. Student ministry is even less predictable than other ministries, in that teenagers tend to require immediate responses to life's questions. If we are not available when a question arises or a situation presents itself, we have often lost the opportunity to speak into a young person's life or to walk alongside him or her.

While this does not mean that youth ministers should be on call twenty-four hours a day, seven days a week, or that they should abandon their families every time teenagers send them text messages, neither does it mean that we can always put teenagers off until a more convenient time in our schedules. When a married couple stops the pastor after church and explains that they are having marital problems, the pastor can ask them to call the church office and make an appointment for the following week. When a teenager stops a youth leader after the youth meeting and asks to talk about a troubled relationship, the youth leader can hardly respond the same way. Teenagers' lives happen at warp speed, and next week would likely be too late to talk to this teenager about this troubled relationship.

I once had a volunteer pull me aside just as our group had started singing to begin our youth club. She explained to me that a student had just told her that she had been raped the night before and she was afraid to tell her parents. This sort of issue cannot wait for a scheduled appointment next week. In this case, it required swift action and a very long night for me and a couple of volunteer youth leaders who had to get up for work the next morning. Another time, a student in our ministry, frustrated after a basketball game at the church, kicked over a big blue mailbox on the street corner—just as a police officer was driving by! Unable to talk the officer out of arresting him for destruction of government property, I spent the rest of that Saturday afternoon in the police station with the student and his parents until bail was posted. This is the kind of commitment youth leaders make. They are often unsung heroes, and the church does well to sing their praises with support and celebrations.

We often commission short-term mission teams in church before they depart, but we rarely have an annual commissioning of volunteers working with children and teenagers. Showing such appreciation and affirmation goes a long way in filling the sails of volunteers for the next leg of their journey with teenagers. When parents invite youth leaders to share a meal with the family, it allows parents to build a relationship with youth leaders and also demonstrates a high level of appreciation. Often families in the church have resources to show appreciation to youth ministers without costing the church anything. Offering a youth minister the use of a vacation home, a recreational vehicle, a boat, tickets to a ballgame or a musical or the symphony, or frequent-flier miles or hotel points is a great way to show appreciation to a youth minister and his or her family.

Providing support for professional development is important in any profession, but it is exponentially important in student ministry because

Evaluating the Health of a Ministry

I have worked in all types of ministry situations, some healthier than others. Right now I am in a very healthy church. Yet I still get flashbacks about the unhealthy staff situations that I have encountered. It has always been difficult to evaluate the situation myself. I make the most of what I have, and sometimes I become too proud to realize there is a better way. We need constant reminders from people inside and outside of our church to help us see what is effective and what is ineffective. This pruning can create health and growth!

Chad Fransen, Bidwell Presbyterian Church,
Chico, California

most churches have only one full-time youth minister. In a public school, a teacher has the opportunity to dialogue with several department members who are all committed to the same subject; within the math department or the English department, teachers have a built-in support system. This is true in most professions: people work alongside others in the same vocation who are committed to the same goals and struggling with the same issues.

While a church often has several staff members, the positions are very different—complementary, but different. Hence, pastors need to spend time networking with other pastors who are dealing with similar issues. Likewise, children's ministers and youth ministers need to network with other professionals in the same positions in other churches who are dealing with similar issues. It is a gift to all ministers when the culture of the church supports staff networking with ministers in similar positions at other churches. Many communities have local networks of youth workers who support one another and often plan cooperative events together. The National Network of Youth Workers strives to develop and support local networks of youth workers across the country.[19]

In addition to local networking, professional development conferences are an essential resource afforded student ministry staff in churches that prioritize student ministry. A variety of national conventions for student ministry and ministry leadership are appropriate for student ministers and volunteer staff. While it can be expensive to send a whole student ministry team to a national convention, there are also regional and sometimes local conferences, symposiums, or forums on student ministry that are very valuable for youth ministers to attend with their teams of volunteer leaders.

Thriving in Student Ministry

We often joke about the great challenges of student ministry, saying, "If you can survive student ministry, you can survive anything!" While this is often hyperbole mixed with a dash of truth, youth ministers serving in churches that make student ministry a high priority tend to thrive rather than just survive, because they are well resourced on a variety of levels.

Several years ago Kevin Lawson conducted a classic study of associate staff ministers that included children's ministers, youth ministers, music ministers, and other associate ministers.[20] Rather than conducting exit interviews with those who had burned out in ministry to discover what went wrong, Lawson aimed to determine the factors associated with those who believed they were thriving in ministry. The first step in the study was to identify those who were truly thriving. Once those ministers were identified, Lawson asked them to describe the factors that contributed to their high level of satisfaction in ministry. Not surprisingly, there was no secret, three-step plan. Lawson was able to identify eight factors, however, that were common to those thriving in associate staff ministry regardless of the particular position they held. These eight factors have withstood the test of time, and many of those in the study were in fact serving in student ministry.

Each of these factors requires contribution from the individual as well as from the church leadership and the congregation. The achievement of these eight factors is not the sole responsibility of an individual but the result of a community working together. Individuals must strive to build these attributes into their own lives, while the senior leadership of the church must work to create an environment in which these attributes may be fully realized. It is interesting to note that many of these attributes are not confined to the work of ministry, or even full-time work, for that matter. Wherever you find yourself in life at this moment, as an employee or volunteer in any organization or group, most of these attributes are relevant to your situation. If you are a leader or a manager, you will find most of these attributes helpful in creating a workplace in which your staff will flourish.

Consider the following attributes and the ways in which youth ministers and churches contribute to each. Also, consider how each attribute relates to your current work and how you might use these attributes to create a healthier work environment.

Satisfaction in Following God

Lawson found that those who were thriving in ministry found satisfaction in following what they perceived to be God's direction for their life and ministry. When staff felt confident in their call to ministry, they tended to have a "peace of mind and confidence that this work is what they should be doing."[21] Those with a genuine sense of calling to their position were passionate about their ministry and seemed to persevere even in the midst of stress and adversity. In those challenging seasons of ministry, staff with a strong sense of calling sought out God as commended by the great preacher Phillips Brooks: "Do not pray for tasks equal to your powers. Pray for the powers equal to your tasks!"[22] Lawson suggests that such confidence in one's calling leads to joy, fulfillment, and contentment in ministry.

While much of understanding one's calling is personal, there is a community element as well. For youth ministers to be confident in their calling, there must be a confirmation of that calling from the faith community. Richard Niebuhr describes this as the "ecclesiastical call."[23] Formal, isolated instances of confirmation—in hiring a youth minister, for example, or at a service in which the minister is installed—are not sufficient. Instead, the senior pastor, elders, and members of the congregation should regularly assert such a confirmation. We are reminded by the wisdom of the Proverbs that "anxiety weighs down the heart, but a kind word cheers it up" (Prov. 12:25).

The installation of a minister—whether it occurs in a special worship service or in a special moment within a regular worship service, which is more typical for associate staff—is a communal act of support and affirmation. It should be viewed as the start of an ongoing process of affirming the minister's calling throughout her time in ministry at the local church. When the church provides regular, informal support and affirmation of the minister's calling, it helps to solidify the confidence of the individual in her own assessment of God's direction in life and ministry. Paul reminds the churches of the Epistles time and time again to encourage one another and build each other up. We too must encourage and build up those who serve in student ministries so that they may be confident in their call.

Collegiality among Staff

Lawson found that among those who were thriving in ministry, the ability to work well with their supervisor and other staff members was vital. Few understand the importance of relationships in ministry more than youth ministers. Relational ministry has been a hallmark of student ministry for decades, but often we forget that relationships are important in every area of life, including the workplace. Reflecting on the insights of his research, Lawson states, "Great work relationships with a ministry supervisor and other staff members do not just happen. They take commitment, effort, an awareness of those things that nurture or interfere with the health of these relationships, and the willingness to forgive. The issue is not so much finding a great staff to join as it is learning how to encourage good work relations as a priority and acting on what you as an individual staff member can contribute to staff harmony."[24]

Building a healthy staff community is everyone's responsibility. Once again, encouragement and affirmation are important, but staff relationships also include issues of trust, loyalty, and credibility. When the leadership of a church creates an environment that fosters such attributes, staff members tend to be more willing to contribute to healthy collegial relationships, which in turn contribute to satisfaction in ministry. Likewise, when the leadership of the church allows the environment to become laced with cynicism, betrayal, and insincerity, building healthy relationships and being good citizens of the community become very difficult for staff members. Staff members become suspicious, turn to gossip, and engage in competition with one another rather than working in supportive cooperation.

Lawson draws heavily on the Proverbs in discussing this issue, as they are loaded with wisdom for developing healthy staff relationships:

Trust—"Many claim to have unfailing love, but a faithful person who can find?" (Prov. 20:6).

Loyalty—"One who has unreliable friends soon comes to ruin, but there is a friend who sticks closer than a brother" (Prov. 18:24).

Mentoring—"As iron sharpens iron, so one person sharpens another" (Prov. 27:17).

Partnership—"Two are better than one, because they have a good return for their labor" (Eccles. 4:9).

Credibility—"A good name is more desirable than great riches; to be esteemed is better than silver or gold" (Prov. 22:1).

Honest Evaluation—"Wounds from a friend can be trusted, but an enemy multiplies kisses" (Prov. 27:6).

A church can offer a youth minister nothing more valuable than a healthy work environment in which she can be herself, share freely and honestly without condemnation, and contribute to an atmosphere that strives for unity within the diversity of the ministries in the church.

Positive Attitudes and Commitments

Lawson found that among those who were thriving in ministry, attitudes and level of commitment were highly correlated to the degree of satisfaction they found in fulfilling their ministry responsibilities. When one's attitudes are poor, the chances of finding satisfaction in one's work are very slim, and the quality of the work is likely to suffer. While everyone becomes frustrated at times, maintaining a healthy attitude can mitigate feelings of being overwhelmed by moments or even seasons of discouragement.

Lawson found that those who had a strongly positive attitude in ministry maintained a strong sense that their ministry was valuable both to those they served and to God. Often in the early years of ministry with students, youth leaders enjoy the work they are doing. They love the students, enjoy creating programs, and appreciate being part of a student ministry team. While they believe from the onset of their work that the ministry is important, it is often not until youth leaders see transformation in the lives of students and families that they begin to truly value the ministry to which God has called them.

The significance of a ministry must also be affirmed by others in the youth leader's community, such as parents, elders, senior pastors, other staff, and people in the congregation who may have no direct connection to student ministries. If the youth minister is the only one in the church who believes the ministry is valuable, he or she may begin to feel delusional. Doubts begin to creep in, and the minister starts wondering if the hard work of ministry is worth the investment. Hence, ministry leaders must surround themselves with people who will affirm the ministry as valuable and be supportive when they are in need of a second wind.

Closely related to finding value in ministry is finding contentment in ministry. Student ministry is not often the most visible ministry in the church. Sometimes youth leaders can begin to feel their work is invisible, which may lead to a desire for a more visible role, more affirmation, and the feeling of a greater level of importance. Innate confidence in one's call to student ministry is essential to maintaining a positive attitude. In Lawson's words, "It is hard to thrive in ministry if you find yourself wishing you were doing something else or serving somewhere else. It's hard to give yourself to your work if you find no real joy in doing it well. A spirit of contentment where you are, doing what you are doing, is critical if you are going to find satisfaction in your ministry."[25]

Paul reminds us of the importance of learning to be content in every situation. Contentment is often a matter of perspective and of taking the broader view of the situation, as Paul does in his Letter to the Philippians.

> I rejoiced greatly in the Lord that at last you renewed your concern for me. Indeed, you were concerned, but you had no opportunity to show it. I am not saying this because I am in need, for I have learned to be content whatever the circumstances. I know what it is to be in need, and I know what it is to have plenty. I have learned the secret of being content in any and every situation, whether well fed or hungry, whether living in plenty or in want. I can do all this through him who gives me strength. (Phil. 4:10–13)

Finding the type of contentment that Paul describes takes a tremendous amount of tolerance and resolve. Student ministry is not a sprint but a marathon, and maintaining the long view requires a high degree of persistence. In most situations, it takes three years in a full-time student ministry position to begin seeing the fruits of one's labor. Those who do not have the fortitude to run the race will bail out, missing the opportunity that God has set before them.

Tolerance is the ally of patience, though the term has been perverted in our culture. Tolerance is often understood to mean acceptance. In reality, tolerance requires disagreement: I cannot tolerate your position on an issue unless I disagree with it. When we agree to disagree, we have entered into an acceptable state of tolerance with one another. Developing the patience to graciously tolerate the views or decisions of others fosters an attitude of generosity that makes it easier to navigate challenging situations.

In addition to maintaining a positive attitude in the midst of ministry, Lawson found four essential commitments that contributed to satisfaction in ministry. Commitments to growing, to people, to longevity, and to supervisors are essential. Each of us is constantly growing and learning and becoming more of a kingdom-building person. When we decide that we have it all figured out is precisely when we begin to fall short and question the value of our involvement in ministry. Ministry, like faith, is a journey, and it is essential to find significant ways to continue growing in ministry. Professional associations, conference meetings, seminars, networking, and reading are all essential elements of professional growth and development. Churches that make professional development opportunities available—for example, by providing funding for conferences and time for study leaves—create an environment that fosters satisfaction in ministry.

The church can become program driven very easily and student ministry can be very prone to overprogramming. It is essential to "keep focus on the people served, not on the programs or activities organized and run."[26] There is nothing wrong with celebrating a well-run retreat, and there is great satisfaction in finally getting the small-group Bible studies working well, but programs are constantly changing and will never provide enough satisfaction for one to persevere in long-term ministry. It is essential to remember that our true satisfaction is found in participating in the story of God's people and in the transforming work of God's Spirit in the lives of those we are privileged to serve.

In addition to focusing on the people involved in one's own student ministry, it is equally important to serve people outside the student ministry. This may take the form of volunteering in another ministry inside or outside of the church, mentoring others who are in ministry, or serving the local community in various ways. Contributing to others outside of student ministries can generate creative thinking, reenergize dormant passions, and encourage youth leaders to understand their own ministry in the larger context of the church and the community in which they live.

Lawson suggests that becoming committed to longevity in ministry is also critical. Maintaining an attitude of perseverance requires a commitment to longevity. In addition to the youth minister's need to maintain this commitment, there must also be a commitment of the church leadership. People want to be in a place where they are wanted. When staff members are affirmed regularly and told by supervisors that they hope they will be in their current position for a long time, then staff members tend to make stronger commitments to longevity in ministry. Making a commitment to stay in a ministry for a significant period of time encourages growth and maturity in life and ministry. Skipping around from one ministry to another, year after year, because of conflicts or because the grass looks greener elsewhere, only leads to wounded relationships and self-destruction. Commitment to longevity in a particular context "reinforces stability and contentment, and helps the staff member deal with frustrations, challenges, and tempting job offers."[27] Youth ministers who maintain a high level of commitment are not easily frustrated, and they are slow to jump at every new job opportunity that appears. In many ways, commitment to longevity provides a safeguard that ensures a thoughtful process as one discerns the possibility of moving to another ministry.

The last area of commitment Lawson observed in those thriving in ministry was the commitment to support their supervisor. Often in student ministries this is the senior pastor, while in larger churches this may be another associate pastor. Valued staff members always support their supervisors publicly and discuss matters of disagreement privately. This creates a strong sense of loyalty and builds a spirit of partnership. Once again, this is a two-way street and calls for mutual support, one for the other, with the aim of achieving maximum effectiveness in ministry. Such loyalty, respect, and support are developed over time and are another testament to the value of commitment to longevity.

These attitudes and commitments serve as a foundation for thriving in student ministry. Churches that desire their staff to find satisfaction and meaning in student ministries create a culture in which these attributes are naturally fostered. Youth ministers desiring to thrive in ministry must constantly check their attitudes and commitments toward the church in general and toward their specific student ministries.

Healthy Church Environment

Throughout this section, I have suggested that thriving in ministry requires commitments from both the youth minister and the church leadership. In Lawson's findings, the health of the ministry environment was so critical that it was found to be one of the eight attributes of those who thrive in associate staff ministry. While it would be nice to advise people, "Go find a healthy church, and you will thrive in ministry," this simply is not the case. Every church has issues, and there are no perfect congregations to serve. While the community of faith creates the church environment, church leadership plays an essential role in fostering a healthy environment. Lawson found three essential areas that contribute to a healthy church environment for ministry.

General Characteristics of the Church

The first area involves the *general characteristics of the church* itself. Ministry staffs tend to thrive in churches that are healthy and growing. In this sense, a healthy church is one that functions in a manner characterized by unity, which is marked by love for God and others. Healthy churches offer people the opportunity to serve based on their gifts and talents, in order to build up the body of Christ (Eph. 4:11–16). Most important, healthy churches, as discussed in chapter 1, have a clear vision and purpose. This vision is clearly communicated to the congregation, and the congregation is united in moving forward in the same direction.

Lawson also found that support of particular ministry areas, in this case student ministry, was an essential component of a healthy church environment. This may seem obvious to the casual observer, but it is not unheard of for a church to hire a youth minister to care for the teenagers as a problem-solving tactic rather than to achieve a prophetic vision for the church and the community. Youth ministers in healthy churches feel that the congregation, elders, and staff believe in them and their ministry. They feel supported in their efforts to reach out to teenagers in the community and nurture those within the ministry. Garnering such support is achieved through clear communication between the ministry and the church community. Often people wish to be supportive, but they are not aware of what is happening in the student ministries. Communicating to the congregation and staff regularly is important for developing the support that is essential to a healthy environment.

Healthy churches are also open to new perspectives. Most youth ministers are either creative themselves or build a team of volunteers that includes a few very creative people. Churches that are open to fresh ideas attract staff members who are passionate about building ministries rather than maintaining programs. These churches offer a "supportive environment for the creative associate staff member to take risks and try out new ministry approaches without fearing that failure will result in rebuke or diminished congregational support."[28]

There are few aspects of a church more encouraging to a youth minister than a cohort of enthusiastic, engaged, and committed volunteer leaders. Healthy churches create an environment in which volunteers thrive. Serving as a volunteer in ministry is a joyful experience laced with appreciation and support. In turn, having highly committed lay leaders who are faithful and dependable provides strength for the church staff. It is not uncommon for a church to have one or two areas in which volunteers make significant contributions, but when serving becomes part of the ethos of church life and volunteering in ministry is viewed as a normal expectation of the congregation, then the health of the church's ministry environment grows exponentially.

Nature of the Ministry Position

The second area that Lawson identified concerning the church environment is the *nature of the ministry position*. Church job descriptions run the gamut and are not always well written—especially job descriptions for student ministries. On one end of the spectrum are job descriptions that are so open ended that no direction is given and the youth minister is left experimenting with various approaches to ministry until finding one that satisfies the church leadership and the congregation. On the other end of the spectrum are job descriptions that are so prescriptive and focused on programs that the youth minister is essentially charged with maintaining the ministry as it has existed for many years.[29]

Lawson found that those who are satisfied in their positions are afforded dynamic job descriptions that provide opportunities for increasing responsibility, creativity, and strategic ministry development. Such positions allow staff members room to experiment in their own areas of ministry and contribute to the broader ministry of the church. Youth ministers often have keen insights to contribute to the church leadership team, and in churches with dynamic ministry positions, youth leaders have a seat at the leadership staff meetings. This is essential if youth ministers are to be able to offer teenagers opportunities to contribute to the life of the church broadly, rather than stationing them in the student ministries corner of the church throughout middle and high school.

Such a dynamic ministry position is healthy in that it creates a greater sense of teamwork among the staff. It is important, however, to guard

Cultivating Mind, Body, and Spirit

A while ago I went out to lunch with my senior pastor. It was encouraging and life giving. But it's not like we go out to lunch every month or anything, so when we do spend time together, I listen carefully. He was asking me about my Sabbath and explained to me that my mind, body, and spirit are closely connected. He went on to explain that if you compartmentalize those three parts, it leads to unhealthiness. For example, it's been proven you feel better about yourself the more you exercise. Often we focus on cultivating our spirits more than our bodies and our minds. We need to be diligent in taking care of all of the parts of our selves. Are you seeking emotional health? Are you exercising and eating in healthy ways? The answer to these questions affects your spiritual vitality.

Andrew Breton, Grace Chapel,
Lexington, Massachusetts

against "job creep," in which significant time is diverted from the mission of student ministries toward other ministries of the church. When a youth minister is giving more than ten hours a week to other ministries in the church on a regular basis, the church does not have a full-time youth minister. If the church is hiring another youth minister as part of a strategic staff development plan that compensates for that time, then it may be prudent for the youth minister to expand on his or her position. For example, some youth ministers grow into a position in which they begin overseeing a college or young-adult ministry; others see the need to develop a ministry for fifth- and sixth-graders. This is all well and good, but it is likely that youth ministers can add such new ministry areas to their job descriptions only with additional staffing.

ENVIRONMENT OF SUPPORT FOR STAFF

The third area that Lawson identified as a mark of a healthy church for associate staff is an overall *environment of support for the staff member*. This is more than the congregation's affirmation and the church leadership's valuing of the ministry that was mentioned earlier. The support here is specific to the ministry position and essential to the well-being of a youth minister. Communication with the elder board is essential, as the board serves as overseers for the church and its ministries. This may come in the form of meeting regularly with the board as a whole or of having one or two elders assigned to the area of student ministry who meet with the youth minister regularly.

Churches must support youth ministers and their families with adequate compensation to meet their needs (as discussed in the last section), opportunities for professional development (as mentioned earlier in this section), and flexible work schedules to address family needs. This issue of family needs and work schedules is crucial, and far too many youth ministers have wrecked their marriages by ignoring their families in the name of ministry. Church leadership must provide support for fostering healthy families among the staff and hold ministers accountable for giving their families the time and attention necessary. It is very easy to spend every night of the week out with students in the name of ministry, but boundaries must be established. A wise friend of mine once advised that I had better be home more nights than I was out. This is sage advice, and those who are out more than two or three nights a week on a regular basis are asking for trouble on the home front. One brave woman recounts her story of living with a workaholic in student ministry.

My husband is a full-time youth director. He is extremely dedicated and spends between 50 and 70 hours a week with young people.

I think the reason he's so successful with kids is that he's always available to them, always ready to help them when they need him. That may be why the attendance has more than doubled in the past year. He knows how to talk their language. This past year he was out two and three nights a week talking with kids until midnight. He's always taking them to camps and on ski trips and overnight campouts. If he isn't with kids, he's thinking about them and preparing for his next encounter with them.

If he has any time after that, he's speaking or attending a conference where he shares with others what God is doing through him. When it comes to youth work, my husband has always given 100 percent.

I guess that's why I left him.

There isn't much left after 100 percent.[30]

This is a sad tale that is repeated far too often in ministry. Healthy churches foster healthy families, and that includes staff families. Generosity of vacation time, flexible schedules, and a "family first" mentality is essential in creating an environment where youth ministers thrive.

Spiritual Vitality

Often in ministry we become so busy working *for* God that we forget that it is God who works *through* us. This happens when youth ministers fail to give adequate attention to their own faith formation. Among the ministers that Lawson studied, those who claimed to be thriving in ministry also felt that they were growing in their faith. They made it a priority to seek God first and to remain open to the work toward which God was leading them. This was most evident in the prayer lives of these ministers. One youth pastor described the importance of a daily devotional time. "I know it sounds like a cliché, but my own quiet times are critical. It's a roller coaster. There are ups and downs, but there have been seasons of really rich times in the Word and just being quiet where the Lord has refreshed me. And if you don't have that, you are going to dry up. It's as simple as that."[31]

Max Lucado once said in an interview that we study the Bible for both information and inspiration. Each is equally important, and yet much of our study revolves around the educational component because we are predisposed to the teaching of others. When we miss the inspiration of Scripture in our lives, we are missing out on the full message that God is desperately trying to communicate to us. When we find ourselves in a dry season, we have most often missed God's inspirational message. Likewise, when the Scriptures appear to be dry, we have likely focused solely on the instructional component of the message and neglected the inspirational component.

Intimacy with God comes in different ways for different people. The key is to understand what spiritual disciplines help you remain in vital union with God. Some people love to journal, while others prefer discussion with an accountability partner. Some find personal retreats alone with God inspiring, while others prefer a regular routine of fasting. There is no magic formula; we are all created in the image of God, and we are all uniquely created. Understanding the habits that will maintain your spiritual vitality is essential, and it takes some time and exploration to work out an appropriate scheme.

One area that can be extremely difficult in the midst of ministry is engaging in worship. Often youth ministers assist in leading worship or have other duties that preclude them from engaging in worship on a regular basis. Even when youth ministers are in a worship service, they are often not engaged in worship because of the many distractions that are on their minds or that physically surround them if they are sitting in worship with a group of teenagers. Engaging in worship may require attending an evening service or an early service that is removed from the student ministry duties of Sunday. Some youth ministers have even found it helpful to worship at the evening service of another congregation when it is impossible to engage in worship at their own church. While perhaps not the best solution, maintaining spiritual vitality often requires some creativity.

The spiritual vitality of youth ministers is both individual and corporate. Church leaders must hold staff accountable for their faith formation—without becoming legalistic—while affording staff members the time and space necessary to engage fully in the faith formation process. Taking staff on soul-care retreats once a year is an excellent way to model, encourage, and highlight the importance of both individual and corporate faith formation. Over a period of time, one should be able to recognize the spiritual growth of a ministry team that is greater than the sum of the individuals. The same is true for the spiritual growth of the congregation.

One essential aspect of resourcing student ministry is providing resources for the spiritual growth of youth leaders. This begins at the top, with church leadership resourcing the staff's faith formation, but it must also flow through to the volunteer student ministry leaders. One of the most important responsibilities of a youth minister is to nurture the faith formation of volunteer leaders, both directly and indirectly. Youth ministers can speak directly into the lives of volunteers, but perhaps even more importantly, they can come alongside volunteers with suggested resources that will stimulate growth.

Multiple Supportive Relationships

Student ministry staff can never receive too much support from too many people. We have looked at the importance of relationships with colleagues and senior pastors, but supportive relationships do not end there. Lawson found that those thriving in ministry found support in multiple areas of life and ministry. "One of the strongest and clearest messages from this research is that the ability to thrive in associate staff ministry is greatly strengthened by our relationships with others who support, encourage, challenge, comfort, pray for, and believe in us."[32]

Such support may be found in numerous places. Over 90 percent of those in Lawson's study reported that they had developed close relationships with members of the congregation. These relationships provided the greatest encouragement and support when members of the congregation served as volunteers striving toward a common aim in student ministry. In addition, many staff found casual friendships within the congregation to be very supportive, as people would offer words of encouragement, thanks, praise, or a new perspective on a particular issue. One youth pastor described the importance of congregational support this way: "I moved into the youth ministry department and had three very frustrating years. There were four men on the youth committee, and they became my covenant group. Each one of them had a different task, and if it hadn't been for those four men I never would have survived. One called and told me the joke of the day, the chairman would take me out to lunch every once in a while, and another one would just give support. I think a support group like that is so important."[33]

While friends within the congregation are important, supportive friendships outside the congregation and outside of student ministry are also critical. Friends outside the church can bring fresh perspectives to particular situations and can be more objective than parishioners, who may hold prescribed views. Friends who work in other professions can provide a clarifying perspective from their fields. If a youth minister is having trouble with conflict among volunteer leaders, it may be very instructive to hear from a friend in engineering how a supervisor handles personal conflicts that arise in the department, or how a principal handles conflicts among teachers in a school, or how a manager handles conflicts among salespersons in a department store.

Supportive relationships may be found in the form of faithful prayer partners, generous accountability partners, peer support group members, wise mentors, and trusted counselors. Such relationships are treasured for their support and honest perspective. While such honest feedback may be difficult to hear it is essential to the growth process. We are always better for humbly accepting constructive criticism as well as heartfelt praise and affirmation.

Networking with others in student ministry is essential, especially for someone who is the only youth minister in a congregation. Those who have gone before have a responsibility to contribute wisdom to those who are following in their ministry footsteps. Few people understand what youth ministers experience better than those who are colaborers in student ministry. Networking with others also provides the opportunity to cooperate in ministry, accomplishing more together than any single ministry could accomplish alone. This often evolves in the form of a service project or social concern issue. When several student ministries in a community rally together, they bring all of their resources to bear on an issue or a project that none of them could conceive of tackling alone.

When church leadership supports, encourages, and affords youth ministers the time for networking with other like-minded congregations, everyone tends to thrive in ministry. The broader community and the congregations are the beneficiaries of such lavish support and cooperation.

Strong Family Support

No strength can compare to the support of a family. This may come in the form of support from a spouse and children, or from parents and relatives, or both. For those in Lawson's study who were married, an overwhelming 97 percent named the support of their spouse as a significant reason for their satisfaction and longevity in ministry. Sometimes a husband or wife serves alongside a spouse as a direct partner in student ministry; other times the spouse may serve in other areas of the church that are more suited to his or her gifts and talents. Regardless of how much direct involvement spouses have in the student ministries, their support and encouragement are invaluable.

The support of parents or a spouse is essential as one pursues a call in ministry. Their ability to listen, encourage, offer perspective, and understand the innate gifts and talents of their adult child or spouse is unmatched by others. Family members can offer the kind of personal care that is found only in a close-knit family through prayer, constructive feedback, and hospitality. There is nothing quite like returning from a retreat with teenagers to the comfort of home. Whether it is your home, your parents' home, or your grandparents' home, this oasis from the harried life of ministry offers rest and relaxation that is rarely found outside of the family.

Unfortunately, some ministry environments are toxic to family life, and everyone in ministry must be aware of the telltale signs of this type of environment. Lawson has identified several significant areas that threaten family life in ministry. Time management, for one, is a never-ending challenge. There are always more teenagers to reach, more students to disciple, more families to embrace, and more events to plan. Most full-time youth ministers can expect to work fifty to fifty-five hours a week on average and to be engaged in meetings or programs a couple of nights a week. When these numbers begin to increase beyond the norm, spouses, children, friends, and roommates begin to feel neglected. Along with the time commitment comes the emotional drain of student ministry. Caring for people can take a toll on emotions and manifest in a lack of patience and the need for withdrawal to decompress. When youth ministers arrive home without any energy left for their families on a consistent basis, the well-being of the families will inevitably suffer.

Many in ministry feel the pressure of unrealistic expectations from the congregation. Living in a fishbowl, with one's personal life in full view, can bring pressure to fulfill the often unspoken expectations of the congregation to live a perfect life, raise perfect children, maintain a perfect marriage, and make perfect social choices. Spouses of youth ministers sometimes feel the pressure to engage in ministry duties that are outside of their area of interest or giftedness. Even those who mean well can drain those living in the public arena by constantly asking how they are doing, what's new, or how they can pray for the youth minister and his or her family. Often life just does not change as much from one week to the next as some people think, and these well-intentioned questions can be draining.

It is essential for those who wish to thrive in ministry and for those in church leadership who desire a healthy staff to protect time for staff members' families. While there will always be seasonal demands in student ministry, it is important to prevent such demands from becoming routine and to compensate for the high-demand seasons when they do come. Being intentional about scheduling date nights and family nights, getting away together, having meals together, and listening to one another is essential in maintaining a healthy family life in the midst of serving in student ministry. There will always be more ministry to accomplish, but it should never be done at the expense of family priorities. Many people can come alongside those who minister to young people and even replace them in order to achieve the goals of student ministry, but those who are married are the only ones who can be a spouse to their husband or wife. Those who have children of their own are the only ones who can be a mothers or fathers to their children. The God-ordained roles of spouse and parent should never be compromised. These roles are irreplaceable, and when student ministry begins to infringe upon them, it is time to reevaluate everything.

Youth ministers rarely realize that ministry is compromising their family relationships until a spouse suggests there is a problem. When that moment happens, it is essential to drop everything, sit down, and listen to the person you trust more than anyone in the world. This is the first step in strengthening the family.

Ability to Savor Joys and Weather Storms

While the aim of student ministry is always life transformation, there are numerous ups and downs along the way. Challenges emerge from every corner of the ministry landscape, and no one is immune from riding the roller coaster of highs and lows in student ministry leadership. The final characteristic of associate staff members who thrive, rather than merely survive, in ministry is their ability to rejoice in the joys of ministry and press on through the inevitable storms without being overwhelmed.

Lawson found that those who thrive in their positions find joy in a variety of aspects of ministry. While many reported finding joy in using their God-given gifts for the work of the kingdom, they also find joy in the experiences of fellow staff members and volunteers. While this may be seen as vicarious joy, it is no less real. Few aspects of ministry are more rewarding than seeing students and volunteers becoming fruitful in ministry as they grow in areas of responsibility that reflect their unique gifts and talents. One minister put it this way: "My job is to equip people to do the work of ministry. And so whenever we see people succeed and get to the point where they can be ministers and are equipped to do that, that is very rewarding. People coming to know Christ and then being built up and equipped to do ministry, and then doing it."[34]

It is often necessary to weather some storms before developing real joy in ministry. The greatest joy—seeing ministry multiply as students who have been nurtured in their faith begin contributing to the ministry of the church in adulthood—takes years to realize. Only those who stay in ministry over the long haul can experience the exhilaration of serving alongside adult leaders who were once students in their ministry.

Weathering the storms is highly related to savoring the joys. Many people in Lawson's study maintained what he calls a *joy file*. This is nothing fancy—just a box or file folder or desk drawer in which one keeps notes of thanks, words of affirmation, and highlights of ministry. When trials come, this collection of memories is a tremendous source of encouragement. Likewise, a picture is worth a thousand words. Placing pictures of cherished people and moments in ministry on your office wall, in the youth room, or on your computer desktop or screen saver is an important daily reminder of the value of ministry with adolescents.

Sometimes navigating the turbulence of ministry requires more than joyful memories. Those who thrive in ministry are not shy about seeking the advice and wisdom of others. Often simply talking out loud to a trusted friend about a difficult situation brings peace and clarity. It is also helpful to remember that everyone is on a journey of growth and formation. Often the greatest growth in our lives occurs when we find ourselves in challenging situations. While we may not recognize this in the moment, understanding this process and remembering that God is in the business of redemption allows us, even in the midst of turmoil, to ask: *What might I learn through this? What might be redeemed through this?*

Serving in student ministry is an adventure like no other, and mountaintop experiences can be followed quickly by dark valleys. This is the nature of life in ministry. Learning to be content in every situation is about learning to "be quick to listen, slow to speak and slow to become

Keeping the Body Together

When Paul describes the church body as a unit in 1 Corinthians 12, each member is indispensable to the body, its function, and its growth. When we segregate our ministries by age, or exclude certain parts from contributing, it is like tearing appendages off the body and scattering them to corners of the building! If this is a consistent habit of the church, those appendages are in critical danger because they've been separated from the rest of the body. While there is certainly room for segregated ministries in the church, we often exclusively default to this ministry model because it seems like the easiest way to grow each member of the body. But God intentionally made our body parts with different functions, and in the same way, church leaders should create opportunities for each Christ-follower to contribute his or her strengths and talents to the body of Christ, displaying all its diversity.

Andrew Beach, First Evangelical Church,
Memphis, Tennessee

angry, because human anger does not produce the righteousness that God desires" (James 1:19–20).

As I have mentioned numerous times, thriving in ministry is a communal responsibility. While youth ministers contribute much to their own satisfaction in ministry, church leadership must create an environment in which ministry staff can thrive. Youth ministers' supervisors, be they senior pastors or senior associate pastors, contribute significantly to an atmosphere conducive to thriving in ministry. Those who were identified as thriving in ministry reported twelve actions and attitudes that they highly valued in their supervisors and that contributed to their satisfaction in ministry.[35]

- Treating staff members as partners in ministry, not just subordinates.
- Leading the ministry team through a vision-casting process.
- Demonstrating trust and belief in staff members' ministry abilities.
- Being available and approachable to discuss ministry issues.
- Being supportive and encouraging, both privately and publicly.
- Demonstrating care for the minister as well as the ministry.
- Demonstrating loyalty in the midst of ministry challenges.
- Maintaining open and honest lines of communication.
- Providing constructive feedback that fosters growth.
- Being a spiritual leader and mentor in ministry proficiencies.

- Encouraging and supporting personal and professional development.
- Praying for staff and praying with staff, privately and publicly.

Supervisors and church leaders who engage in these behaviors create an environment in which people are able to find great satisfaction and truly have the opportunity to thrive in ministry.

Resourcing student ministry is not a simple undertaking and should never be taken for granted. Developing a comprehensive ministry in which all students matter and youth ministers, paid and volunteer, thrive in their ministry among teenagers requires a calculated and strategic plan of action. Funding must be adequate, staff must be developed, vision must be cast, and ministry must be implemented and constantly evaluated. Anything less is not worthy of the call that God has placed on us: to engage in and foster the transformational stories of adolescents.

Are You Thriving in Ministry?

Based on the eight factors for thriving in ministry, how do you score? Answer each question below with *no, sometimes,* or *yes.*

1. Do you have a strong call to ministry?
2. Do you feel like your church believes in your call to ministry?
3. Do you receive regular informal support and affirmation?
4. Do you work well with your supervisor?
5. Are expectations for you clear?
6. Do you work well with *all* of your coworkers?
7. Do you feel that your ministry is valuable?
8. Do others feel that your ministry is valuable?
9. Do you meet with other people not connected with your church?
10. Are your volunteers highly committed to the ministry?
11. Do you have a healthy balance of life and ministry?
12. Does your church *really* encourage you to find balance?

Give yourself one point for each *no* answer, two points for each *sometimes,* and three points for each *yes.* Now add up your score.

If you scored:
30–36 points: You are thriving!
20–29 points: You have some issues that need to be addressed.
12–19 points: You need to make some significant changes to begin thriving in ministry.

Discussion Questions for Student Ministry Leaders

1. Do you have the resources to reach both students within the church and students outside of the church? What are some creative ways to reach both groups within the constraints of current resources?

2. What are ways you can better equip, encourage, celebrate, and support your volunteer staff? How are you investing in people around you such as current volunteers, future volunteers, future youth ministers, and parents? How would your congregation respond to commissioning volunteers who work with youth and children?

3. Where are you thriving in ministry, and where are you merely surviving? How does your church prepare you and support you in raising leaders to do ministry?

4. Take inventory of four areas of your ministry. Are you being a good steward of the finances currently available? Are you developing people around you? Are you adding to the health of your ministry environment? Are you taking care of yourself physically, emotionally, and spiritually?

5. What tools do you have in place to guard your family life? If you are married and have children, what do your spouse and children say about the amount of time and commitment you invest in the ministry? How can you guard your spouse from possible expectations from the church to be involved in student ministry?

Discussion Questions for Church Leaders

1. If you are reading this book, you likely have a desire for a strong student ministry in your church. What are some limitations that prevent you from resourcing your student ministry as a mission of the church to teenagers outside the church family?

2. Many church leaders would say their churches are committed to reaching students. But do you have the courage to advocate and appropriate at least 10 percent of your church's total budget to student ministry? Keeping in mind the suggestions in this chapter for increasing financial resources for the student ministry, how could your congregation realistically invest in a comprehensive student ministry?

3. What are some ways that you could inspire the church leadership to creatively offer stronger support to student ministry staff and volunteer leaders?

4. Based on the leader-to-student ratios, is the student ministry properly resourced with paid staff and volunteer leaders for the current number of students? (Refer to table 3.1.) If not, how could the gap be bridged? How could the ministry be staffed for growth, with a vision of reaching 20 percent of teenagers in the local community?

5. Are you creating an environment in which your student ministry leaders are merely surviving or truly thriving? Answer this question by surveying parents, interviewing students, and having conversations with student ministry leaders.

6. How important is student ministry in light of the church's vision and values? If student ministry is highly valued in your context, how might your church need to reallocate funds, encourage current volunteers and future volunteers, and support your student ministries staff?

7. Most times we like to think we are doing well, but we can always do better. How can you make an honest assessment of student ministries in your church, and how can you humbly initiate change where it is needed?

4

When Teenagers Matter:

THEY BECOME PART OF THE CHURCH

Time and again people say, "We are losing our young people from the church." It's time for a reality check. In many cases, our young people have never been part of the church. Even when we have developed seemingly strong comprehensive student ministries, we often relegate teenage contributions to areas of service within the student ministries themselves.

More often than not, teenagers are segregated from the adult population of the church into specialized, "age-appropriate" programs and are only occasionally put on display for the adult congregation during a Youth Sunday or a mission-trip commissioning ceremony. They have grown up in the church building week after week. They know the church property like their home. They participate enthusiastically in their specialized programs. But they have never been assimilated into the larger intergenerational community of the church.

Many teenagers in the church rarely attend an intergenerational worship service, opting instead for the homogeneous youth worship program that has become a church of its own within the church. In at least one instance, I have witnessed a church move Sunday morning student ministry programs to the same hour that the contemporary worship service was being held in the sanctuary for logistical reasons. The result was that the vast majority of teenagers no longer attended the church worship service, rejecting the earlier traditional style service and choosing their youth program—consisting of worship, teaching, and small groups—over the contemporary service in the sanctuary.

This phenomenon is nothing new to student ministry, as the seeds of this separatist culture are planted early on in children's ministry. In decades past, it was common for children to participate in the first part of a worship service, come forward for a children's sermon, and then leave for their age-appropriate programs. While some churches still follow this pattern, more and more churches—often growing churches in need of seating for adults—have chosen to remove children from the worship service altogether. Children are provided with their own specialized programs that include worship, teaching, and small groups. Parents drop their children off before the worship service and retrieve them afterward, thus providing both adults and children with highly satisfying worship experiences on Sunday morning, albeit in different locations.

The pattern then becomes one in which children grow up in a "children's church," then move into the "middle school church," and then to the "high school church." The tragic result of this trend is that students graduate from high school having outgrown the "high school church" and having rarely experienced an intergenerational worship service or "adult church" and they have no place to go. If they go to college, they may replace their student ministry with college Christian fellowship but rarely attend church.[1] Once they graduate from college, with few age-appropriate options remaining, these emerging adults find themselves orphan Christians without a faith community.

Integrating Teenagers into the Church

The movie *Failure to Launch* is a romantic comedy about three men in their thirties who, having failed to take the leap into adulthood, are still living at home with their parents. They are not ready to engage fully in adult society, and, in many respects, the adult world is not ready to embrace the three of them. They just refuse to grow up and embrace the transition from adolescence to adulthood.

This transition is less mysterious than once imagined. The reality is that *we are who we were*, and our faith commitments tend to follow a rather predictable pattern. The research of the National Study of Youth and Religion, led by Christian Smith, found a significant amount of religious stability and continuity among those moving from adolescence to emerging adulthood. Even those who are likely to decline in their religiosity as young adults can be identified in the adolescent years by observing key factors related to religious decline. Smith writes that "the lives of many teenagers who are transitioning into the emerging adult years reflect a lot more religious stability and continuity than is commonly realized. Everything simply does not change. The past continues to shape the future. This is important to know, because it means that religious commitments, practices, and investments made during childhood and the teenage years, by parents and others in family and religious communities, matter—they make a difference."[2]

While Smith has identified several factors that contribute to high levels of faith among emerging adults, personal relationships with adults (parents and other caring adults) who connect teenagers to the faith community in the middle and high school years is necessary in almost all cases.[3] Further, Lisa Pearce and Melinda Lundquist Denton found that teenagers who were the most committed to their faith reported that, in addition to having parents and close friends who shared their beliefs, they were also connected to a faith community that provided "a welcoming, challenging atmosphere that *values and integrates youth.*"[4]

Transformation happens most deeply in the lives of teenagers when they are engaged in the broader life of the church and connected to a network of caring adults. This is not meant to minimize the role of student ministries, which are the launching pads of adolescent faith transformation. Nothing is more reflective of healthy student ministries than students who launch into the full and robust life of the church. In order for this to happen, though, the broader church must be prepared for and committed to receiving teenagers into its midst by valuing them for who they are and allowing them to contribute to the whole life of the church. This is a very countercultural perspective, as few institutions embrace the notion of allowing students to contribute to the adult world.

Dave Coryell suggests that most churches view students from one of three perspectives.[5] Churches that view teenagers as *rocks* do not see much, if any, value in their young people. Adolescents are understood to be adults in waiting, who need to patiently wait their turn to take on significant roles in the church. Their opinions on leadership decisions in the church are not valued, and they typically have few meaningful relationships with adults. Worship services are rarely designed to engage or involve teenagers.

Churches that view teenagers as *receivers* foster "passing" language, which places adolescents as recipients of the church programs, values, norms, ethics, traditions, and beliefs. Students become static receptacles of the church's teachings and are offered few, if any, avenues of contribution outside of the student ministries programs. While there is much for teenagers to learn, faith formation requires contribution and involvement that is more significant than a faith passed down from the previous generation.

Churches that view teenagers as *reservoirs* understand that students have much to contribute to the life and ministry of the church. Adults in these churches are willing to build relationships with teenagers and invest the time necessary in developing their gifts and talents, encouraging them to contribute in nearly every aspect of church life. In this sense, students are contributing and connected to the life of the whole church.

Making Connections

In our technological society, life is predicated upon connections. Ted Gregory, a reporter for the *Chicago Tribune*, suggests that we are *hyperconnected*.[6] His interviews with college students reveal that it is not uncommon for students to have three to five electronic devices, including a laptop, smartphone, e-reader, and multiple iPods (one for the car and one for the gym). We are constantly connecting with people via text messages, cell phones, email, video chats, and Facebook. As long as these connections remain viable, all is well. But as soon as a network drops a call or a server goes down, interrupting the internet feed for email or Facebook, we feel helpless and disconnected. All of this technology certainly makes connecting easier, when it works, but it also has the potential to proliferate superficial connections. Before we consider the connections between teenagers and the adult population of the church, it is important to ponder the issue of community fellowship in a high-tech, low-touch culture.

A strong and active fellowship among believers in a faith community is an essential component of a healthy church. Our technology certainly keeps us connected with more people faster than ever before, but what level of connection is being maintained? Is the church increasing or decreasing in its ability to live out the "one another" passages in Scripture? More than fifty times following the ascension of Christ, as the early church is being established, the Scriptures remind God's people how to live in community with one another. For example, we are called to:

accept (Rom. 15:7), admonish (Col. 3:16), build up (Eph. 4:29), care for (1 Cor. 12:25 KJV), comfort (1 Thess. 4:18 KJV), confess to (James 5:16), be devoted to (Rom. 12:10), encourage (1 Thess. 5:11), fellowship with (1 John 1:7), forgive (Eph. 4:32), greet (Rom. 16:16), honor (Rom. 12:10), love (Rom. 13:8), pray for (James 5:16), serve (Gal. 5:13), and submit to (Eph. 5:21) one another.

Living in community is different today than it was in the early churches of the New Testament era. Life is demanding and fast paced, but in some ways our technology helps us to stay connected and live out these "one another" passages. In other ways, our technology interferes with our ability to live out these commands. No matter where we land in such a conversation about things that compromise community, it is important to realize that we are not the first generation to struggle with the issue. As the letter's author encourages the Hebrews to persevere in their faith, he emphasizes the importance of community. "Let us hold unswervingly to the hope we profess, for he who promised is faithful. And let us consider how we may spur one another on toward love and good deeds, not giving up meeting together, as some are in the habit of doing, but encouraging one another—and all the more as you see the Day approaching" (Heb. 10:23–25). Staying connected is essential to caring for one another, and churches that care for one another are churches in which people are connected to one another in authentic and meaningful ways.

In order for students to become connected to the whole church, the whole church must highly value community. Many churches, large and small, work tirelessly to ensure that everyone feels connected and welcome in the faith community. For churches of only a few hundred people, this is easier, as everyone knows everyone and gathering the whole fellowship together in one place is not too difficult. Churches that number more than a thousand people tend to develop small groups, regional groups, or some kind of community group system that helps people to connect with others who live in close proximity, or who are in a similar stage of life, or who are interested in similar issues. There are myriad strategies for fostering fellowship in large churches, and most make community development a priority because of how easily people can fall through the cracks of a large church.

Churches that are most at risk for failing in the area of fellowship are those in the five- to eight-hundred-persons range. These churches, which are often growing fast, have outgrown the small, family-church size, in which connection and community happen almost naturally. Yet they may not have realized that people are falling through the cracks. Once they begin pushing the one-thousand-persons size, it will become

Intergenerational Bonds

For twenty years, our church has run a midweek K–6 program during the school year called LOGOS, a program of GenOn Ministries. This program incorporates anyone of any age in the faith formation of all who are involved. There are parents and grandparents who help out in the kitchen or serve as a table parent during dinner, teachers from thirty-five to eighty years of age responsible for Bible study, music teachers who help to teach worship skills, and a "young-at-heart" fifty-four-year-old who creates and runs games for the kids. After around eleven years of the LOGOS program, teenagers who had aged out of the program didn't want to quit coming to LOGOS. They decided to help and become Living LOGOS (living out God's Word). Teens teach and participate in Bible study, help to run games, assist with music and worship skills, and set up for dinner. College kids return on breaks and seek out the eighty-two-year-old woman who has always been a kitchen helper or the fifty-four-year-old dad who creates energy and excitement no matter what he's doing. All ages contribute to this intergenerational ministry, and lifelong bonds have been developed.

Niki Brodeur, First Presbyterian Church,
Pittsford, Massachusetts

obvious that a community strategy is essential. In the meantime, they are in danger of believing that everyone is connecting as if they are still a small family-church.

To place a high priority on connecting students to the larger congregation, the church must be committed to the value of community and "one anothering" among its adults. Such modeling is essential to the success of inviting adolescents into the fellowship of the whole church. Once a church has established a deep commitment to community, the assimilation of adolescents becomes the responsibility of the entire community, the whole pastoral staff, and all parents of teenagers. This is not an endeavor that can be executed by the youth minister alone.

Making connections usually begins in the student ministry itself, as faithful adult leaders connect with students. It is essential that these connections happen not only at the regularly scheduled programs but also between programs. Adults make connections with teenagers by demonstrating a curiosity about the interests of teenagers. This type of relational ministry is often the lifeblood of student ministries. In order to engage all the students in this relational manner, it is essential to maintain a 1:5 leader-to-student ratio, as discussed in the last chapter. This ratio helps students remain connected to leaders, to small groups, and to the student ministry. This ratio doesn't always translate to assimilating students into the life of the broader church, however, unless leaders intentionally make assimilation a priority and the church develops environments that are welcoming and engaging to students.

Recently Chap Clark and Kara Powell have suggested that we consider flipping the ratio from 1:5 to a ratio of 5:1 that strives to have five adults caring for one student.[7] While this is not a new suggestion—Chap Clark first wrote about it in 2004 and Jim Burns declared its importance in 2008—it seems to be gaining greater traction in our relationally starved culture today.[8] This is not to suggest that the student ministry should have five times as many volunteer leaders as students, or that a small group of ten students would have fifty adult leaders! The idea is that teenagers need multiple adults speaking into their lives.

Many teenagers already have multiple adults in their lives. They have teachers, coaches, youth leaders, scout leaders, and music instructors. My daughter is regularly connecting with her small group leader at church, her flute instructor, her track coach, her yearbook adviser, and her Young Life leaders, all of whom are wonderful role models. They are not all part of our church community, and there is nothing wrong with that. But what if there were another two or three or four adults from our church with whom she was connected as well? In fact, there are, and I will talk about them a little later. Each of these connections, large and small, help teenagers feel engaged and connected to the local congregation that is their church home.

Clark and Powell give an excellent example of how parents can foster these adult connections through small groups, or what we call *life communities* at my church. The idea behind the name is that the group is more than an adult Bible study; it is a group that actually does life together.

> Early on, [this small group] decided that they wanted to do more than study the Bible together every week or two; they wanted to be families who stuck together.
>
> Every three months, they bring their calendars to their small group meeting. As is typical in small groups of busy families, they plan several months in advance when they are going to meet. But unlike most small groups, they have taken calendaring to a new level.
>
> This small group has covenanted to make each other's family events a joint priority. So during their quarterly calendar review, not only do they plan their meetings, but they also share important upcoming family dates and events. All five families mark the Sunday afternoon when Claire has her piano recital. All five families make a note of Mario's Eagle Scout

ceremony. All five families jot down the date and time of Isabella's middle school graduation. And as much as possible, the five families try to attend these milestone events.

That's 5:1. That's kingdom community.[9]

Consider for a moment the places in which teenagers make connections with adults on a Sunday morning at church in addition to the student ministries venue. Perhaps each week at the front door they shake the hand of the same greeter, who knows them by name. Perhaps they sit in the same seat of the sanctuary each week with family or friends, surrounded by the same adults who know them and who offer a friendly inquiry into the happenings of their week.

A few times every year most churches baptize or dedicate children, depending on the tradition of the church. The occasions are marked by the joy of parents and grandparents, the endearing innocence of babies, and often a baby's surprised reaction to the experience. One aspect common to all such rituals is the asking of a question to the congregation. The question is always something like: "Will you promise to love, support, and care for these children as they live and grow in Christ?" To which the congregation gives a rousing: "We will!" But do they? And how? Unfortunately, if you asked most church members to name the children they had promised to love and support, they would be at a loss for words.

But what if in that moment, rather than everyone in the congregation (especially a large congregation) pledging to love and support every child, a small handful of adults pledged to love and support one child, or one adult small group pledged to care for one child and their family? Children's baptism and dedication pledges were designed in the context of small, family-style congregations and still function well in that context. Larger churches, though, need to consider adapting these pledges for their context in such a way that it is truly meaningful. Imagine a family coming forward with their child *and* ten or fifteen other adults and children that compose their life community or small group, who commit to walking alongside this child in faith for the next two decades.

Connecting children and teenagers to a broad range of adults in the church must be done with great intentionality. Yet connections alone are not enough. While it feels very supportive for students to be known by other adults in the congregation, formation of individuals and communities requires contribution. When teenagers matter and student ministry is a priority of the church, students are afforded opportunities to contribute to the whole life of the church.

Making Contributions

After every big win, the stars of a sports team always say the same thing: it was a team effort, and everyone contributed to this win. Sure, some players may contribute more than others, but in order to win in team sports, everyone must contribute. This is not just a phenomenon in sports. The same is true in the arts. There may be lead actors in a play or musical, but the whole cast contributes to the performance. Leonard Bernstein, the great conductor, was once asked which instrument in the orchestra is the most difficult to play. His quick-witted response was "second fiddle." Bernstein went on to explain that he had no problem recruiting people to play first violin, but finding someone to play second violin, or second trumpet, or second flute with as much enthusiasm was always a challenge. Yet if nobody played second, there would be no harmony in the music.[10]

Every instrument contributes to the majesty of a concert. Every player contributes to the beauty of a game. Every believer contributes to the splendor of the church. Without the contribution of every person of every age group, gender, ethnicity, and stage of life, the church does not radiate her full splendor as the bride of Christ. It is as though players have been left in the locker room or musicians have been left backstage, and while the spectators may not notice their absence, the coach and conductor are keenly aware of the deficiency. Coaches and conductors quickly recognize when something is missing from their group because they understand what a complete team or orchestra looks and sounds like. I fear that we have forgotten what the splendor of church looks and feels like because we have segregated age groups for so long. We have accepted a new definition of normal, in which children and teenagers are spectators in most settings and contributors only in their age-appropriate contexts. Sometimes children and teenagers remain spectators in their age-appropriate contexts as well.

Allowing teenagers to contribute is not only important for the faith formation of adolescents; it benefits the entire community and the faith formation of everyone who is a part of it. We hear this truth whispered on a regular basis from volunteers in children and student ministries when they say: "I get more out of teaching Sunday school than I give"; "I learn more from the teenagers in my small group than they learn from me"; "Those young people keep me young at heart." These are testimonies to the mutual contribution that is apparent in our lives. A few moments of reflection bring a sea of examples of how numerous people younger, older, and of the same age contribute to our lives. Theologian

Marcia Bunge reflects on the important contributions children make to adult faith formation.

> Many Gospel passages turn upside down the common assumption held in Jesus' time and our own: children are to be seen but not heard; and the primary role of children is to learn from and obey adults. In contrast, the New Testament depicts children in striking and even radical ways as moral witnesses, models of faith for adults, sources or vehicles of revelation, representatives of Jesus, and even paradigms for entering the reign of God. . . . Viewing children as models for adults or vehicles of revelation does not mean that they are creatures who are 'near angels,' 'closer to God,' or 'more spiritual' than adults. However, these passages [Matt. 18:2–5; 19:14] and others do challenge parents and other caring adults to be receptive to the lessons and wisdom that children offer them, to honor children's questions and insights, and to recognize that children can positively influence the community and the moral and spiritual lives of adults.[11]

Bunge further suggests,

> The idea that children can be teachers, bearers of revelation, or models of faith has often been neglected in Christian thought and practice. However, throughout the tradition and today, we do find theologians who have grappled seriously with these New Testament passages, forcing them to rethink their assumptions about children and exploring what adults learn from them. For example, Friedrich Schleiermacher emphasized that adults who want to enter the kingdom of God need to recover a childlike spirit. For him, this childlike spirit has many components that we can learn from children, such as 'living fully in the present moment,' being able to forgive others, or being flexible.[12]

The church is a wonderfully multifaceted community in which there is great opportunity for individuals of all ages to contribute. When I was a teenager, my family belonged to a church that had blended services long before blended or contemporary worship was popular. One of the more traditional aspects of the service was the processional, in which the choir and clergy marched down the center aisle during the opening song and took their seats on the platform. In the procession were teenagers who served as acolytes and carried crosses or flags. One acolyte led the procession with a cross just ahead of the choir, two others served as flag bearers just behind the choir, and the fourth acolyte processed just behind the flags and in front of the clergy. I remember as a teenager thinking that I was playing an important role in the worship service. No doubt the choir could find their way down the center aisle and into the choir stalls without me leading them with a cross in hand. But in my teenage mind, I felt that the worship service could not begin without me leading the procession. I felt like I was contributing to something important and something larger than myself.

When I was serving as a youth minister, I regularly received calls from people in the church asking if some teenagers could help with the women's luncheon, or the men's breakfast, or child care for an event, or the annual fall festival that raised money for missionaries. My response was always the same: "I can think of several students who would do a great job for you. I'll send you a list of their names and phone numbers so that you can contact them directly."

This simple yet strategic response accomplishes several things. First, when youth ministers are constantly asking students to do things, they communicate the subtle message, "He or she only calls me when they want something." That's not healthy for an authentic relationship, and this strategy cuts down on the amount of asking that the youth leader has to do. Second, this gives other adults in the congregation an opportunity to connect with teenagers. By naming a specific person to contact (not the whole student ministry mailing list), a youth minister is placing a high level of confidence in the student, and the adult's connection to the student will likely be a positive experience. Third, students are empowered when other adults see value in them and reach out to them. Time and time again, I would walk into a youth meeting and a student would come up to me, saying, "You'll never guess who called me last night!" The notion that another adult in the church—worship pastor, children's minister, chair of the women's guild—would ask them to contribute to a church program outside of student ministry blew their minds. Students feel valued, empowered, and honored when other adults ask them to contribute to meaningful ventures.

As the parent of two teenagers, I continue to find ways, large and small, for my son and daughter to connect with other caring adults and contribute to the ministries of the church. When my kids were younger and my wife and I were part of the communion-serving team, we would involve our kids as well. When we left our seats in worship to acquire the communion trays, they came with us. My wife and daughter would take one aisle as my son and I took another aisle, moving the communion trays from one row to the next. After the service we all helped to wash the dishes in the church kitchen, along with other adults. This monthly act of service offered a brief, simple, and stress-free moment of connection with caring adults and the opportunity to contribute to the ministry of the church.

Both of my kids know and are known by our pastor of adult discipleship, Doug Whallon, who has nothing to do with the student ministries of the church. Because I regularly teach or host an adult Sunday morning class, our family tends to arrive at church early. I ask Kasey and Ryan to help set up the room by distributing handouts around the tables while I am fussing with the technology and my wife is organizing the food. Each Sunday, without fail, Doug and often his wife, Mary, come by the room, thanking all of us for our service and taking an interest in the happenings of Kasey's and Ryan's life that week. Each fall Doug and Mary have a picnic for the adult discipleship committee members *and* their families—yet another opportunity for children and teenagers to connect with adults of the church.

My daughter serves with the student worship team in the high school ministry. Every few months, that worship team leads music for the church worship service. This is not designated as a Youth Sunday; in fact, the high school pastor will not let the teenagers be introduced as if they were guests leading worship. He wants teenagers leading worship to become the norm, not the exception. Students have the opportunity to contribute to worship among their peers in the student ministry as well as to the all-church worship service. This brings a unique life and vitality that would otherwise be absent from the congregation.

My son has been obsessed with acting since he was in elementary school. By the time he finished his first year of high school, he had performed in a dozen plays or musicals. From time to time the worship arts ministry of our church performs short dramas to frame the sermon, so I asked the drama leader if she would consider casting teenagers in some sketches. She agreed to give Ryan an audition, and he was cast as an iPhone-wielding teenager in the Christmas Eve drama about a family struggling with the real meaning of Christmas. The role required weeks of rehearsals on Wednesday evenings and performing in five Christmas Eve services over the course of three days. This is a significant commitment, but for the last few years he has been a regular in the Christmas Eve dramas. I am thankful to the worship arts ministry for helping him to connect with other adults in the church and allowing him to make a significant contribution to the most well-attended services of the year.

Other students in our church serve in the nursery, children's ministry, Vacation Bible School, and the café. From time to time students play in the orchestra in worship. My hope is that as time goes on, other avenues for students to contribute will emerge. There's nothing to wake you up on Sunday morning like a high five from a teenage greeter at the door. And what teenager wouldn't want to tell adults where to park their cars?

Students Finding Their Niche

One of the ongoing conversations we have as a youth staff is about innovative and practical ways to better engage each year's senior class. Henry is one of our students who found his niche early through volunteering for the tech team. Over time, Henry was recruited to help run media for the main church services. A member of our church's staff, Dave, who runs an incredibly organized and well-executed media ministry, took Henry on as an intern during Henry's senior year. Being a student and a learner of the trade, Henry may not have been the most efficient, the most skilled, or even the most predictable person for the job. But Dave valued Henry above a perfectly orchestrated production and saw the significance of giving Henry real, concrete ownership. For the church to invest in Henry has meant church is not just a place he comes to participate, but is a family where he finds value and belonging.

Leah Knight, Grace Chapel,
Lexington, Massachusetts

Some churches have been even more strategic in assimilating teenagers into the life of the church. From the very start of North Point Community Church in Atlanta, Andy Stanley and his team decided not to offer any programs for high school students on Sunday morning. They have a great high school ministry on Sunday afternoon, but Sunday morning is designed for high school students to contribute to the ministries of the church. Most students contribute to the nursery, children's, or middle school ministries during one hour of the morning and attend the worship service during the other hour of the morning. Their vision for high school students on Sunday morning is for them to serve for an hour and worship with the whole church for an hour.

People often suggest that there simply are not enough roles for all the teenagers to have an opportunity to contribute to the faith community. At Second Presbyterian Church in Memphis, Todd Erickson is so committed to having every teenager contribute to the church that he pulled the staff together and they took the time to identify all the possible areas where teenagers could contribute. Eventually they came up with enough areas that every one of the hundreds of students in their church has the opportunity to make a significant contribution each year. Todd believes that discipleship is an active, not passive, process, and that real success in student ministry is plugging students into the church in such a way that they are contributing to the church family. As in many churches that value the contributions of teenagers, Todd has dozens of high school juniors and seniors serving on the middle school ministry team, with the mentoring of adult volunteers. Freshman and sophomore high school students take responsibility for leading the Vacation Bible School program, under the mentoring guidance of caring adults. These students don't simply show up for a week to serve as counselors. They are involved in the entire ministry development process, beginning with planning meetings in the winter and making significant contributions to creating and implementing the VBS program in the summer. Another group of students leads the sixth-grade transition program, which includes several events throughout the year designed to help kids make a smooth transition from children's ministry to middle school ministry. They have created a tradition of Tuesday morning prayer groups, which are organized and run by teenagers. The church is committed to a local community program for tutoring the refugee population in Memphis, and teenagers are fully integrated into the leadership of that program.

Likewise, Jim Byrne at The Falls Church in Virginia seeks every opportunity for teenagers to contribute to the ministries of the greater church body. In the summer, numerous high school students serve as leaders for the middle school day camp operated by the church. In worship services, some students play in the worship band while others serve as acolytes. In this Anglican church, Jim has created an acolyte program that is respected by teenagers and parents alike, raising its level of importance and allure. While in many churches mission trips are segregated by generation, Jim took the forward-looking approach to short-term mission trips by emphasizing family mission trips and mainstreaming students into adult mission experiences. While he occasionally still offers a mission trip just for teenagers, the emphasis is on encouraging people to contribute to church missions as a family, with parents and teenagers experiencing outreach together.

Perhaps the boldest strategic decision Jim made, with the full support of the church leadership, was to eliminate the high school Sunday school class in favor of offering students opportunities to contribute to the Sunday morning experience. Students serve in the children's ministries, set up various rooms for Sunday morning programs, and direct traffic in the numerous parking areas surrounding the church.

When students contribute to the church, they become an authentic part of the family, and once you are part of a family, you go where the family goes. One of my mentors taught me long ago that people do something for one of two reasons: either because it's fun or because it's important—and fun never lasts! While there's nothing wrong with using fun and entertainment to engage students in ministry, at some point ministry, church, and faith have to become important as students genuinely become integrated into the family of God. When I call my kids for dinner, they show up because it's dinnertime, not because of the great entertaining meal that is being served. As Todd Erickson says, "When kids are coming to contribute, the church becomes family, and they show up for family dinner no matter what we are serving."[13]

When students are invited to contribute to the life of the church, they are afforded opportunities to put their faith in action and experience meaningful engagement with the broader community of faith. Inviting students into this kind of contribution must be done intentionally, and it is the responsibility of the entire leadership of the church.

Communication Is Key

Churches communicate in numerous ways, both overtly and subtly. We are typically so accustomed to the patterns of our home church that we quickly overlook many of our own subtle messages. The best way to experience this subtle messaging is to visit an unfamiliar church. Undoubtedly all of the subtle messages will appear as you experience the church as a visitor.

Pulling into the parking lot, you may get a sense of the economic status of the church by the context of the neighborhood in which the church is located and the types of cars that fill the parking lot. Strolling through the lobby of a church, you may pick up on the degree to which a visitor is welcome by its decor, greeters, and even the way people are dressed. It doesn't take long for people to decide whether or not they fit into their new surroundings. I attended a church once where the associate pastor made an announcement that was specifically designed for visitors. He said, "For those visiting with us today, you will find more information about our church on the table in the narthex." Narthex? What is a narthex and how would a person visiting—especially a person who has not grown up in church—ever find it?

Now think of the church from the vantage point of a teenager. What does it say to teenagers when there are signs on the church building facing the parking lot that read: "No Skateboarding Allowed"? That communicates to teenagers that they are not welcome. Even though the finance committee may have good reasons in a litigious society to erect such signs, that doesn't change the meaning to teenagers. In one church, a group of students was meeting one evening on the second floor, directly above a room in which an adult committee meeting was being held. Growing weary of the noise from above, one of the adults went upstairs and told the teenagers to quiet down. The pastor happened to be walking by at the time and, catching the tail end of the exchange, he interrupted the conversation. He admonished the adult that this was the teenagers' room and the teenagers' night, and they could make as much noise as they pleased. If the noise was disturbing the committee, they could move to another room in the building or relocate their meeting to a committee member's home. The committee and the pastor communicated two very different messages to the teenagers that night—one of exclusion and one of inclusion.

Faithful and effective inclusion of teenagers in the life of the whole church requires an intentional effort to communicate that teenagers matter in the church. From the quality of the student ministry rooms to the welcoming nature of adults in the lobby, everything matters. In an effort to make life easier for people, some churches have designated parking areas for a host of special people: visitors parking, handicapped parking, single parent parking, and parking for families with young children. Imagine what it would communicate to high school students if the church designated a student parking area. Would that create a sense of elitism and entitlement? Perhaps. But it would certainly communicate that high school students are welcome and that the church leadership wants them to participate in the life of the church.

Too often, teenagers are treated as second-class citizens of the church and are given the leftovers after the adults are finished. When the adults get new chairs for the fellowship hall, the students get the old chairs. When the sanctuary gets an upgrade in technology, the youth rooms get the old equipment. When the student ministries rooms need maintenance and repairs, they are often deferred until the adult and children's areas are taken care of. When the large LCD video screen in the middle school room of one church died, the middle school couldn't project anything for six months. If a screen or projector in the worship center had died, it would have been repaired or replaced in a matter of days.

Communication in the worship service is critical to creating an intergenerational environment. Announcements that are spoken from the platform and printed in the worship bulletin should include information that is of interest to teenagers as well as to adults. Worship directors must work with youth ministers to ensure that some of the music in every service is from the playlist of teenagers. If the teenagers' music is played only when teenagers lead worship, then the service is not intergenerational; it is alternate-generational. Intergenerational worship includes music that resonates with all ages at every service.

Perhaps the most challenging aspect of communication in the worship service is preaching across the age spectrum. Even pastors who work at it find it challenging, as they tend to picture an adult audience when they are preparing their weekly message. Without being arrogant, a youth minister needs to present the pastor with a photograph of teenagers, perhaps from a retreat or mission trip, and ask the pastor to place that picture on the desk where sermons are written, to serve as a reminder of who is in the congregation. One simple trilogy that is a helpful start to preaching intergenerationally is to infuse every application of the message with the contexts of work, home, and school. In other words, during sermon preparation the preacher is constantly considering ways in which the message connects with the everyday lives of people in their homes and neighborhoods, in their workplaces, and in their educational environments. All three contexts can include illustrations that speak to both adults and teenagers. Teenagers certainly have a home life with siblings and parents, many teenagers have part-time jobs, and of course schools are the primary domain of teenagers and are where they engage with both peers and adults. It is hard to imagine a sermon that could not connect with each of these contexts in which a living faith is so vital.

Membership Matters

Once upon a time, membership in a local church had its privileges. Members were afforded certain accommodations that were not available to visitors. Old North Church, one of the oldest remaining church buildings in Boston, is famous for its two lanterns, which signaled Paul Revere that the British were heading toward Lexington by sea as he rode his horse through the county warning the patriots. Revere was never a member of Old North Church, as his family was Congregationalist, not Anglican. But those who were members in 1775 were able to purchase a pew for their families. Not unlike purchasing seats for a concert or ball game today, the practice of purchasing church pews assumed that the better the location of the pew, the higher the price. Touring historic churches on the East Coast reveals that church members often owned family pews. Ownership was indicated by a brass medallion, engraved with the family name and affixed to the pew.

Another historic example of privileged membership in the church was the common policy of church members receiving discounted fees for church events. I remember churches offering member prices and non-member prices for attending Vacation Bible School as late as the 1970s. One would be hard-pressed to find churches with such a fee structure today. On the contrary: as evangelicalism became more popular, churches began to eliminate as many barriers to attendance as possible. Programs such as VBS became outreach-oriented, and everyone was charged the same price or none at all.

Likewise, participation in nearly every aspect of the church has been opened to regular attenders rather than limited to members only. No longer does a person need to be an official member of the congregation to sing in the choir, contribute to the worship team, join a pastoral care ministry, or almost anything else. In many churches nonmembers can participate and serve in nearly every aspect of the church except on the church board. Even the way churches determine their size has changed from the number of members to the weekend worship service attendance number. Denominational churches often have a greater number of members on the rolls than people in worship, while independent churches often have far more people in worship than they have members. All of this raises the question: does membership matter?

Anyone who has led a confirmation class or a baptism preparation class for teenagers (depending on your tradition) has faced this question of the relative importance or unimportance of membership for teenagers. Rarely do teenagers see any value in becoming official members of the church, even when they have grown up in the church. Their posture is typically that there is no payoff for them to become members. Why bother to become a member if the only reward is being allowed to vote at the annual congregational meeting? This is a self-centered response, to be sure, but few churches have offered teenagers any other significant reasons for engaging in the membership process. When churches ignore the issue of membership, they communicate to young people a poor understanding of theology and a poor understanding of community.

Theologically, membership is about belonging and contributing to a community of faith. Our misunderstanding of the very nature of membership is exposed regularly when we ask one another, "Where do you go to church?" Fundamentally, we must understand that the church is not a place to which we go. The local church is not a building or a location; it is a community of believers committed to the work of God's kingdom. In one of their final gatherings with Jesus, the disciples asked if he was about to restore the kingdom of Israel. His response was that they were to be his witnesses in Jerusalem, Judea, Samaria, and to the ends of the earth (Acts 1:6–8). They were looking for Jesus to establish a kingdom, and he said, essentially, "*You* are the kingdom, *you* are the church, *you* are the community of God." The kingdom of God is nothing less than the community of God's people, committed to one another and empowered by the Holy Spirit. Mark Dever describes the importance of church membership:

> A temple has bricks. A flock has sheep. A vine has branches. And a body has members. In one sense, church membership begins when Christ saves us and makes us a member of his body. Yet his work must then be given expression in an actual local church. In that sense, church membership begins when we commit to a particular body. Being a Christian means being joined to a church.
>
> Scripture therefore instructs us to assemble regularly so that we can regularly rejoice in our common hope and regularly spur one another on to love and good deeds (Heb. 10:23–25). Church membership is not simply a record of a box we once checked. It's not a sentimental feeling. It's not an expression of affection toward a familiar place. It's not an expression of loyalty or disloyalty toward parents. It should be the reflection of a living commitment, or it is worthless.[14]

The New Testament never makes a dichotomy between membership in the church universal—that is, a believer's commitment to Christ along with all believers, past, present, and future—and membership in the local church. Once people professed their faith in Christ they were baptized, symbolizing their new life in Christ *and* their commitment to the community of faith. Membership in the early church was never a second step after baptism. When people accepted Christ they also accepted his bride, the church, and they immediately entered into fellowship with other believers in the local church. Today membership has often become an entirely separate process from confirmation or baptism, suggesting that a personal commitment to Christ is more important than a commitment to the community of faith. New life in Christ is viewed as essential, while commitment to the church is seen as optional. This dichotomy further undermines the value of community in the church by creating a system of elitism. When we do not enthusiastically view teenagers as potential members of the church, we communicate that they are not worthy of such a status. This is expressed in teenagers' response to the question of why they do not become members of their church: "Because nobody really cares if I'm a member." Once again, the church becomes another institution in teenagers' lives that is perceived as not caring about them.

Becoming members of the local church upon their profession of faith in Christ is an important aspect of assimilating teenagers into the community of faith. Membership matters for teenagers for a variety of reasons, which require us to rethink membership as an important aspect of the assimilation process.

Taking a Stand

Membership declares before God and others that we are part of a particular local faith community that has been entrusted with the gospel, and it is through the visible church that God expects us to live out our faith. The majority of Paul's Letters are written to local congregations or to their pastors. Nowhere in the New Testament are there individuals floating around in "just me and J. C." land. Yet that is exactly what many faithful teenagers are doing, because the church has not embraced them as committed, contributing members of their fellowship. Christians have always belonged to a local church, because the visible church is a witness to the invisible body of believers.

Membership provides a visible commitment to Christ and his people in the same way that a marriage covenant provides a greater level of commitment than simply living together. As a wedding ring is a clear and public statement concerning one's identity as a committed spouse, so church membership makes a clear and public statement about one's identity as a committed Christian. This commitment is directly tied to the "one another" passages mentioned earlier. We are called to love, comfort, serve, forgive, admonish, and exhort one another, among other things. This only occurs among those who are committed to one another in a healthy faith community. Such a community provides a place where we can live out these characteristics of a life in Christ, with real people who have real needs and real problems and real faith. While this often happens within a student ministry group, it must also happen throughout the church. Teenagers must become members of the larger church community, "one anothering" the whole family of God and demonstrating their commitment to the bride of Christ, not just to the youth group.

Living in Obedience

Paul uses the image of the body as a metaphor for the church (Rom. 12; 1 Cor. 12; Eph. 4). Being a part of the body requires connection. An arm that is not connected to the body is not part of the body. The family of God is connected to and belongs to one another: "For just as each of us has one body with many members and these members do not all have the same function, so in Christ we, though many, form one body,

and *each member belongs to all the others"* (Rom. 12:4–5, italics added).
Membership is a visible sign of being connected to the body and a commitment to obey all that Christ has commanded. Joshua Harris suggests
that the best thing the church does is bear witness to new life in Christ,
and that is best done in community. "One thing a local congregation
does best is to show your non-Christian neighbors that the *new life* made
available through Jesus' death and resurrection is also the foundation for
a *new society.* By living the Gospel as a distinct community, the church
down the street accomplishes the important mission of displaying the
transforming effects of the gospel for the world to see. Others won't be
able to see this larger picture if we remain detached from each other and
go our separate ways."[15]

Scripture contends that believers are to submit to and obey the leadership of the community of faith (Heb. 13:17), and the only people who
are charged with being accountable for leading God's people are pastors,
elders, and overseers of the local church. Chuck Colson writes, "Of course
every believer is part of the universal church. But for any Christian who
has a choice in the matter, failure to commit to a particular church is
failure to obey Christ."[16] Without being a faithful member of a local
church, it is impossible to follow this model of Christian community.

Further, the leaders of the church are instructed to care only for those
who have committed themselves to their care and become faithful members of the local church (Acts 20:28). Without making a commitment to a
local faith community, it is impossible to function as part of the body and
enter into a caring community that provides the accountability essential
to fostering faith formation. As Mark Dever suggests, "The practice of
church membership among Christians occurs when Christians grasp
hold of each other in responsibility and love. By identifying ourselves
with a particular local church, we are telling the church's pastors and
other members not just that we are committed to them, but that we are
committed to them in gathering, giving, prayer, and service. We are telling them to expect certain things from us and to hold us accountable if
we don't follow through. Joining a church is an act of saying, 'I am now
your responsibility, and you are my responsibility.'"[17]

This is a countercultural statement that says we are committed to
one another and we are more interested in giving than receiving. When
this attitude is reversed and membership is more about receiving than
contributing, we become a reflection of our consumer-driven culture,
focused only on engaging others for what they can do to benefit us. There
are few areas of our contemporary culture that challenge students to
sacrifice for the good of the community, and the church should take its

rightful place at the head of that line. Holding students accountable in a manner that offers grace and truth contributes to their humanity and to the common good of the church and society at large.

Building Up the Body

It is hard to imagine effectively contributing to the growth of a local church as a detached and autonomous attender. The church comprises many people with a variety of gifts and talents for the clear purpose of equipping one another and building up the body of Christ (Eph. 4:11–16). We understand the growth of the church to be the continual transformation of lives, as more people come to faith and faithful people are continually sanctified. The strength of the body determines the power of our witness to the gospel. A church that is a strong and faithful body of believers is a powerful witness, while a church that is weak, divisive, and self-centered produces a poor witness. The unity of a faith community is a strong witness of Christian living in a secular culture. Together we proclaim to the world about the character of God by loving one another, persevering through tough times, and serving the community at large as the bride of Christ.

Together we grow in maturity by building each other up, challenging one another, and learning from one another, "attaining to the whole measure of the fullness of Christ" (Eph. 4:13). Only then are we no longer susceptible to false teachings and evil temptations. Rather, we become a community marked by Christ and held together by every supporting member as each person contributes to the body of believers. Thus we become a community that is greater than the sum of its parts. Building up the body must include the teenagers of our community: without them, the body is incomplete and weaker than it should be. Every teenager should be encouraged to become a fully contributing member of the body of Christ that is the local church.

Practices of the Intergenerational Church

After Walt Disney had attained success producing animated movies in the 1920s and 1930s, he began focusing on his dreams for an amusement park. By all accounts Disney was a workaholic, but he never neglected his family. He spent every Saturday with his daughters, although finding activities to do on their special days together became increasingly frustrating, as there were few places for parents to have fun with their children. That became his driving motivation for creating Disneyland Park in California, which opened in 1955. Disney declared, "I felt that there should be someplace where the parents and the children could have fun together."[18]

On a recent family vacation to Walt Disney World in Florida, I was struck by how the parks are seamlessly designed with children, teenagers, and adults in mind. While some rides have particular height requirements, there are no special "Kiddyland" sections with children's rides, no segmented areas especially designed for teenagers, and no distinctive areas for adults. The parks are fully intergenerational and designed for adults, teenagers, and children to spend time together. Imagine a family arriving at a Disney park and spending the day moving throughout the park together as a family. Now imagine a family arriving at a typical church, where they are instantly segregated into specialized areas by age and reunited only as they leave. Some churches do a better job of integrating adults, teenagers, and children than others, but few have achieved something similar to Disney's vision by creating a church where parents and children can grow and serve and worship together.

The concept of being intergenerational is often viewed as simply gathering more than one generation of people together for a program. Intergenerational *ministry*, however, requires an intentional interaction among generations that promotes the faith formation of all ages. Hence, it is essential to comprehend the differences between multigenerational and intergenerational. Most churches are multigenerational: many generations are represented in the congregation and through the ministries of the church. Such congregations strive to create ministries for children, adolescents, and adults, but they may not integrate these age groups. Intergenerational ministries strive to integrate multiple generations through meaningful conversations, interactions, and service on a regular basis.[19]

Brenda Snailum found that intergenerational ministry bridges the generation gap, improving connections and reducing the detrimental effects of generational disconnectedness. Her exhaustive review of intergenerational research literature showed that churches committed to intergenerational ministry create environments of nonparental and nonfamilial intergenerational relationships that contribute significantly to the faith formation process of adolescents. Snailum names the following benefits of intergenerational relationships:

- Promote individuation and identity development
- Increase social capital

- Promote overall well-being and healthy development
- Promote positive behavior
- Influence religiosity, intrinsic religious motivation, and faith maturity
- Influence experience of God and/or relationship with God
- Influence church attendance and participation during adolescence and adulthood
- Facilitate and promote the transition to adulthood
- Provide modeling for a variety of life and faith issues
- Have reciprocal benefits that strengthen the congregation as a whole[20]

Snailum further explains the importance of developing a congregational environment that promotes a confluence of peer, parent, and other adult relationships, which provide genuine support for adolescent faith formation. "One of the strongest implications of this research is that the influence of parents, peers, and non-parental adults exists in a complex interrelated system that greatly impacts all adolescent development. The way they interact with one another can be depicted as three separate streams of influence that exist in a confluent and synergistic relationship."[21]

Figure 4.1. Contributors to Healthy Spiritual Formation[22]

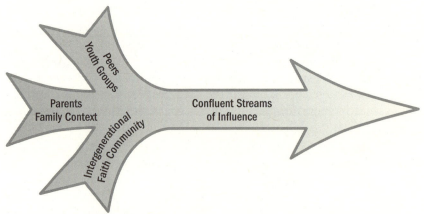

Each stream of influence makes a unique contribution but also interacts with the others, making the total greater than the sum of the parts. Several studies indicated that all three forms of influence combined (parents, peers, and non-parental adults) were significantly related to many important benefits including increased social capital, positive youth development, faith maturity, and church program participation. The same can be said when comparing the overall context of age-specific youth groups and intergenerational church community approaches. Each approach interacts synergistically with the adolescent's home environment, and all three contribute in important but unique ways to an overall social ecology that greatly impacts adolescent development.[23]

In her Delphi study of intergenerational ministry and student ministry, Snailum found seven common practices that best serve congregations that truly want to become intergenerational.[24]

Establish Intergenerational Community as a Core Value

For a church to become intergenerational, the whole staff and the whole community, not just the student ministry, must own the initiative. This movement requires more than simply the addition of multigenerational activities. It requires a philosophical shift in the congregation's understanding of ecclesiology. Establishing intergenerational ministry as a core value necessitates a fresh discussion of the church's vision, values, and purpose. As one intergenerational expert in Snailum's study commented, "Intergenerational is not something churches *do*—it is something they *become*."[25] Another intergenerational specialist said, "It is a focused *mindset*, not a new *model* for ministry."[26]

This new mindset highly values community by moving beyond the individualism of the popular culture. Once there was great hope that the millennial generation would be far more community-minded than previous generations, and yet they appear to have fallen prey to the same individualism as their elders.[27] Shifting from an ingrained individual mentality to an intergenerational perspective is more than a challenge—it is countercultural. Teenagers have to change their views of adults, and adults have to change their views of teenagers. All generations must be seen as possessing intrinsic value to the community. As Snailum asserts, "Ultimately, the goal is that all members of the congregation so fully embody intergenerational values that it spills out far beyond the church walls and infiltrates their daily, ordinary lives."[28]

Balance Intergenerational Values with Age-Specific Ministry

There is a strong consensus among intergenerational specialists that while the church embraces intergenerational values, it is also essential to maintain important age-specific ministries. One intergenerational expert asserted, "Believing in intergenerationality does not mean we swing to the other end taking away all separate programming environments.

. . . There is a healthy balance allowing youth to be youth, but the local church has separated too far and we need to bring intergenerational concepts back to our understanding of ecclesiology."[29]

Snailum found that it was essential to hold age-appropriate ministries in balance with intergenerational ministries, as the two are not mutually exclusive. For example, students benefit from worshiping with their peers as well as worshiping with the whole congregation. Likewise, peer small groups and intergenerational small groups both have benefits. In the words of King Solomon, "There is a time for everything, and a season for every activity under the heavens" (Eccles. 3:1). While Solomon never discusses the issue of age segregation, I am sure he would agree that there is a time for peer gatherings and a time for congregational gatherings. The artistry of ministry is in identifying those times, places, and seasons in which such gatherings are mutually beneficial to the individuals and the community. While everyone needs to be incorporated into a network of relationships that crosses generational boundaries, each age group must also be afforded a homogeneous context for developing peer relationships and working through issues relevant to their particular life stage.

Ensure That Leaders Are Fully Invested

Those who have made the transition from an age-specific mindset to an intergenerational mind-set agree that such a transition requires the uncompromising commitment of the church leadership. Senior pastors, associate pastors, elders, deacons, small group leaders, Sunday school teachers, and other key leaders must all be dedicated to the vision from the start. They must champion the value of becoming intergenerational until it becomes an irreplaceable mark of the congregation's identity. Such leadership requires actively promoting intergenerational initiatives and teaching the value of intergenerational community throughout the congregation. Snailum advises, "Unity and harmony among the leadership team is critical to a successful transition, which requires high levels of trust and humility. A youth pastor wanting to create intergenerational community must begin by casting vision and winning over the key leadership in the church."[30]

Begin Where You Are

Prior to teaching about intergenerational ministry or implementing a series of intergenerational activities, it is prudent to assess the current

The Value of Older Adults as Volunteers

We have a retired guidance counselor who has been a volunteer leader in our ministry for many years. The perception at first from our students was: "What does this old guy know about me?" Teenagers seem accustomed to interacting with their elders generally for one of two reasons: either they're being instructed, in some form or another, or disciplined. Rarely do teenagers expect to be understood by adults, particularly senior adults. Allan has over time become one of our most beloved leaders, not only because he is a consistent advocate for and voice in our students' lives, as so many of our leaders are, but because his life and presence broadens their somewhat limited perspectives. Often the perception in churches is that teenagers need contemporaries, people who understand them, to walk with them. The thinking is that younger adults best fit that criterion. But what if teenagers regularly experienced relationships with adults, young *and* old, who not only offered a breadth of life experience but accepted and supported them as they navigate their own unique (but perhaps not-so-different) journeys?

Leah Knight, Grace Chapel,
Lexington, Massachusetts

conditions of the church ministries, beginning with existing structures that may be ripe for an infusion of intergenerational thinking. Assessments of the reasons that the church desires to become intergenerational, and an honest examination of whether the leaders and members of the congregation perceive age-specific ministries as valuable, are essential. The level of openness to change among the leadership and members should also be considered in order to determine the pace of change required for a successful transition, as moving too quickly could prove counterproductive.

Becoming intergenerational is about changing the culture of the church and must take into account the church's history, location, staff, membership, and vision. Ministries that are currently effective and ready to move to the next level are often most suited to becoming intergenerational. For example, one intergenerational expert in the study suggested, "If you already have a small group strategy, recruit a few older leaders and train them to invest in youth. Or if your church sends different age-level ministries to serve in a local homeless outreach [or on short-term mission trips], experiment with going together instead, or pairing up kids with one particular older group. Try a four-week series where different age-level Sunday school classes mix together, perhaps during a particular season like Advent."[31]

In keeping with this logic, it may not be wise in a traditional church to start a contemporary service just so that teenagers can lead in worship. If a contemporary service already exists, though, adding some teenagers to the worship team would be an excellent strategy.

Educate the Congregation

Teaching the value of becoming intergenerational is an essential step in the process. People who naturally gravitate toward individualism and homogeneous groupings need to learn how to understand and appreciate other generations and why an intergenerational community is valuable. Such education requires continual communication and emphasis on the philosophy, principles, and goals of becoming intergenerational. Snailum discovered the challenge of becoming intergenerational in our contemporary context. "Our modern culture lacks models and language for what intergenerational means," she writes. "People need to be taught the differences between generations and learn to love and value other people who are not like themselves. The congregation needs to be made aware that 'intergenerationality' emphasizes interaction that builds relationships between members of different generations, which goes beyond attending a multigenerational worship service or event in which various generations simply gather together but do not interact."[32]

Congregations must also learn that intergenerational relationships have reciprocal value. This is not a transmissive process, in which older people pass on knowledge and goods to younger people for the sole benefit of the younger generation. Intergenerational experiences are crucial to the faith development of everyone involved as they encounter one another in the context of community. Such encounters require communication, and everyone must learn to communicate across generational barriers and identify the shared story that exists among generations. Every generation contains stories that are both unique to that generation and similar to the stories of other generations.

Finding the similarities in one another's stories is essential to rich and vibrant communication. One intergenerational specialist in Snailum's study suggested that "we need older generations telling 'God stories' to younger generations and for younger generations to breathe life and passion for the older generations. . . . I really think the key here is for older generations to take the lead and younger generations will begin to reciprocate the relationship over time."[33] While noting the similarities of generational stories is important, it is equally crucial to preserve and honor the unique aspects of each generation rather than trying to make the church a homogeneous community in which the diversity of age groups disappears.

Be Intentional and Strategic

Creating an intergenerational culture will not happen by chance. Such a paradigm shift requires leaders who are committed to the value of becoming intergenerational and who champion strategic planning and intentional modifications. Without strategic intentionality, the result of an intergenerational initiative is often nothing more than getting generations to rub shoulders in the same space. Becoming a church that genuinely engages "one another" across generations for the mutual benefit of the whole community requires great intentionality as people begin to move outside their homogeneous comfort zones. Such changes are often best accomplished incrementally, as changing everything at once can be too much of a shock to the community. Casting vision, educating the congregation, and implementing small changes that the community will embrace provide an on-ramp for culture creation. Sharing stories of successful intergenerational engagement, testimonies of the meaningful contributions people have made to one another, and celebrating small intergenerational moments provide encouragement to the whole community and show that people value one another.

Sustaining such cultural change requires commitment and patience over a long period of time, and commitment requires systems of accountability and support. To move toward authentic intergenerational community, leaders must be held accountable for examining every ministry initiative through an intergenerational mindset. Creating an intergenerational team that examines all initiatives according to intergenerational values and supports the intergenerational efforts of all ministries can be very helpful for creating the momentum necessary to produce change. Regularly asking ministries to consider infusing current activities with a dose of intergenerational flavor is essential.

For example, one church's objective for their annual youth retreat was to engage parents at a greater level, rather than just dropping their children off and picking them up a week later. They asked the question of their leadership team, "How do we do this in such a way as to engage the parents in this event even though they will not be there with their children?" This launched an entirely new conversation with the leaders who had previously been focused on making sure that the students had a great experience. It resulted in an amazing effort to bring the parents into the process and actually help them be a part of the retreat even though they were not physically present.[34]

When an intergenerational mindset is established, such questions become the norm for every discussion of ministry activities. Often the answer is that this particular activity should not be intergenerational, but consciously choosing to make an activity age specific is just as important as choosing to make it intergenerational. An intergenerational mindset requires a deliberate and authentic decision.

Include All Generations and All Ministry Venues

Intergenerational ministry is not simply about adults and teenagers. Every generation represented in the community of faith—including children, teenagers, college students, singles, young adults, parents, and seniors—should be in relationship with one another. It is the development of authentic relationships among generations that love and value one another that is important. Intergenerational programs can provide structures to facilitate these relationships, but programs are not the goal. Teenagers and senior adults are often the most marginalized groups in the church, yet they often have much to contribute to one another. One expert in Snailum's study recounted the benefits of an intergenerational small group that incorporated multiple generations. "Most importantly, the children came to know the teens, the young adults came to know the older adults, the middle adults came to know all the children and the teens (not just their own); everyone heard each other's stories. We came to care for each other. . . . *All* of us were participating—actively, authentically—in each other's spiritual formation."[35]

While incremental change is a wise approach to becoming an intergenerational community, the goal will never be fully realized until all ministry venues—including worship services, small groups, Sunday school, Bible studies, outreach events, and mission trips—become intergenerational to one degree or another. Identifying a community need and gathering together multiple generations for service or advocacy can often be a good starting point. In order for worship services to become truly intergenerational, they must be designed so that all generations can participate, engage, and contribute. The worship service is an important venue for intergenerational ministry; however, intergenerational worship must be understood as more than simply requiring teenagers to attend the adult worship service. Initiatives must be taken to integrate teenagers into the service in a manner that allows them to fully participate in a service they find engaging and to which they have the opportunity to contribute. Yet intergenerational worship is not enough. Teenagers must also be integrated into other ministry areas of the church in order to truly create an intergenerational community.[36]

One intergenerational expert in the study asserted that small groups are a helpful starting point for intergenerational engagements. "In my experience, the best way to involve youth (and children) with *all* generations of the church on a regular basis is through intergenerational small groups. I was involved in an intergenerational approach to church for several years. The members of our church met together on Sunday mornings for our weekly celebratory worship service and teaching . . . but on Sunday evening the members of our church met in small groups—around 20–25 people with children and youth present."[37]

Because age-specific contexts are as valuable as intergenerational contexts, not every activity must be intergenerational. However, within every ministry area of the church there should be intentional intergenerational opportunities for generations to contribute to each other's life and faith.

These seven practices of intergenerational ministry, derived from Brenda Snailum's research, suggest that intergenerational ministry extends well beyond student ministries and incorporates every generation and all ministry areas of the church. This confirms the essential notion that the term *intergenerational student ministry* is an oxymoron; intergenerational ministry must always be owned by the entire leadership of the church and infiltrate the entire faith community.

Discussion Questions for Student Ministry Leaders

1. Does the vision of the student ministry support or counteract the vision of the congregation of which it is a part? How can you develop a vision and mission for student ministry that supports and is supported by the staff and leadership of the church, as well as the church's vision?

2. Think about your ministry. Are teenagers involved because it is important or because it is fun? How can you constructively capitalize on the importance factors and build bridges from fun to importance? How can the church as a whole contribute to this?

3. How do you envision your students contributing to the church? What existing structures within student ministry and the church are ripe with possibility for intergenerational integration? Which

opportunities listed in the chapter could be incorporated into your church culture?

4. How are you calling and equipping adults in your church, other than youth leaders, to invest themselves in teenagers? What could you do to rally churchwide involvement in student ministries for both teenagers inside the church and outside the church?

5. What are some concrete steps you can take to involve teenagers in the larger church body?

6. How do adults perceive the teenagers in your church? How do teenagers perceive the adults? What is feeding these perceptions? What would need to happen to bridge barriers or bring unity among generations within your church?

7. How can a 5:1 ratio, in which five adults care for every student, become a greater reality in your church? Are there opportunities for the older generations to take the lead in engaging the younger generations? How can you bring other generations into student ministry?

8. A community of Christians more interested in contributing than consuming is very countercultural in North American society today. How can student ministry better encourage students to contribute to the greater community of the church without feeling that they have lost the joy of belonging to their age-specific group?

Discussion Questions for Church Leaders

1. Does your church primarily send a message of exclusion or inclusion to teenagers? What are some signifiers? Think about your programs, events, announcements, relational connections, and even the building layout. How do other pastors in the church include teenagers in their ministries?

2. What value do you see in having students contributing to the life of your church? Where can they constructively contribute? What are some fears about allowing them to have real ownership?

3. Intergenerational ministry is possible only alongside a wholehearted commitment to community. Is genuine community a practiced value (not just a theoretical one) of your church? What are ways you can confront the rampant individualism of our culture with a renewed vision for community? What are some obstacles you would have to face in order to do this?

4. Who are some key people in your congregation who would help connect the generations of your church? What opportunities are there to include teenagers in your church services and ministries?

5. Look at your church's membership process to see what is required for adults and for teenagers. If the process is different, try to discern why this is the case. How can the process be adjusted for more "equality" in membership between teenagers and adults?

6. Does your church have a program—such as a midweek program, Sunday school classes, or worship—that is specifically intergenerational? If so, how might that program affect an intergenerational mindset of the congregation? How can that program be leveraged to create a stronger intergenerational culture in the congregation?

7. How does your church predominantly view teenagers? As *rocks*: those awaiting their time to have significant roles in the church? As *receivers*: passive consumers of church ministry? Or as *reservoirs*: contributing members of the church who are highly invested and highly valued? What factors have contributed to this view of teenagers in the church?

8. If intergenerational ministry is only a ministry model that you implement and not a core value that seeps into all aspects of your church, intergenerational endeavors will be just another program and will never truly influence your culture. What would it look like for your church staff and eventually the larger church community to make intergenerational integration a core value? How might that influence the purpose and vision of your church? What changes need to happen? What might practically need to be added or even removed?

5

When Teenagers Matter:

PROGRAMMING IS SIMPLE

Nearly two decades ago, Mike Yaconelli raised the provocative question, "What have we done to make youth ministry so complicated?"[1] If he were living today, I suspect he would still be asking that question, because student ministry seems to be more complex than ever. Is it possible that, in the midst of our complexity, we have robbed volunteers and students alike of the joyful wonder of a faith adventure that is absolutely messy?

When Peter Schreyer explained the design philosophy of Kia Motors' new K9 sedan in comparison to similar cars offered by BMW and Audi, he said, "Simplicity, balanced proportions, and attention to detail are important features for the new model."[2] Those powerful words—*simplicity, balance, detail*—reflect the very core of student ministries. We desire to present the message of the gospel with clarity and to provide students with a simple path that directs their faith journeys. We want to ensure that student ministries value all students and engage them at their current point of faith formation, which requires a constant evaluation of each aspect of the ministry to ensure a balance that leads to transformation. We must pay close attention to the details of ministry to ensure that students are not falling through the cracks, that everyone is safe, and that programs are implemented with excellence.

In many ways, student ministries often resemble one of the most disturbing and heartbreaking television reality shows of the twenty-first century. *Hoarders* chronicles the lives of people who cannot bring themselves to throw anything away. For many people, this is a serious pathological condition that results in a life paralyzed by the accumulation of so much stuff in their homes that they can barely move. Each episode features the assistance of health-care and organizational professionals who help people break their hoarding addictions. Following an intervention, some people are able to keep their hoarding behavior under control, while others fall back into the debilitating disease.

At the root of hoarding is often a deep-seated need for control and the fear of losing that control if one gives or throws away meaningless objects. In student ministry, this compulsion arises when we continually add programs to student ministries in order to gain greater control over the faith formation of students. We believe that if we have enough programs to meet the needs of all students, then we can control their development. When a new need arises, a new program is created. Like a hoarder of clothing who has long ago run out of closet space and who adds new clothes to the collection without discarding any old clothes, we tend to add programs to our ministries without discarding any old ones. The net result is a complex maze of ministry programs that become overwhelming to staff, volunteers, students, and parents. Our tendency to hang on to programs too long is usually driven by one of two beliefs: that discarding a particular program will upset parents or students, or that if a program helps just one student or one family, it should continue regardless of the resources necessary to keep it going.

Complexity in student ministry rests on a philosophical understanding of ministry as program driven. Programs are visible, goal oriented, scheduled, promoted, organized, attended, and controlled. Thus, they help us maintain an image that something is happening, people are busy, and ministry is occurring in a clean and organized manner. Whenever we create a video to promote student ministry among elders, parents, or students, the video is filled with programs, because they are the most visible and tangible aspect of the ministry. While programs certainly help to facilitate ministry, much ministry should be happening between the regularly scheduled programs. This aspect of ministry is not very visible, not as high energy, and does not make great promotional videos.

When I was a youth minister, my church would consistently stop all of our student ministry programs for about six weeks from the middle of December until the first of February, with the sole exception of an outreach ski trip in January. No youth club, no Bible studies, no prayer meetings, no leadership meetings—no regularly scheduled programs. This provided an opportunity for volunteer leaders to take a break from the regular routines of ministry, gave students a chance to consider what they were really committed to, and, most important, gave leaders an opportunity to reflect on their personal ministry.

During this break I would ask leaders: "If there were no programs, would you still have a ministry?" The program-free period was meant to emphasize the value of relationships with students. Leaders who were fostering relationships with students were thankful for the extra time to spend with teenagers individually or in clusters of two or three. Leaders who were not sure what to do without the programs were challenged to reconsider how they were building authentic relationships with students. Yes, ministry can happen without programs. While some aspects of ministry, such as community building, necessitate a collective environment, an overreliance on programs can quickly shift our attention from the genuine needs of teenagers. This brief, six-week break in the middle of the ministry season each year provided an essential reminder of the importance of relationships in ministry. It also served as a caution to never become so burdened with programs and overwhelmed with planning that there is no time for relationships.

Build a Ministry without Clutter

Those of us in student ministries have plenty of arrows in our quivers to shoot at everyone—from the senior pastor to the custodian to the budget committee—to explain the shortcomings of our ministries. Before pointing a finger at others, however, student ministry leaders should consider some ministry modifications that have the potential to greatly increase the effectiveness of our work.

Over 150 years ago, long before all of our modern technology and consumer obsessions, Henry David Thoreau wrote from his cabin near Walden Pond, "Simplicity, simplicity, simplicity! I say, let your affairs be as two or three, and not a hundred or a thousand; instead of a million count half a dozen, and keep your accounts on your thumb-nail."[3] Sometimes less is more. In our quest to provide the very best ministry for students, we often program students right out of the church. Andy Stanley said, "Complexity dilutes your potential for impact."[4] When the church strives to "keep up" with the fast pace of a technological society, we often begin teaching students (and adults) to become consumers of the church in the same way that they are consumers of the secular culture. Events begin to replace relationships, and students eventually feel abandoned by the church in the same way they have been abandoned by most other institutions.[5] Too often we believe that more is better, and before long programming has become so complicated and overdeveloped that students, parents, and youth leaders are left dazed and confused.

There was very little "programming" in the ministries of Jesus and the apostle Paul, yet scores of lives were transformed. Yes, that was a different time and a different culture, and they were not dealing with adolescents. But the simplicity of their ministries is worth consideration. In order to develop a comprehensive ministry that brings students into the presence of Christ and connects them to the community of faith that is the church, we must elevate some core commitments in student ministry. We must value people over programs, conversations over conversions,[6] and relationships without abandonment.[7]

Prioritize Process

The first area of consideration is the tension between process and programs. Faith formation is a journey that begins when a person is motivated to investigate the faith, proceeds through the process of salvation, and continues for a lifetime of sanctification. God is in the transformation business, and our task is to place people in what Andy Stanley calls *environments* where they can reap the transforming power of God. Stanley prefers the term *environments* to *programs*, because programs often feel cold and static, while an environment feels more inviting, engaging, authentic, and dynamic. Creating environments is important, but it is essential to maintain focus on the process of moving students forward in their faith formation. When the process is the primary focus, then dynamic environments can be developed to support the process. When programs become the focus, a convoluted process is created to justify numerous programs. When student ministry development focuses on process over programs, the ministry will develop environments that support the faith journey process.[8]

Maintaining a focus on process requires a keen awareness of where our students are in their faith journeys and a clarity regarding where we want them to go. The first task is to define "our students." Who are we truly concerned about? If we define "our students" as only teenagers in the church, or only those students who actively participate, then we may not be too concerned about moving students from a position of being far from God toward embracing God's saving grace. However, if we define "our students" as all those in the local community in which our church is situated, then it is likely that the majority of "our students" will be far from God and in need of moving toward God's saving grace. The former results in a "good enough" ministry for the discipling of the teenagers in the church; the latter results in a comprehensive ministry that embraces the missional mandate of Jesus and is concerned for all the teenagers of the community.

The Threefold Process

Thom Rainer and Eric Geiger have researched and written extensively on the matter of simplifying ministry. They suggest that *simple ministry* is "designed around a straightforward and strategic process that moves people through the stages of spiritual growth."[9] They point to Jesus' ministry of mentoring his disciples along a threefold process based on Luke 5–9, which includes *calling*, *building*, and *sending*.[10]

CALLING

In Luke 5, Jesus calls the first of his disciples during a fishing expedition, and upon returning to shore the men follow Jesus and leave their fishing boats behind. Jesus begins the process by introducing himself to his would-be disciples, and they respond by following him. Likewise, the student ministry process begins by introducing students to Jesus in the hope that they will begin following his call on their lives.

BUILDING

In Luke 7–8, the disciples are educated in the ways of Jesus. Building them up, Jesus teaches them about the critical issues of the kingdom as they accompany him day after day and observe his ministry among the people. They learn what it means to have great faith from the centurion's friends, who ask Jesus to heal the centurion's servant. They learn to have compassion as they see Jesus' compassion for a widow whose only son has died. They witness the saving grace that Jesus offers the sinful woman. They come to understand that Jesus is the Messiah John the Baptist has taught about. They learn the secrets of the kingdom of God as Jesus explains the parable of the sower, and they embrace the importance of living a faithful life for all to see. They learn that the family of God is greater than a nation or a people group or blood relatives. In a boat on the stormy waters of a lake, they learn how little faith they actually have and how far they have to go to be like Christ. They learn that even invisible and marginalized people are worthy of Jesus' time, as he attends to the unclean woman in the crowd who touched him—again pointing out to his disciples what true faith looks like. Jesus teaches and trains his disciples in preparation for sending them out into the world to do the work of the kingdom.

Sending

In Luke 9, Jesus begins to give the disciples some ministry responsibilities. They are sent out to preach about the kingdom of God and heal the sick. When they return from preaching and healing, he asks them to feed five thousand people with five loaves and two fish. Jesus steps in and helps them out when they have trouble casting a demon out of a little boy. Peter comes to understand that Jesus is the Christ, and Jesus continues to teach them the depths of genuine discipleship and the true cost of following him. Jesus never stops training the disciples. But he quickly sends them out to engage in ministry themselves, that they might gain confidence through contributing to the kingdom and gain even greater wisdom for the days ahead.

The disciples participated in a simple process with Jesus. He *called* them to follow him, he *taught* them the ways of the kingdom, and he *sent* them to contribute to the ministry. Throughout this process, they certainly worshiped together, prayed together, fellowshiped together, and grew in their passion for the gospel that Jesus was teaching. A similar threefold process is found is Acts 2, which was discussed in chapter 1. First, they became a *community* of believers who fellowshiped together, supported one another, and had everything in common. They ate common meals together in one another's homes and cared for one another. They prayed, worshiped, and celebrated the Lord's Supper together. Second, the people of the early church *learned* everything that Jesus commanded through the teachings of the apostles. They were not casual learners; rather, they were devoted to the teachings of the apostles and to learning the ways of the Lord. Third, as they learned how to live a life of faith, caring for one another and those around them, they began carrying out the *ministries* of the church and reaching out to the larger community. The apostles continued to heal people, and everyone sold their possessions and goods so that they could faithfully serve those who were in need with compassion and mercy. This community, which numbered more than three thousand people at the time, lived a vibrant, faithful life in both word and deed, so much so that everyone who encountered this group of people was amazed by what they experienced. Intrigued by the authenticity of the faith of this community and the work that God was doing through them, others began to trust in the message of the gospel, and new believers came into the fellowship every day.

Exemplary Student Ministries that Value Simplicity

Simplicity can be applied to the church as a whole, any ministry within the church, or even parachurch ministries. For the purposes of this book, we are concerned specifically with student ministry in the context of the local church. Based on the principles discussed in this chapter, what does simplicity in student ministry look like? Eric Geiger and Jeff Borton have devoted an entire book to this topic with helpful case studies.[11] Throughout their research, they found that many of the most effective student ministries share common approaches to the faith formation process.

The threefold process is almost always at the heart of effective student ministry, though the environments for each aspect of the process will vary. Geiger and Borton cite five churches, City Church, Christ Fellowship, Community Christian Church, Grace Baptist Church, and First Baptist Church, as examples from their research.[12] To add to these, I will reflect on the examples of three churches, Grace Chapel, Second Presbyterian Church, and The Falls Church, that I learned about in my own research. Each of these eight churches is located in a different context with a variety of dynamics. Some are in the city and others are in the suburbs or in rural locations. Some are neighborhood churches and others are regional churches. The designs of their environments differ, but they all focus on three primary aspects of ministry engagement: entry points, growth points, and contribution points.

CITY CHURCH

For City Church in Simpsonville, South Carolina, the trilogy is: encounter God, connect with others, and serve the world. They begin by creating an environment on Sunday evenings in which students genuinely encounter God through worship, teaching, testimony, and prayer in a large group setting. Students move from this large group gathering into life groups, which meet throughout the week in homes and enable students to connect with others. Life groups are segregated by age and gender and are led by volunteers who create an environment that fosters fellowship, Bible study, prayer, and doing life together, which includes serving together once a month in the community. Finally, students are encouraged to take another step toward serving the world. Service opportunities are promoted at the Sunday evening meetings and modeled in the life groups. For City Church, serving the world includes a broad range of service, from weekly local service to annual mission trips. This is where the congregation begins to integrate teenagers into the life of the church by providing opportunities for them to contribute. Students serve in children's ministries, older students serve with middle school ministries, and some connect with a variety of adult ministries. Beyond the church, students serve in the local community, meeting a variety of needs and living out their faith in practical and meaningful ways. Not only is "encounter, connect, serve" the trilogy for the student ministries of City Church; it is the ethos and process of the whole church. When the church and student ministries are promoting the same simple system of ministry, there is great synergy, as adults and students are moving through the same process together. When the church at large does not have a simple system, the same level of synergy may not be present. Even so, there is still great value in championing simplicity for the student ministries.

Christ Fellowship

At Christ Fellowship in Miami, Florida, the theme of connecting is also central. They strive to connect students to God, others, ministry, and the world. While their list includes four goals, the threefold nature of the process is still evident. On Saturday evenings they connect students to God through a large group gathering that provides a creative environment for singing, teaching, games, and videos that are all designed to connect students to the person of Christ. Sitting at tables (rather than on the floor or in rows of chairs) creates a relational environment for discussion led by volunteer leaders, as well as for the integration of new students to the community. While the table groups are helpful in connecting students to one another, that is only the beginning. Students genuinely connect with one another in small groups that meet at various times during the week and in which students feel free to discuss spiritual issues, study Scripture, and support one another. Small groups are encouraged to think beyond themselves by serving in the community in tangible ways. As students learn, play, and serve together, they begin living out their faith in everyday life, growing in their relationships with one another and with God. Connecting to ministry is all about making a contribution, and at Christ Fellowship teenagers serve in children's ministries, media ministries, drama ministries, worship teams, and welcome teams. Those involved in service garner ownership of the student ministries and the church as they invest in and contribute to the greater community of faith. Connecting to the world is the fourth aspect of the student ministries at Christ Fellowship, but this is not a regularly scheduled program. This is really an extension of connections to ministry that further encourages students to share their faith with others locally, nationally, and globally. Students are encouraged to invest in relationships with friends and invite them to the large gathering that serves as the entry point for newcomers. Through caring for those around them and sharing their stories of living in the presence of God, they witness to the grace of God in their lives. Students are also invited to invest in people and share the message of the gospel with people in cross-cultural settings around the country and the world through short-term mission trips. The heartbeat of Christ Fellowship is connection. The church connects people to God, others, ministry, and the world through three simple environments, which include large group gatherings, small groups, and ministry teams.

Community Christian Church

At Community Christian Church in Naperville, Illinois, the mantra of the whole church is celebrate, connect, and contribute, again providing great synergy throughout all the ministries of the church as everyone engages in the same process. Everything in the church, including the student ministries, revolves around the 3Cs. They create an environment on Wednesday evenings in which students gather to connect to God and one another. This is a large group gathering that is high energy, creative, and relevant to the lives of students. Students play games, hang out in the café, worship together, laugh together, and encounter a relevant message of God's grace. It is truly an environment that promotes the celebration of God and one another. Moving from the large group gathering, students are connected into small groups by age. Middle school small groups meet on Sunday mornings at the church, while high school small groups meet during the week in homes on various nights of the week. The small group environment focuses on building healthy relationships and strong Christian communities in which students learn together, care for one another, and support one another. The curriculum for the small groups is based on the teaching from the large Wednesday night gatherings. In the small groups, questions can be raised and clarity can be brought to the teaching. Small groups also serve together in the church or in the community. Having received a taste of serving in small groups, students are encouraged to contribute to the various ministries of the church along the lines of their particular gifts and talents. One of the goals of encouraging students to contribute to the church at large is to ensure that the student ministries never become silos that are disconnected from the rest of the church. Once again, through contributing to the larger church, students develop a sense of ownership of the church beyond the student ministries. This commitment to the local church pays significant dividends in maintaining the connection of students to the local church after they graduate from high school. Students are also given opportunities to contribute to the local community, meeting the needs of people in their own backyard.

Grace Baptist Church

Grace Baptist Church in Cedarville, Ohio, follows a pattern similar to the previous churches but with some differences in timing and locations. This congregation's threefold process is gospel, grow, and go. Wednesday evening is the *gospel* environment where they gather as a large group for a high-energy time of fun, fellowship, worship, and biblical and life-application teaching. This is a gracious environment to which students invite friends to introduce them to the message of the gospel. At the end of the evening, following the message, students break up into small groups to answer questions about the lesson that night. The small groups also provide a safe place for visitors to connect with other students and leaders as they begin to assimilate into the ministry. Following the gathering, these groups often go out for food to continue building relationships. On Sunday morning, the *grow* environment of the process for student ministries at Grace Baptist can be found. Each Sunday students gather for Bible study during the church's regular Sunday school time. This is an opportunity for deeper teaching than is provided on Wednesday evenings, and students in this environment are encouraged to serve others in a variety of contexts. The *go* aspect of the process provides students with numerous opportunities to serve in the children's department, media department, landscaping team, orchestra, children's summer camp, and other ministries throughout the church. Going also involves reaching out to the community and meeting the needs of people in the surrounding neighborhoods. Finally, short-term mission trips provide students with faith experiences in cross-cultural settings that emphasize the importance of incorporating missions into the daily lives of students.

First Baptist Church

At First Baptist Church in Oviedo, Florida, the process is described as expose, equip, experience. While the names are different, the pattern of a large group gathering, small groups, and service is the same. The large group gathering occurs on Wednesday evenings in an environment that begins with games, hanging out, snacks, and videos. Then the group gathers for a time of singing, games, skits, and a message that exposes students to the message of the gospel. Following the meeting, students spend time hanging out at the adjacent shopping center, skate park, or snack bar until it's time to leave. The casual beginning and ending of the evening is designed for relationship building as leaders engage students in conversation. These conversations and relationships can lead students into a small group environment that First Baptist calls Bible fellowship groups, in which students grow deeper in their faith. These are offered on Sunday mornings and are facilitated by volunteer leaders. In these small-group environments, leaders emphasize the importance of spiritual disciplines, accountability, Bible study, prayer, Scripture memorization, and community. The goal is to equip students as lifelong followers of Christ. As the small groups emphasize the importance of putting faith into action, students begin to move into areas of service through the *experience* part of the process. In this environment, students work out their gifts and talents and join an E-Team, which serves in the student ministries, the greater church, or the community. Students in this experience phase meet together on Sunday afternoons to discover more fully their gifts and talents, meet and plan with their E-Team, and receive some leadership development.

GRACE CHAPEL

At Grace Chapel in Lexington, Massachusetts, the threefold process is called growing deeper, growing closer, and growing wider. This trilogy is exemplified in the student ministries. On Wednesday evening for middle school and Friday evening for high school, the ministry provides an environment with doors wide open for all to enjoy. This environment offers students a safe and compelling place where they can bring their friends and introduce them to the message of the gospel and the student community at Grace Chapel. These evenings are packed with high-energy games, videos, food, hangout time, singing, testimonies, and a message. Sunday morning provides a greater opportunity for growth and fellowship as students begin in a large group for worship and teaching, then break into small groups where they discuss the morning's message, pray for one another, and support each other. Each small group also plans a special time together each month that may involve serving or fellowship. Out of these small groups, students begin to serve on worship teams, drama teams, tech teams, orchestra, café, or the children's ministry.

SECOND PRESBYTERIAN CHURCH

Comprehensive does not have to be complicated, as the first six examples demonstrate. Earlier in this book I extolled two churches, Second Presbyterian Church in Memphis and The Falls Church in Virginia, for exemplifying a comprehensive student ministry reflective of Jesus' Great

Commission. These two churches also employ simple ministry models that move students through every aspect of the Great Commission. At Second Presbyterian everything is about growing: growing in Christ, growing in community, and growing in outreach. Wednesday evenings focus on outreach in a safe, dynamic environment, to which students can bring their friends and in which they can introduce them to the transforming message of the gospel. On Sunday mornings, students are immersed in dynamic Bible study with a gifted communicator, and on Sunday afternoons, students gather in small groups to process what they are learning so they can assimilate it into everyday life. Students grow in community by serving all over the church and the city of Memphis, caring for others and using their gifts and talents for the work of the kingdom.

THE FALLS CHURCH

At The Falls Church in Virginia, student ministries are committed to connecting students with God, helping them grow in their faith, and assimilating them into the broader community of the church. The Sunday evening environment is an amazing time of fellowship, teaching, worship, and small groups. Students bring friends and make new friends as the evening begins with dinner and is followed by games, laughter, singing, and teaching. The message is followed by small groups, in which students have the opportunity to discuss the teaching, ask questions, and process the experience. Students grow deeper in their faith during the week in the environment of breakfast Bible studies located near the schools that students attend. (Breakfast gatherings with students never seem to go out of style.) As students begin to put their faith in action, they become involved in serving throughout the church and the community.

Characteristics of Simple Ministries

Each of these student ministries has created a process that provides clarity, simplicity, and sustainability. Each has created a dynamic, friendly, and engaging large group gathering to which students can invite their friends. This is a place where students far from God can connect in a natural and relational way with Christian adults and other students who are genuinely interested in their stories. It is a place where the person and work of Christ is presented in a compelling manner, and caring adults and students alike share how their stories have merged with God's story. Out of the larger gathering, students are connected to a small group, in which they can grow in a close-knit community, study Scripture, serve, and fellowship together, all the while growing deeper in their relationships with God and others by striving for the fruits of the Spirit. Finally, each of these student ministries strives to move students from being consumers to being contributors through service in the student ministries, the broader church, and the greater community. The greatest opportunity to contribute to the work of the church is usually on Sunday mornings. There is a trend in student ministries toward deprogramming Sunday morning for high school students. This way teenagers are free to serve somewhere in the church for one hour and to worship in an intergenerational environment at another hour.

The ministries are limited to two or three programs at the most, each clearly fostering one of the three aims: outreach, discipleship, and service. Community is clearly accomplished across all three of these aims, and worship is typically part of the large group gatherings. While worshiping with peers in student ministry is important, each of these ministries also strives for students to engage in one of the intergenerational worship services of their churches. Students who are serving and worshiping in the larger context of the community of faith are far more likely to continue on their faith journey into adulthood than those who are confined to a silo of student ministries set apart from the life of the congregation.

If this all sounds terribly familiar, it should. Those 120 disciples of Jesus in the upper room were in awe at the response to Peter's message to the crowd on Pentecost. Seemingly before he could even finish his sermon, the crowd asked him what they should do. He told them to repent of their sins and be baptized in the name of Jesus. Amazingly, three thousand of them did as he said! The apostles had to figure out what to do with a faith community of some 3,120. They had clearly outgrown the upper room in a single day. The apostles could not simply send everyone home and instruct them to grow on their own—"Read the Torah and figure it out." Nor could each apostle mentor 250 new converts! So they created a community consisting of two environments. They gathered together as a large group in the temple courts, and they gathered together in small groups in their homes. Out of those gatherings they served those in need, shared stories of God's goodness, and every day more people were drawn into their community of faith. It was a simple process that transformed the world.

Prioritize People through Simplicity

With all of our technology and multisite campuses, there is still something very satisfying about simplicity. When we make teenagers a priority in the church, we are making humanity a priority. We are valuing people over tasks. When ministry becomes too complex, filled with events and programs, the first thing to go is relationships. We become task driven rather than people driven. We spend far too much time locked away in the office and not nearly enough time out among the people—teenagers, parents, and volunteer leaders—who make up our ministry.

Leadership guru Hanz Finzel argues that one of the top ten mistakes leaders make is putting paperwork before people.[13] We can become so program driven and task oriented that people fall by the wayside. Finzel offers a simple, unscientific test to determine whether a person is task oriented or people oriented. When you are in the midst of planning, writing, or studying in your office and a person requests to have a conversation with you, are you more likely to view that person as an interruption or an opportunity? If your inclination is to keep the conversation as brief as possible and get back to the task at hand, you may be task oriented. If you engage in the conversation with delight until the exchange naturally concludes, then you are more likely a people-driven person. Henri Nouwen suggests that people's interruptions are the most important task we can engage in. "A few years ago I met an old professor at the University of Notre Dame. Looking back on his long life of teaching, he said with a funny twinkle in his eyes: 'I have always been complaining that my work was constantly interrupted, until I slowly discovered that my interruptions were my work.' This is the great conversion in our life: to recognize and believe that the many unexpected events are not just disturbing interruptions of our projects, but the way in which God molds our hearts and prepares us for his return."[14]

In an age of increasing complexity and bureaucracy, factors to which the church is not immune, we need to focus on streamlining everything. The information explosion has drawn ministry leaders into being task driven. With the barrage of information, there is more to read, more to write, more to blog, more to respond to than ever before. A friend of mine who is a business executive asked his adult son one night why he was at work so late. His son replied with exasperation about the number of emails he had to respond to each day in his corporate setting. My friend asked his son one question: how many of those email responses will help you become a vice president of the company? That is a ruthless question, but it makes a great point. How often do we spend time on tasks that do not contribute to our goals? How many of the tasks we engage in actually contribute to the faith formation of students?

Jesus spent more time talking, touching, teaching, and connecting with people than on any other activity in his ministry. He was highly people oriented. He was constantly pressed by friends and foes alike to engage in a variety of tasks, and his greatest task was to train the apostles to carry on the ministry of the gospel after his ascension. Yet he never became program driven or task oriented. He remained faithful to the people.

Thomas Watson was the founder of IBM, and he was fastidious about serving his customers. In the early days of the company, Watson attended a meeting in which his managers were reviewing some customer issues.

> On the front table there were eight or ten piles of papers, identifying the source of problems: "manufacturing problems," "engineering problems," and the like. After much discussion, Mr. Watson, a big man, walked slowly up to the front of the room and, with a flash of his hand, swept the table clean and sent papers flying all over the room. He said, "There aren't any categories of problems here. There's just one problem. Some of us aren't paying enough attention to our customers." He turned crisply on his heel and walked out, leaving twenty fellows wondering whether or not they still had jobs.[15]

Watson understood the importance of being a people-oriented company. His company never offered machines for rent; rather, they offered machine services that included the equipment, servicing the equipment, and the counsel of the IBM staff. Watson certainly produced products, but the people his company served were his top priority.

When our ministry model is simplified, we are free to invest in the people of our ministries. We are free to reach out to new people and draw them into the community of faith. Simplicity is a great gift that allows us to invest in the lives of the people we have been called to serve. Without simplicity, we become directors of programs and events in the hope that students will engage and find meaning in the programs we develop. I have never liked the title "director of student ministries," because directors run programs, while ministers care for people. If we are going to minister to students, volunteers, and parents, then we must approach our ministries with the simplicity that affords us the time to make genuine relationships our highest priority.

Organize for Simplicity

Clutter can be overwhelming no matter where you find it. In our homes, offices, or ministries, it is often so overwhelming that we ignore the clutter rather than deal with it. Leo Babauta is an expert on clutter and suggests remedies to deal with the mess. He offers four laws of simplicity that can be applied to almost any area of life and work, from a cluttered drawer to a cluttered ministry.[16] Imagine two things: the actual drawer in your house or office that is cluttered, and the ministry that you feel is overly cluttered. Let's de-clutter both of them using Babauta's four laws of simplicity.

Collect Everything in One Place

When tackling a cluttered drawer, one must take everything out of the drawer and place it in a pile on the floor or a table. Wipe out the drawer so that it is clean and totally empty of any item, dirt, or dust.

For student ministry, the same principle applies. Collect all programs in one place. Write the name of every program on an index card or sticky note, and then pin the index cards to a foam board or post the sticky notes to a large wall. Be careful to break down large programs into their component parts; for example, rather than posting a card with "retreats" on it, post one card for each retreat. Likewise, post one card for each small group rather than representing all small groups with one card. Be sure to include items that may not typically be considered programs but that nonetheless take up valuable time, such as staff meetings, contact work with students, parent meetings, and planning meetings.

Now stand back and survey everything that is included in the student ministry. This can be overwhelming, but it is absolutely necessary to take inventory of what is happening and where precious ministry time is being spent.

Choose the Essentials

Now that the clutter of the drawer is spread out, it is easy to see what is there. Survey the pile and choose only the items that are essential, the things that are really important to keep. Place these important items in a separate pile, which will obviously be smaller.

Likewise, survey all the cards containing ministry items that you have posted on a wall or board. Move those that are truly essential to the far side of the surface. To determine if each ministry item is truly essential, ask these questions: What purpose does this item serve? Are multiple items serving the same purpose? What items deliver the greatest impact? What has the most long-term impact? What activities *need* to be done, and what activities do we just *want* to do for various reasons? Do we really need to do this in order to be faithful and effective in student ministry? If we could only do three things in our ministry, what would they be? This process will only be effective if you are highly selective about choosing the absolute essentials for ministry.

Eliminate the Rest

The clutter of the desk drawer is now separated into two piles: the original pile and the new pile of essentials. Hopefully the essentials pile is smaller than the other pile; at worst, the piles are the same size. Now comes the real challenge: throw away what is left of the original pile of clutter. This is not the time to be sentimental over those stickers from Disneyland or that collectible key ring. If some items can be recycled or donated to charity, put the recyclables in one box and the charity items in another, and then take those boxes to the recycle center and the charity within forty-eight hours! The rest goes in the trash.

Now approach the clutter of student ministry with the same tenacity. If the items on the cards did not make the list of essentials, seriously consider eliminating them. Clearly, this is more complicated than cleaning out a desk drawer. While the church staff meeting may not have made the essentials list, you might be out of a job if you stop attending staff meetings. So now we need to fine-tune the essentials list by adding a few items that may not be essential to student ministries per se but are essential to our broader ministry in the church. While some items of the cluttered drawer could be sorted into piles for charity or recycling, some of the nonessential items on the ministry list might be sorted into piles for gradual phase out or reassignment. Many things in ministry can be brought to a screeching halt, but others need to be phased out gradually to avoid causing a train wreck with parents, students, and leaders. People need to understand why a particular aspect of the ministry is no longer viable, and that can take some time. Often the best time to put a program to rest is over the summer, when certain aspects of ministry naturally slow down. To accomplish this in a timely manner, it is important to define the time frame of the phase out so that everyone knows a particular program will no longer exist in September, or after the first of the year, or once school is out for the summer.

Occasionally aspects of ministry are very important but can be reassigned either within the church or outside of the church. For example, the short-term mission trips may be very important to student ministries, but perhaps the time has come for intergenerational mission trips. Perhaps student ministries should stop leading mission trips and allow the missions pastor and missions committee to coordinate all the mission trips, with the youth minister serving as an adviser to the missions committee. Another good example of reassignment involves retreats. Perhaps the winter retreat is considered essential, but the planning of the retreat by the student ministry leaders may not be essential. When we take students to a winter retreat where the camp does all the planning and provides all the programming, it offers leaders more time to spend with students and it frees up an enormous amount of time on the front end for other aspects of ministry. Of course, the downside to outsourcing the retreat programming is that we no longer have control over the theme, activities, music, or messaging of the retreat. This is why *you* have to decide what is essential for *your* ministry context. In some instances, it is essential to plan and execute one's own retreat in order to accomplish specific goals. More often than not, however, it is more beneficial to attend a retreat programmed by the camp and leverage the precious time of the youth leaders more effectively.

Unlike removing the junk pile, recycling pile, and charity pile within forty-eight hours, it takes time to phase out and reassign various aspects of ministry. That said, if it takes much more than six months to phase out or reassign aspects that are cluttering the student ministry, then we need to question the seriousness with which we are approaching the process.

Organize the Essentials

Now that there is so much room in the empty drawer, the temptation is to simply throw the items from the essentials pile back into the drawer and be done with it. In doing so, we simply create an environment that is a starter pile for clutter. The essentials should be placed back into the drawer neatly and in an orderly way. Common items should be grouped together, leaving a little space between groupings. The spacing offers a clean look, makes everything easy to find, and allows the beautiful woodwork inside the drawer to be seen.

Once again, organizing student ministry is more complicated than organizing a cluttered drawer, but the principle remains the same. How can the essential programs continue in a manner that is most effective, scalable, and sustainable over the long haul? Rather than simply continuing the essential aspects of the ministry, each item on each card should be analyzed for maximum effectiveness. Perhaps there is a better way to organize the media or music for the youth club. If music is an aspect of multiple ministry programs, perhaps all the music can be clustered together and creating music teams and rehearsals can be made more efficient. Cluster all the small groups that were determined to be essential and consider the curriculum being used for each. Should all groups use a common curriculum? Do some need a specific curriculum? Cluster all the trips and assess the efficiency and effectiveness of transportation planning, scholarships, and the relative timing of each trip throughout the ministry year. Organizing the essentials of ministry brings simplicity to life and ministry, allowing for greater time to invest in relationships with students, leaders, and parents.

Responding to Those Who Resist Simplicity

Until they hired Sharon as their first full-time youth minister, Hope Community Church had always maintained a student ministry through volunteers and seminary interns. Sharon felt very welcome during her first month on the job. She began building relationships with the youth leaders, most of whom had grown up in the church. She visited students, engaged the church staff, and made some keen observations about the student ministry programs. Sharon quickly concluded that some things had to change, but that there would also be great resistance to change. She knew that she was in an environment that embraced the status quo. So rather than raise the flag of change herself, she wisely called on a consultant to meet with the student ministry advisory committee and the volunteer leaders.

Bob had been the regional director of Christian education for the denomination for nearly twenty-five years, and he had literally seen it all. When Sharon approached him with her dilemma, he was delighted to assist and had the perfect exercise for the ministry leaders. Sharon called her committee and leaders together for a meeting in the hopes that Bob could bring them into the twenty-first century of student ministries. Bob arranged the room with four large flip-charts and asked the group to create four lists. The first list contained everything that they remembered about being teenagers. The second list contained everything they knew about the growing pains of contemporary teenagers. The third list contained everything that they could remember about the student ministry in which they grew up, and the fourth list contained everything they knew about the current student ministry that they were leading.

With wisdom and grace, Bob stepped to the front of the room and noted that the first list and the second list were very different. Growing up had changed dramatically over the years, and he applauded the group for recognizing this important shift. Then the moment Sharon had been waiting for finally arrived: Bob observed that the third and fourth lists were nearly identical. The student ministry had not changed in decades.

Coffee with Parents Goes a Long Way

I've had a few parents who could be a proverbial "thorn in the side." When major programming changes needed to be made in order to align student ministry with the direction of our church, I invited those parents out for coffee. We discussed a few of the new ideas, and I was able to gain their support. What had traditionally been a painful process went smoothly, and I even gained a cheering section. Because I put my frustration aside and took the time to win these parents over, everyone benefited from the program changes. This was a huge learning experience for me.

Kori North, Grace Fellowship Church,
Latham, New York

This group of bright and talented people had clearly recognized the change in youth culture, but they continued to minister through programs that were designed to meet the needs of a previous generation. The youth leaders quickly admitted that they felt some things needed to change but that they were afraid of what a new model of ministry might look like. They had continued with the same approach for years primarily because they were afraid of change.

Most people resist change because they are afraid of the unknown, and even talking about innovation makes people nervous. It is usually more comfortable to maintain the status quo than to take the risk of implementing change. Effectiveness in student ministry—and the church, for that matter—is predicated on innovation. We must constantly cast visions for new ways to provide transformational environments that will engage the hearts and minds of students. When implementing change in ministry, especially moving toward simplicity, three constituencies (church staffers, parents, and students) will typically express their fear of the unknown.

Church Staff Fears

Senior pastors, associate pastors, secretaries, custodians, elders, officers, committees, and volunteer leaders may resist a movement toward simplicity, as they fear the unknown. The resistance among church personnel is typically the fear that, in one way or another, the bright ideas of the youth minister will affect others in negative ways.

In my former church, Gary, the youth minister, proposed that the student ministry hold a coffeehouse gathering in the church gym, which was also the fellowship hall, to create an entry-point environment for outreach. At his proposal, the normally tame staff meeting exploded with questions.

Custodian: Who will clean the building late Saturday night so that the church is ready for Sunday morning?

Secretary: Does this mean I have to send yet another mailing to students and families?

Pastor: Will the noise be disruptive to the neighbors? I don't want the neighbors complaining to me on Sunday morning about these coffeehouse gatherings.

Business Manager: What liability risks are we taking if the coffeehouse gets out of hand? I will have to check with our insurance company before you do anything.

Music Director: How will this affect the students who need to attend the Sunday morning worship team rehearsal?

Each person raised legitimate concerns that were rooted in their fears about what might happen. These fears grew out of their lack of experience with such a ministry program. Other concerns are often raised regarding expenses, theology, staffing, community image, or even the value of the proposal. Often this resistance is alleviated when a detailed plan of implementation demonstrates that the new idea will not have a negative impact on the responsibilities or ministries of colleagues.

In the end, Gary was allowed to implement the coffeehouse because he had completed his research *before* he presented the new idea to his colleagues. He had spoken with the three neighbors adjacent to the church who might raise concerns about the noise and parking issues. All the neighbors agreed that the coffeehouse would be fine as long as it was over by 11:00 p.m. He had arranged to pay the assistant custodian for working late Saturday night out of the proceeds from the coffeehouse. He had spoken with the local police, who agreed to drive by the church a few extra times on Saturday evening to curb any trouble that might arise from a large crowd of high school students. He had recruited a few parents to prepare some extra mailings to promote the new outreach environment, and he had made a deal with the students serving on the worship team that if they were late for the music rehearsal on Sunday morning, there would be consequences.

Over the years, the coffeehouse environment attracted hundreds of unchurched teenagers who came to know Christ and became active in growing environments of the ministry. The innovation was possible because Gary was able to relieve the fears of his colleagues in a single staff meeting.

Parental Fears

When parents are faced with a new idea that challenges the status quo, they typically raise one question: How will this affect my kid? Just a few years ago, the pastor of student ministries at my church faced this very situation. Todd proposed that the high school students embark on a mission trip to Mexico, where he had taken students many times while serving in his previous church. Parents who had nurtured, cared for, protected, and loved their children were now being asked to send their kids to a part of the world that was experiencing an increase in violence from drug cartels. It seemed that just prior to each information meeting about the mission trip, another story about shootings in Mexico hit the news. Todd asked some parents to research the situation, contact the State Department, and make a realistic assessment of the risks. He spoke about the dangers with the missionaries where they would be going in Mexico. Like Gary, he did his research before a final decision was made.

While the missionaries assured him that their area was safe, and the parents' research affirmed that the violence was taking place far away from the mission site, the team did have to travel past one of the cities that were experiencing increased violence on their way to the mission site. All this time, Todd was researching other possible mission trip locations. In the end, it was decided that he would take the students to New Orleans and serve in the continuing restoration of the city ravaged by Hurricane Katrina.

The trip to New Orleans was transformational in the lives of many students. Many had never realized that such devastation existed so close to home. They were amazed at the grace and compassion of the people they were serving, who had lost everything. Todd had to change the location in order to ease the fears of parents, but the resulting experience could not have been any better. Doing the necessary research and involving parents in the process resulted in a transformational mission trip that was highly supported by parents who had confidence in the student ministry leadership.

Student Fears

Students often resist change when they feel comfortable in an environment and wish to keep it that way. Unfortunately, an attitude of us-versus-them arises even in the church. Some people are as excited about the people they think will not be in heaven as they are about the people they think will be there. Students often think the same way about their student ministry environments. They love the large group or the small group environments because of who is *not* there as much as who is.

When Leah delivered a message to her students about reaching out to their peers and a list of ten ideas for growing the ministry, she was met with a lot of resistance. They did not want to invite other students to their large group meetings; they did not want to go on retreats with other groups. They wanted to keep their Sunday evening youth group all to themselves. Moving out of their comfort zone was not appealing to them.

Most people need to move out of their comfort zone to grow in faith, and Leah knew that to be true. She had to find a way to help her students understand the benefits of doing so. Often student resistance can be overcome through communicating a compelling vision that offers a clear picture of the future—a future that is better than the existing status quo. If the picture of the future is meaningful to students, they will often make sacrifices to move in that direction.

Leah realized that she had jumped the gun and needed to set aside her list of ten ways to grow the ministry. Instead, she began teaching through Ephesians to her students. As she highlighted the importance of sharing their faith with their friends, they began to catch the vision. Students still raised concerns about inviting friends to the group. Some were a little embarrassed that they met in the musty basement of the church, while others were concerned that their friends who were really into music wouldn't like their style or quality of singing. Leah agreed to move the meeting upstairs to a new room and commissioned a group of students to work with her to create a welcoming environment that they could be proud of. Likewise, she asked a few volunteer leaders to work with a group of students to improve the music. Once students caught the vision, they realized that some things needed to change. After the new environment was launched and students began inviting their friends, the ministry doubled and tripled in size, and more small groups were created as new students wanted to explore the faith more deeply.

Moving from the burdensome complexities of ministry to simplicity is not easy, and many people will express their fears about change. Doing the research ahead of time and anticipating as many objections as possible is essential. Compromise is often necessary and, in the long run, strengthens the ownership of the ministry among everyone involved, as others in the church become more supportive when they feel that they have a stake in the ministry. But most important in leading change is casting vision with great clarity. When colleagues, parents, and students begin to envision the sophistication of simplicity and contribute their own ideas for simplifying the ministry process, the momentum of change becomes a natural outgrowth of desiring something better for all students and their families.

Adding New Programs Carefully

The twenty-first century has been marked by the inundation of tablet computers and e-readers. While the iPad, Kindle, Nook, and Galaxy are currently the most popular, there are over three dozen such devices available. Corporations are rapidly moving from laptops to tablets and, in the process, making costly mistakes along the way. In ministry we tend to adopt new programs in order to "keep up" with what is perceived to be trendy at the time. In so doing, we can easily make mistakes and waste resources. On this matter we can glean some important lessons from the mistakes corporations have made as early adopters of tablet computers.[17]

Create a Plan

Many companies began using tablets before they had an implementation plan. Price Waterhouse purchased twenty thousand tablets for their employees without any idea how they might be used. They just waited for employees to report on how the tablets were helpful. In the end, it was a waste of money and caused great frustration. They quickly learned that they could not simply hand tablet computers to people and say, "Go for it!" The best practice, much like a focus group, is to give tablets to a small number of staff members and let them discover what works best.

Likewise, in student ministry we are wise to experiment with and test new programs, new curricula, new structures, and new models with a handful of students and leaders before rolling them out for the entire ministry. Alternatively, a new program can be tried with everyone for a limited period of time as an experiment, before making it a permanent fixture. Valuable feedback can be gained from such focus groups and short-term experiments, helping youth ministers craft informed decisions about adjustments to existing programs and adoptions of new programs.

Understand Strengths and Weaknesses

Tablets are very powerful, but they cannot do everything, and at this point they are not a replacement for laptop and desktop computers.

American Airlines learned early on that one device would not work for all their needs. Pilots wanted vivid graphics to replace maps and charts. Mechanics wanted something strong to withstand their rugged environment on the tarmac and in the workshops. Flight attendants wanted something small and light to meet their needs.

Everything has strengths and weaknesses, including ministry programs. Middle schoolers need some high energy; high schoolers need some thoughtful engagement. Girls need time to talk; boys need time to do something. Urban, suburban, and rural students have different needs. Homeschool, private school, and public school students all have slightly different needs. In student ministry there are no silver-bullet programs that will meet the needs of all students—hence the importance of personal relationships and authentic engagement between the regularly scheduled programs. Before implementing a new program, we must always consider the strengths and weaknesses as if we were doing a cost-benefit analysis. If the benefits do not outweigh the costs, perhaps the program is not the right fit for the ministry context, even if it has worked well somewhere else.

Consider the Software

While the tablets may be powerful, often software or apps necessary for the task are not available. At other times the apps on a tablet will not receive information in the proper format from the software of a desktop or laptop. Hyatt Hotel employees became frustrated, even with virtual desktop apps on their tablets, because they were so accustomed to using a mouse and keyboard that navigating the tablet app was nearly impossible. Some companies were surprised to find that tablet applications with the same functionality as computer software did not exist, rendering the tablets useless.

This is akin to starting new programs in student ministry without the necessary resources. A strategic plan to launch a mentoring program is wonderful, but without the human capital of mentors, the program will never leave the design board. Many in ministry have wisely advised that a new program should never be launched until new leadership has risen up to lead the program. Alternatively, perhaps a new program should not be launched until an existing program is disbanded, freeing up the leadership necessary for the new program. Sometimes the resources necessary are in the form of human capital, and other times they are financial. Either way, Luke reminds those who would follow Jesus to count the cost, just as people building towers first determine if they have the resources to complete the task (Luke 14:28). What is true of counting the cost of following Jesus is equally true of counting the cost of undertaking ministry. Dave Rahn, senior vice president and chief ministry officer of Youth for Christ, has said, "If you are in a ministry that raises the dead, you can raise the money for your ministry." I couldn't agree more, but we need to determine the cost in order to raise the resources.

Think about Stewardship

While tablets are cheaper than laptops, they reportedly do not last as long. Software giant SAP distributed fourteen thousand tablets to their employees and expects to replace them within eighteen months in order to take advantage of the latest software and hardware improvements. That is half the lifetime of a good laptop. Given the relatively short life expectancy, for tablets to be cost effective, they need to have greater benefits than a lower price tag.

Similarly, in ministry, we often ignore the ideas of *sustainability* and *scalability*. Sustainability questions the life expectancy of a program. Is the program designed in such a way that it can be sustained with the given resources for an extended period of time? Or will it be a once-and-done program? Sometimes we create programs that take an inordinate amount of time and energy and that are impossible to sustain or repeat. While some will benefit from the short-term endeavor, there is little long-term benefit to the ministry. Almost anything is sustainable with enough resources, but resources are rarely unlimited. So the sustainability question becomes: can we keep running the Friday night programs at this level every week with current resources? If the answer is no, then the solution is to either gain greater resources or perhaps cut the program back to once a month. Scalability questions the ability of the program to handle more people as the ministry grows. Small group programs often run into scalability issues when there are not enough leaders for the number of small groups needed. Can you recruit, train, and nurture enough small group leaders to keep pace with the demand? Physical space is often another scalability issue. Is there enough space for the program if is doubles or triples in size? If a program is not scalable, then there is no room for growth. In this case we end up settling for a ministry that is good enough but never pushing for a comprehensive ministry that fully reflects the Great Commission. Scalability issues are typically resolved by gaining more resources of one kind or another.

Focus on Support and Security

Many companies have found that tablets do not fit into their existing IT support and security systems. Hyatt thought they could manage all their tablets within their existing support systems, only to realize that they were dealing with different operating systems, compatibility issues, and security risks. The addition of the tablet devices required a new mobile-device management system to deal with technical support issues more efficiently.

In student ministry, we run across the same issues when we add programs without considering the support and security issues necessary to implement the new programs. Support comes in a variety of shapes and sizes. We may need support from the elders, other staff members, volunteers, parents, students, or community leaders before implementing a new program. Security and safety have become increasingly important issues in student ministry. It is no longer possible to declare that all the high school students are going to work with the children's ministry starting next week, because first everyone needs to have a background check. When taking students away to a camp, a retreat, rafting, skiing, paintballing, or on a mission trip, safety concerns must be addressed up front. Considering the support and security necessary for the implementation of a new program is essential to the viability not only of the new program but also of the entire ministry—if not the entire church. One accident, one scandal, or one breach of trust can bring down a ministry and sometimes even a church.

Any new program, event, or environment that is created in a student ministry should be done very thoughtfully. There are always tradeoffs whenever something new is created, because it will require resources: time, people, money, facilities, and probably equipment. Can you deliver the new initiative without robbing resources from existing programs in the ministry process? Will the new environment replace an existing environment? What aspect of the ministry process will the new program support? If the new program does not enhance the ministry's ability to connect students to God, help them grow in their faith, or empower students to contribute to the work of the kingdom, then perhaps the new idea is not worth implementing. There are millions of great programs in student ministries, but ministry is always contextual, and not all programs are effective in every context. Therefore, it requires great wisdom to determine what programs, events, and environments are best suited for a particular ministry context that will support the ministry process.

Simplicity as Stewardship

In the final analysis, simplicity is about stewardship. We have been given gifts and talents and resources to further the kingdom of God here on earth as it is in heaven. When we promote simplicity in student ministries, we are striving to be good stewards of what God has provided for the work of the kingdom. The psalmist declares, "And David shepherded them with integrity of heart; with skillful hands he led them" (Ps. 78:72). Leaders are called to feed their flocks and guide them in the ways of the Lord. When ministry becomes so complex that we are not feeding or guiding students, then our ministry is no longer faithful to the mission of the gospel. When feeding and guiding students becomes so inefficient that it is no longer scalable or sustainable, issues of stewardship must be considered and ministry must be streamlined. Effectively deploying the resources at hand is an important part of the kingdom-building efforts to which we have been called.

Discussion Questions for Student Ministry Leaders

1. Is your ministry driven by values or by programs? Are there programs within your ministry that lack a foundational purpose, even though you believe they are important programs in the ministry?
2. What does the threefold process—calling, building, and sending—look like in your ministry? What would need to happen in your ministry for you to develop the threefold process?
3. How long would it take for you to describe your student ministry to someone new to your ministry context? If it would take more than three minutes, maybe your ministry philosophy needs to be simplified. What are some possible consequences of an over-programmed ministry?
4. What keeps you from eliminating the clutter from your student ministry? How do you keep regular, meaningful programs from falling into the status quo trap?
5. Have you settled into status quo programs because of past conflicts when you tried to bring about change? When simplifying your student ministry, whose fears should you be mindful of, and why should you take them into consideration?
6. When you read the question, "Can you deliver the new initiative without robbing resources from existing programs in the ministry process?" what example comes to mind? How will simplifying

your student ministry make you a better steward of the resources you have been given?

Discussion Questions for Church Leaders

1. Is simplicity a core value of the church that permeates all aspects of ministry? If not, is this a value worth pursuing for your church?
2. How do the ministry goals of the churches referenced in this chapter reflect the simplicity of Jesus' ministry to his disciples?
3. Are you committed to ensuring that student ministry programs attract students from the community, or is your primary concern developing student ministry programs that nurture teenagers growing up in the church?
4. How could student ministries and other church ministries be more effectively aligned in their ministry purposes and values, which would create greater simplicity?
5. Who would need to be at the table to bring about greater unity, cohesion, and simplicity among all the various ministries of the church?
6. Are there ways your ministry could partner with the student ministry to accomplish something neither of you can accomplish alone? (Possibilities might include a parents ministry, local outreach, worship teams, media, or technology.)
7. How can you, in your leadership roles within your church, provide support for your youth minister as he or she begins to simplify that specific area of ministry?

When Teenagers Matter:

PARENTS MATTER

The modern remake of the classic Walt Disney movie *The Parent Trap* stars twelve-year-old Lindsay Lohan in dual roles as cunning identical twin sisters Hallie and Annie. Separated at birth when their parents divorced, the two girls meet at summer camp and devise a shrewd scheme to reunite their estranged parents before their father marries his new girlfriend The twins desperately long to become a whole family and enjoy life together with both of their parents. More than anything, this film demonstrates how much parents matter. Hallie and Annie go to great lengths to reunite their family because of the intrinsic importance of their parents.

Parents matter in numerous ways, and they influence every aspect of their children's lives, including their faith formation. Yet often in student ministries, parents are viewed as part of the problem rather than engaged as part of the solution. "We'll get what we are," Christian Smith declares, arguing that there is nothing more influential in the faith development of teenagers than the modeling of parents.[1]

When I teach a course at my church about parenting adolescents, I often ask parents if they would like to see what their teenager's faith will look like when he or she is an adult. I assure them that I can predict with great certainty what their teenager's faith will look like some twenty-five years into the future. The parents are always both intrigued by and skeptical of my prophetic declaration—until I hold before them a full-length mirror. Look in the mirror, I tell them; this is what your teenager's faith will look like in a couple of decades. His or her faith will look very similar to your faith. Instantly, these parents recognize the power of their influence. Partnering with parents means helping them recognize, understand, and embrace the significant depth of their influence and the numerous modes in which they can contribute to their teenager's development of a sustainable faith.

The importance of parenting cannot be overemphasized. Tony Campolo suggests that many times parents are made to feel that they should apologize for being mothers and fathers, yet in reality, such roles are very noble callings. When he was on the faculty at the University of Pennsylvania, he and his wife, Peggy, often attended university functions. Campolo recalls one such occasion when Peggy defended her noble calling.

> I was once at a very sophisticated gathering at the University of Pennsylvania. I didn't want to be there, and I felt uncomfortable with the kinds of conversations that were going on. A woman colleague who taught sociology struck up a conversation with my wife and me. At one point she turned to my wife and asked, in a very condescending fashion, "And what is it that *you* do, my dear?"
>
> My wife, who is one of the most articulate people I know, shot back, "I am socializing two Homo sapiens into the dominant values of the Judeo-Christian tradition in order that they might be the instruments for the transformation of the social order into the kind of eschatological utopia that God willed from the beginning of creation!"
>
> Then my wife asked politely and sweetly, "And what is it that *you* do?" The woman answered humbly, "I . . . I . . . teach sociology."
>
> We must recognize that raising children is a high and holy task.[2]

Youth ministers, of all people in the church, must champion the role of parents and partner with them to guide students in their faith formation.

Student Ministry and Family Ministry

There is a modest movement afoot these days that suggests student ministry should fall under the umbrella of family ministry. The impetus of this movement is the idea that for too long, the church has divided families into age-specific ministries and parents have delegated the work of faith formation to children's and student ministries. Both are valid critiques, but student ministry is concerned with a broader audience than simply the teenagers of Christian parents in the church. Family ministry should not be thought of as a model for ministry. Rather, family ministry should be viewed as a concept that is an essential aspect of student ministries, as discussed in chapter 4. Mark DeVries, the father of family-based student ministry, puts it this way.

> When I talk about implementing a family-based youth ministry, it's important to understand that I am talking less about establishing specific programs and more about creating an ongoing ethos (what might be called a "new normal") in the ministry. . . . Family-based youth ministry is not, strictly speaking, a "model" but rather a foundation that *every* youth ministry needs to ensure its long-term impact. The specific model of youth ministry a church chooses is almost irrelevant. . . . Family-based principles are an imperative foundation for any of these models, because, regardless of the mode, every ministry must find ways to build on a foundation of parents providing intentional Christian nurture for their children and students connecting to an extended Christian family of faith-full adults.[3]

The importance of engaging, supporting, and partnering with parents cannot be overstated. This is an essential element of student ministry regardless of the particular model of ministry employed.

Notice that the quotation above, however, makes one assumption about family ministry or family-based student ministry in which parents provide Christian nurture for their teenagers. The assumption is that teenagers in student ministries have Christian parents. The reality in a comprehensive student ministry, which is faithful to the Great Commission, is that some students will be blessed with loving Christian parents, and some students will *not* be growing up in Christian homes. Hence, student ministry is broader than family ministry. Yet it embraces the principles of family ministry whenever and wherever possible by partnering with Christian parents in the faith formation of their teenagers *and* ministering to students whose parents have no interest in Christianity or the church. Opportunities often arise to reach out to the non-Christian parents of teenagers, and building trust with those parents is very important. It is essential that the entire church staff, not just the student ministry team, embrace the responsibility of reaching out to non-Christian parents and offering them the support of the church.

One church demonstrated this communal responsibility of reaching out to parents of teenagers in the student ministry who were not connected to the church. Shortly before Easter, the senior pastor asked the youth minister for a list of names and addresses of all the students whose parents were not connected to the church. The senior pastor then sent a personal invitation to each of the parents, expressing how delighted he was that their child was involved in the student ministry and how honored he would be if their whole family would attend one of their Easter services. "If you choose to join us for Easter," he instructed them, "please introduce yourself to me after the service so I can meet the wonderful parents of [name of student], who has become such a valuable part of our student ministry." Now who could turn down such an invitation? The senior pastor and associate pastor followed up with all the Easter visitors, including the visiting parents of teenagers in the student ministry, and warmly welcomed them to the church. Reaching out to families takes teamwork and is the responsibility of the whole church staff working together.

Ministering to families in the church also requires a team effort. Reggie Joiner outlines several systems for family ministry in the church.[4]

The Competing System

The *competing system* emerges in churches that task each department with ministry responsibilities across all ages. The music minister is responsible for music with preschool, children, students, and adults. The Christian education director is responsible for the educational ministries of preschool, children, students, and adults. The missions pastor is responsible for missions across all four groups. At the same time, the preschool director, children's minister, youth minister, and associate pastor are all working to minister to their age-specific constituencies. In a larger church, these seven staff positions may be full time; in smaller churches some of them may be part time or volunteer. However the positions are staffed, people will always be competing for participants in their programs. For example, the music minister schedules the student choir for a choral festival during the same week that the children's minister is trying to sign them up for Vacation Bible School, or the student choir is scheduled to sing in the worship service on the same weekend as the middle school retreat. The department that has the greatest value in the eyes of the church will always win the tug of war over participants, budgets, calendars, and facilities. While this system may look like an impressive attempt at integration on paper, it becomes a cumbersome nightmare in reality.

The Departmental System

The *departmental system* of family ministry is much simpler but equally ineffective. In this system every department—preschool, children, students, music, men, women—is individually tasked with the responsibility to program for families as a whole, in addition to their age-specific groups. In this case, the old adage "when everyone is responsible, no one is responsible" applies. At best, each department may offer random events for the entire family, but there is little coordination among departments or any visionary planning to achieve the goals of family ministry. The result is often a host of family activities sponsored by various departments. This might fill the church calendar, yet it lacks any meaningful purpose.

In order to solve the problems of the departmental system, a church may opt to hire a family ministry pastor to coordinate family ministries across age-group departments. In this scheme, family ministry becomes another department and often begins competing with the age-group departments. For example, family ministry plans a family apple-picking event on Sunday afternoon, but the high school small groups meet on Sunday afternoon. This brings us full circle, back to the competing system of departments.

The Integrated System

Joiner argues that the most effective system of family ministry is an *integrated systems* approach. In this approach, the leaders of the age-group ministries agree on the importance of family ministry and meet regularly to strategize opportunities for making family connections. "The goal is to avoid having any other departments that would create competing programming or strategy for children from birth through graduation."[5] The leader of each age-group ministry serves as a specialist in their area of ministry, while also serving on the family ministry team. Bringing together everyone who has the greatest investments in each age group, while at the same time valuing family ministry, creates synergy. Family ministry then becomes a byproduct of the church staff working together intentionally. Moving toward such an integrated system, which creates an ethos of family ministry, often requires vision casting from the senior pastor or executive pastor in order to move age-group ministers beyond their natural passion for their constituency and to break down the silos that isolate the different groups.

Student ministry and family ministry should never be at odds with each other, but student ministry can never be subordinate to family ministry. When student ministry comes under the umbrella of family ministry, it will only be good enough to serve the students of Christian families in the church and will never reach beyond its walls. Student ministries should always engage parents at every opportunity and partner with other ministry leaders to ensure that the needs of parents and families are being addressed through the collective efforts of the church ministry staff.

What Parents Want

Parents today want a lot. They want good schools, nice neighborhoods, and coaches who are also role models. They want their children to be safe, get good grades, and have nice friends. They want a close-knit family, a caring church, and loving relatives. Underneath all of these desires is a foundational longing for understanding.

Of all the parenting experts in the world, perhaps none have been more insightful than Merton Strommen, founder and former president of Search Institute. Few studies have equaled the thoroughness of Strommen's research on adolescents, parents, and families over the past fifty years. Beneath all of the yearnings of parents, he suggests, is a deep cry for understanding.[6] They want to understand themselves as parents, and they want to understand their teenagers.

Parents Understanding Themselves

The desire to understand oneself does not suddenly emerge at the onset of parenthood. The journey of self-understanding begins in childhood when children begin to ask, "Who am I?" and "Who am I in relation to those around me?" In parenthood the question becomes, "Who am I as a parent?" Even before the birth or adoption of the first child, people begin to wonder who they will be as parents. Often we begin forming this understanding in comparison to how we were raised and how much we desire to be similar to or different from our parents. Before the age of twenty-one, most people will utter a comment and realize, with much surprise, that they sound just like their mothers or fathers. And so the journey of understanding oneself as a parent begins.

Numerous outside influences shape the character of a parent. The influence of the family in which parents were raised cannot be underestimated. So much modeling, good and bad, occurs in a family that it is nearly impossible not to acquire some of the expectations and behaviors of our parents and meld them into our own parenting. For example, as one couple discussed their expectations in pre-marital counseling, the woman declared that she expected her husband to clear the table and do dishes after every meal. Unfortunately, her soon-to-be husband believed that the kitchen would be his wife's domain and that he would rarely set foot in the room. Before glaring looks turned into raised voices, I asked them to share their kitchen experiences growing up. Predictably, the woman grew up in a family in which her father cleared and washed the dishes every evening, and the man grew up in a family in which his father never set foot in the kitchen. The expectations of both had been sown from a very early age, and the couple had to formulate some new expectations for a peaceful marriage.

In addition to the influence of one's own parents are the memories of one's adolescent years. These can be pleasant or painful. They may be experiences that parents desperately want their teenager to encounter or desperately want their teenager to avoid. If a father felt rejected by his peers, he might overcompensate to ensure that his teenager does not feel the same kind of rejection. If a mother came to faith in a particular way, perhaps on a mission trip, she might push her teenager into the same experience, hoping for the same result. In a similar manner, parents often try to live their lives through their teenagers. This may come in the form of attempting to relive the "glory days" of their adolescence.

On the one hand, perhaps a parent was a star athlete, debate champion, or valedictorian and has the trophies to prove it. She may push her child toward the same accomplishments to relive the thrill of victory one more time.

On the other hand, if the parent never realized her dreams, she may see the lives of her teenagers as an opportunity to vicariously accomplish her adolescent goals. Perhaps she never made the varsity team, lost the student government election, or fell just shy of being inducted into the National Honor Society. She may push her child toward achieving some of her unfulfilled dreams. Either way, the teenager feels pressure from a parent striving to satisfy the desires of the person the parent once was or always wanted to become. Parents understanding themselves in healthy relation to their teenagers is critical. A parent's life is not the teenager's life, and living vicariously through one's child only devalues the teenager and stifles the teen's quest for self-identity.

Parents further struggle to understand themselves when they feel that they have somehow failed as parents. This often occurs when parents begin comparing themselves to other parents who seem to be doing a better job. It is important for parents to recognize that they are comparing 100 percent of what they know about themselves to about 10 percent of what they know about other parents. Because we inevitably compare everything we know about ourselves against the very little that we know about others, we always come up short. A parent may fly off the handle and overreact with her teenager in a stressful moment, only to feel like a failure because she believes that none of the other soccer moms ever fly off the handle. This is likely a false perception.

Encouraging parents in student ministry is essential for helping parents understand themselves. This is not so much about giving advice—especially if you have yet to become the parent of a teenager—as it is about showing empathy, compassion, and support. In student ministry, we can encourage parents when they feel they have failed. We can help parents recognize the gifts and talents of their teenagers, which may be different from those of the parents. We can be excellent listeners so that parents can use us as sounding boards in making decisions. We can point them toward great resources to further their understanding of themselves as parents.

Parents Understanding Their Teenagers

Adolescence is a time of transition—physically, emotionally, intellectually, and socially. As teenagers progress on this transformational journey, parents often begin to wonder what is happening to the child they have known and loved over the past ten years. Everything seems to be changing. Strommen's extensive research determined that there are four areas of development that parents must understand in order to relate well to their teenagers.

ATTAIN SUCCESS

First, as teenagers begin the journey through middle school, they typically develop a desire to attain success in some area. This is part of identity development, and the opinions of parents and others are very important. This desire is likely exacerbated by our success-driven culture that constantly rewards people for achievement or even simple participation. From an early age, children are rewarded for playing on age-group sports teams. In elementary schools, students are rewarded for participation more than achievement. In middle school, the tables begin to turn as students are taught the importance of achieving grades and success in sports and the arts. By their first year of high school, they have learned that only the best athletes make the team, the best students make the honor roll, the best musicians make the band and chorus, and the best actors make the musical. Even those who make it into these groups recognize stratification between regular members of the group and starters, soloists, first chairs, or lead actors.

Everyone wants to be at least good, if not excellent, at something. In student ministry, we have the opportunity to help students and parents to discover the gifts and talents of teenagers. When parents begin to recognize the God-given talents of their children and encourage them to pursue endeavors, they begin to understand the personhood of each child. When students begin to discover their talents, they become self-confident and value who they are as they continue to develop into God-honoring people. Student ministry can make a significant impact in this area for both students and parents.

Develop Friendships

The second area in which teenagers want to be most successful is in developing friendships and broadening their social circles. Teenagers have a strong desire to fit in and to belong. While children in elementary school are, for the most part, friends with most people within their classrooms and grade levels, this begins to dissipate in middle school. Students no longer remain in the same classroom with the same classmates all day. Middle schools receive students from multiple elementary schools, thus broadening everyone's pool of potential friendships. That "nice group of kids" that a child grew up with in elementary school is now tossed into a larger sea of students, which is constantly mixed and remixed every time the bell rings to change classes. This creates numerous opportunities to make new friends as well as to be rejected by old friends.

Parents need to be as accepting as possible of the new friendships that their children establish, while at the same time encouraging healthy friendships. The primary group of four to six friends that a teenager spends the most time with becomes incredibly important in building social capital. It is important for parents to be very careful about how they talk about their teenager's friends for two reasons. First, when parents disapprove of their child's friends, they are also criticizing their child. Teenagers believe they are a lot like their friends. If parents do not like their friends, then teenagers assume their parents do not like them either. Furthermore, teenagers whose parents disparage their friends feel that their parents are criticizing their decision-making ability. After all, they choose their friends. Second, when parents disapprove of their teenager's friends, they threaten the social capital of their teenager, and teenagers will fight very hard to maintain the social capital they have attained. Nurturing healthy friendships from the start is much easier than trying to replace bad friendships in the midst of the adolescent journey. Student ministries are in a prime position to nurture healthy friendships and support parents in understanding the importance of primary groups and building social capital among adolescents.

BE UNDERSTOOD

Teenagers want their feelings to be understood. This is the third area of teenage development that parents need to understand. Teenagers are well aware of the process they are going through, and they want others to understand them. The approach to this issue is perhaps the simplest and yet most difficult of all. Parents need to learn to *listen* to their teenagers. Listening sounds easy, but true listening is a very difficult skill to master. Too often parents "listen" while watching TV, reading the newspaper, or cooking dinner. Listening while formulating a response in your head as the other person is talking is not listening at all. Listening requires making eye contact, gesturing affirmatively, and asking gentle, probing questions. Listening to teenage girls is different than listening to teenage boys. Girls will often sit and talk for long periods of time over a meal or a drink. Boys tend to open up more when they are doing something, such as working on a car, riding a bike, playing a board game, or shooting a basketball in the driveway. The activity has to provide regular breaks in the action to allow for deeper discussion. Two people playing basketball in the driveway provides a much better environment for conversation than ten people playing a basketball game. Playing a board game provides a better environment than playing a video game that has no breaks in the action. Student ministries that take the time to teach the fine art of listening to students and parents alike provide a gift of understanding to families.

SEEK AUTONOMY

In the fourth area of development, teenagers seek autonomy and want to take on greater responsibility and decision-making power as they transition from childhood to adulthood. They want to know that their choices matter and are valued by parents and other caring adults. This is a gradual process that parents can either nurture or stifle. The best way for parents to help students begin this process is to offer choices to young teenagers, create boundaries within which teenagers have the freedom to choose. If parents have been encouraging their children to read by giving them a particular book to read over the summer, they might consider offering a choice from a pile of books for the summer following fourth grade. When discussing a curfew for an older teen, the parent may offer a choice of 10:00 p.m. or 10:30 p.m. The teenager will almost always choose the later time, but they have made that choice and taken on the responsibility. When it comes time to get a driver's license, there are myriad choices that parents can offer their child rather than simply laying down the law every time. Ask, for example, "Would you like to help pay for gas or insurance?" They need to pay for something, but parents can let them choose. There may be two or more ways to drive to the mall or a friend's house or church, and parents can ask what the teenager thinks is the best route.

The same approach can be taken in student ministries to support students in taking responsibility and gaining maturity. A small group leader may determine that the group needs to study a book of the Old Testament, but she could allow the group to decide which book. A group of older students might take on the responsibility for determining the destination of the annual mission trip and help with the planning and execution of the trip. Teaching students Mueller's 3(D) process (discover, discern, decide) mentioned in chapter 1 is invaluable for supporting this transformation toward maturity. Allowing students to make decisions within a prescribed framework or set of options develops ownership, responsibility, and maturity.

When parents truly understand themselves as parents and understand their teenagers as transforming into adults, then most often everything else that parents want falls into place. There are always challenges to face and difficult situations to navigate, but confronting them from a foundation of understanding significantly increases the possibility of a positive outcome. In student ministry, it is essential to provide opportunities for parents to learn about themselves as parents and about their teenagers as developing adults. This can be accomplished through parenting seminars or parenting classes. It is often helpful to bring in an outside expert in adolescent parenting or adolescent development, especially if the youth minister is not yet a parent of teenagers. Even youth ministers who are not parents, however, have much to offer in educating parents on the culture in which their teenager is growing up. Without suggesting how they should parent, youth ministers can certainly help parents understand what their teenagers are facing in the real world, offering cues and clues of what to look for in the media, in relationships, and in attitudes.

As helpful as providing parents with information and resources may be, the greatest gift we give parents of teenagers is the opportunity to sit together around a table, in a safe environment, to discuss the challenges of parenting teens in the real world. When parents feel uninhibited about sharing the joys and struggles of raising teenagers in a safe community of fellow believers, synergy arises that fosters healthier parenting throughout the community of faith.

Overflow Parenting

This chapter opened with the unsurprising revelation by Christian Smith that parents are the primary influence on their teenagers' faith. The faith that parents see in the mirror is the faith that their teenagers will likely embrace as adults. Hence, if parents want their teenagers to have a stronger, deeper, and healthier faith, then perhaps the image of faith they emulate needs to be stronger, deeper, and healthier. Whenever we see an image in a mirror that we don't like, often our first reaction is to blame the mirror. We might clean the mirror, step farther away from the mirror, or even find another mirror. Eventually, we come to realize that the mirror isn't the problem. It only reflects the image placed in front of it, leaving us with the reality that we have to change ourselves if we want to see a better image in the mirror.

Similarly, parents must consider the image of faith that they reflect to their teenagers, recognizing that their teenagers will in all likelihood imitate the faith they observe in their parents. Therefore, the church is obligated to support parents in developing the most authentic faith possible so that they might parent out of an overflowing richness of God's love in their own lives.

Rather than parenting with a faith that is half full, we want to encourage parenting with a faith that is overflowing and soaking into the lives of children and teenagers. Smith concludes that by and large, teenagers in the United States today subscribe to a faith he calls *moralistic therapeutic deism*.[7] This view suggests that a deity exists who created the world and watches over humanity from a distance without getting personally involved unless called upon to resolve a problem. This God who lives far, far away wants people to be moral and to treat one another fairly and to be nice to one another. Finally, this far-off God wants the moral people of the world to be happy and feel good about themselves in a way that is comforting and therapeutic. A distant God, the Golden Rule, and a happy life: these tend to dominate teenage religious views as well as the religious views of parents. For parents to raise their teenagers with a faith that overflows, they must move beyond moralistic therapeutic deism and embrace authentic, transformational faith.

Rather than allowing parents to settle for a moralistic faith that offers a reductionist view of being nice and doing good, which can be found in almost any world religion, we must teach parents that God offers us the gift of justification by faith that amazingly makes us righteous in the eyes of the Lord, because of the work of Christ (Rom. 3:9–31). Faith is not about what we have done but about what God has done for us through grace. Teenagers know they are broken and that they will never be good enough, nice enough, or fair enough. When parents acknowledge their own brokenness and recognize their own forgiveness, the reflection in the mirror changes as grace abounds. In turn, teenagers have a healthier image of faith to emulate as they deal with the pain in the world and the pain they cause others.

When parents settle for a God who created the world and watches over humanity from a distance, they miss the redemptive story that God has authored (Luke 24). God is not some sort of divine butler, responding only when called upon to resolve a problem. The story of God includes both the story of creation and the story of redeeming all of creation. God cares enough to come, through the incarnation of Christ, to redeem us and reveal who is Lord over all creation. This is seen throughout all of Scripture and the history of the church. When our story merges with God's story, we become redeemers too, and God becomes our guide personally and communally through the fellowship of the church. When teenagers recognize that their parents have unconditional, personal relationships with God and are deeply committed to a local faith community, they are much more likely to investigate the meaning of such a relationship and connections to the faith community. In an attempt to answer the fundamental questions of identity formation, they will strive to understand where they came from and where they are going.

When parents define their ultimate goals in life as happiness and feeling good about themselves, they perpetuate narcissism and consumerism among their teenagers. When we strive to become more Christlike through the process of sanctification, our lives are transformed and we begin to focus outwardly for the good of others (Phil. 3). Sanctification is a lifelong process that is more of a wild adventure than a smooth escalator ride. When parents model this sanctification journey, which gives honor to God for everything with grace and gratitude and joyful sacrifice, teenagers gain a healthier understanding of life goals, respect for others, and unconditional love. The thirst for instant pleasure becomes the joy of delayed gratification, narcissism becomes selflessness, and striving for self-improvement becomes fostering Christlikeness.

Shepherd Parenting

Shepherding is about showing up. When parents and other adults show up in the lives of teenagers, they are akin to shepherds leading their flocks. "Start children off on the way they should go, and even when they are old they will not turn from it" (Prov. 22:6). Proverbs are not guaranteed promises; rather, they are principles for faith and life. This principle, directed to parents, declares that when children are given a good start in faith and life, they will, more often than not, continue on the same trajectory throughout their lives. Notice that the proverb does not read to start off children on the way *parents* want them to go. It is not a deterministic promise but a general principle that advises parents to identify the gifts and talents of their children and raise them in the way *they* should go, so that they can honor God with all the blessings they so richly embody. Raising children is the most important thing a parent will ever do, because parenting directly influences the future. It influences the future of children, parents, other people, and the world.

Children and teenagers are of immense value, says the psalmist: "Children are a heritage from the Lord, offspring a reward from him" (Ps. 127:3). Yet teenagers—especially middle schoolers—often act a lot like sheep! While sheep do not usually rebel intentionally, run away from home, and find themselves lost in the wilderness, sheep are obsessed with eating lush green grass, and they can only eat the grass with their heads down. This obsession prevents them from looking up very often, so they simply follow the fresh grass one step at a time until, without the guidance of a shepherd, they nibble their way into lostness. One of the saddest sights in the wilderness is a sheep without a shepherd. The prophet Ezekiel reminds us that a sheep without a shepherd gets lost and becomes food for wild animals (Ezek. 34:5).

Likewise, teenagers tend to nibble their way into lostness. It is often unintentional; they just become obsessed with relationships. So they follow the simplest path to relationships and acceptance one person at a time and eventually, without the guidance from a shepherd, they may nibble their way into bad relationships, behaviors, attitudes, and habits. If the saddest sights in the wilderness are sheep without shepherds, then the saddest sights in humanity are children and teenagers without shepherds, for like the sheep they get lost and become food for a crooked and depraved culture. Parents are called to be leaders in the home—shepherd leaders. In the same way that shepherds lead their flocks of sheep, parents are to lead their family flocks.

Our culture has gravitated toward the old adage, "It takes a village to raise a child," attributed to a Nigerian proverb and popularized in 1996 by then–first lady Hillary Clinton in her book, *It Takes a Village: And Other Lessons Children Teach Us.* This is a strong statement about the need for community and extended family, but it has also at times become a justification for parents to abdicate their responsibility for the faith formation of their children to the village that is the church. In our litigious society, we have become accustomed to placing blame on others. McDonald's has been sued for everything from a woman spilling hot coffee on herself and getting burned to people who eat Big Macs every day and gain weight. In other words, it's not my fault I got burned—the coffee was too hot! It's not my fault I gained weight—the food has too much fat in it! In 2012, there was a debate over who should be blamed for causing a car accident. In New Jersey, both a man who was texting while driving when he crashed into another car *and* his girlfriend who was texting him from home were sued for debilitating injuries to the people in the other car. In other words, it's not just my fault that I was texting and driving—she shouldn't have texted me while I was driving!

When student ministry matters, Christian parents are encouraged, trained, and challenged to take responsibility for the identity and faith formation of their children. Snailum's research on intergenerational ministry revealed that churches capable of creating intergenerational community strive to facilitate relationships between teenagers and their parents. One expert she interviewed declared that effective churches "view parents as the primary spiritual influencers of their children (not the children's ministry or youth ministry). This involves high investment in parents."[8] When parents take responsibility for raising their children *and* are supported by the church community, they are able to thrive in their calling.

Parenting in Cultural Context

A great deal has been written about overprotective parenting in recent years. Often referred to as *helicopter parenting* or *overparenting*, the ultimate image of such overprotection was a full-page photograph of a mother wrapping her son in bubble wrap.[9] Can you imagine bubble-wrapping a sheep? The latest in shepherding technology: bubble wrap!

Shepherds offer protection as leaders by providing for and guiding their flock, but they know that it is impossible to always keep them out of harm's way. The psalmist speaks to this very point: "Even though I walk through the darkest valley, I will fear no evil, for you are with me" (Ps. 23:4). Notice that the writer does not suggest that this situation can be avoided. It does not say, "If I walk through the darkest valley" or "If I happen to stumble upon the darkest valley." The writer states that this is a predictable, unavoidable situation. Shepherds know this to be true, as they have no option but to drive their flocks through the valleys of darkness. Sheep are not goats and cannot climb up and over the mountains. They must be guided across the floor of the dark valleys, where they are very vulnerable to dangerous wild animals. Timothy Laniak argues that "this valley symbolizes life's hazardous transitions—occasions when the Shepherd Guide could be trusted without the illumination of daylight."[10] The sheep cannot be bubble-wrapped for shipment through the valley of darkness. As much as parents desire to protect their children from life's vulnerabilities, they cannot bubble-wrap them for shipment through adolescence. What parents *are* called to do is to guide their children, shepherd them through the dark valleys that they surely will encounter. Continuing in the metaphor of Psalm 23, we find that parents maintain two essential roles in the lives of their children: to provide and to guide.

The Parent as Provider

Parents provide for their children is a similar manner that shepherds provide for their sheep, and more! The psalmist writes that the shepherd provides food, water, rest, structure, and protection for the sheep; the sheep lack nothing that is essential. Parents are all too familiar with the role of providing for their teenagers when it comes to food, shelter, clothing, technology, and money for various activities. These are certainly important provisions, especially the essentials of food, shelter, and clothing. However, there is much more to providing than the items money can buy. As a shepherd establishes the environment for the flock, parents set the tone for the ethos of a family by providing a welcoming environment at home where teenagers and their friends feel comfortable being themselves. A welcoming home is a safe home where teenagers are happy to be after school. Unfortunately, not every home environment is a safe place for kids, which is all the more reason for Christian parents to provide a warmhearted environment for their teenagers *and* their friends.

As shepherds provide a structure for the lives of their sheep, leading them through their daily routines, parents also provide structure for their children and teenagers. Every household structure is different, but some type of framework for living helps students to manage their time and their responsibilities. Ecclesiastes reminds us, "There is a time for everything, and a season for every activity under the heavens" (Eccles. 3:1). There is a time to work, eat, sleep, go to school, go to church, do homework, play sports, practice musical instruments, be with friends, watch TV, listen to music, and even play video games. Without a framework to organize the myriad activities and responsibilities, though, the life of a teenager can quickly become daunting and overwhelming. Parents provide the gift of structure for managing life.

As shepherds provide care and protection for their sheep, parents provide love and security for their teenagers. Parents love their children unconditionally. Even in the tough times when a teenager's behavior is abhorrent, the love of a parent for a child triumphs over disdain for the behavior. Love is provided in a variety of ways. Teenagers are never too old to be told that they are loved, and they are never too old for a hug or a kiss from parents—though perhaps not in front of all their friends! Most important, parents demonstrate love through their actions by encouraging their kids, attending their kids' activities, and being present in the painful times of life.

Providing security is a step above providing a welcoming and safe home where teenagers feel comfortable. Security is provided in the midst of threatening situations. When a teenager feels vulnerable or defenseless, parents are there to provide the security necessary. Often this reveals itself more in emotional security than physical security, in times when teenagers are shaken to their core following a traumatic emotional event. Such events can range from a relationship breakup to the suicide of a classmate. While emotional trauma may be more prevalent in the life of a teenager, physical security can also be very important when teenagers are physically threatened or injured. When injuries occur on the ski slopes, at the skate park, during sporting events, or in car accidents, the comfort and security that parents provide is invaluable.

The Parent as Guide

Shepherds do not only provide for their flock. They also guide sheep along a journey that can, at times, be treacherous. The most recognizable symbol of a shepherd is the staff: a long, slender stick with a crook on one end. The staff is what shepherds use to guide their sheep. The crook of the staff is often used to gently draw baby sheep back to their mothers, thus avoiding touching the lamb for fear the mother may reject her baby at the smell of human odor. The staff is also used to draw sheep in and hold them still for a close physical examination. The straight end of the staff is often used to point the sheep in the right direction. The shepherd does not hit the sheep with the staff but instead lays the staff gently alongside the sheep's side and applies pressure. This can guide the sheep through a gate or along a narrow path. In this way, the shepherd reassures the sheep of the proper direction for the journey ahead. Finally, the staff is used to rescue sheep that have wandered down a cliff or fallen into the water. The shepherd simply hooks the sheep with the crook of the staff and lifts them back to safe ground. Likewise, shepherding parents guide their children through the ups and downs of life's journey. Sometimes parents pull children along; at other times they gently push them in a certain direction. Occasionally, they rescue them from a dangerous situation.

Modeling is a powerful way to guide children, and we often forget how much they retain from observation. When my kids were only ten and twelve, we celebrated their grandmother's eightieth birthday at our home. My wife and her sister gave their mother a beautiful wooden box that contained eighty strips of paper. Each strip contained a sentence of thanksgiving that described what she had meant to them over the years. We all sat in the living room as Grandma read each thankful note, all of which brought back many memories from days gone by.

What does this have to do with modeling? Well, just a couple of years later I turned fifty, and without any prompting, my kids bought a box and filled it with fifty thank-you notes: *Thank you for making us lunch every day. Thank you for teaching us to ride a bicycle. Thank you for driving us everywhere. Thank you for taking us camping.* Some notes were from both of them, and some were from each of them separately. Their mother and aunt had modeled for them how to express thanksgiving in a simple and special way.

While modeling is perhaps the most influential type of guidance as parents draw their children into a particular family ethos and set of values and morals, there is also a place for gently pushing children in the right direction. Parents offer this kind of guidance when they steer kids toward developing their natural and spiritual gifts and talents. Parents guide students toward healthy friendships, through educational pathways, and along the journey of faith. Guiding children through the life process requires pushing them to explore new worlds that may lie outside their comfort zone. Such exploration may feel unnerving for parents, but it is healthy for teenagers.

My daughter has been driving for over two years now, and I still cringe every time her phone number appears on my caller ID when she has the car, because I worry that she has had an accident. Bubble-wrapping her to ease my stress would not help her grow and mature, however. Allowing students to explore and discover within a predetermined framework helps them to grow into adulthood.

Teenagers value the guidance of adults—even parents—especially when the advice helps them to achieve their goals. William Damon, director of the Stanford Center on Adolescence, describes the values and the problems with adult guidance.

> Young people treasure guidance from experienced adults who care about them and know more about the world than they do. To be most help-ful—and welcoming—the guidance must speak to the youngster's highest aspirations. . . . Young people do not wish to be shielded from hard realities; they wish to learn to accomplish their dreams in the face of such realities. Informing them of the actual steps they must take in order to achieve their highest aspirations is educative in the best sense of the word.
>
> The problem is that many young people are not receiving guidance that respects their deepest purposes while at the same time providing them with constructive practical advice. Too often what they hear from important adults in their lives are dire warnings and crafty strategies for beating the competition. When this happens young people are not learning realistic ways to pursue their purposes; rather, they are learning that the purposes themselves are unrealistic, without being shown any alternative that could inspire them.[11]

Damon suggests that parents and caring adults can help teenagers pursue their highest aspirations more effectively and, drawing on his extensive research, offers nine crucial factors for parental guidance of teenagers.[12]

Watch Closely for the Spark and Then Fan the Flames

Everyone has sparks of interest that arise from time to time. When parents discover a spark of interest, they are in a prime position to fan the flames and promote the aspirations by helping their teenager articulate their dreams and act upon them. "When it comes to discussing future plans, parents are accustomed to doing most of the talking. For a clear view of a child's innermost aspirations, parents need to practice the conversational art of asking good questions and listening for answers."[13]

Take Advantage of Regular Opportunities to Open Dialogue

Parents need to ask open-ended questions to promote dialogue—just like a good interviewer. Asking *why* questions helps teenagers reflect and think more deeply about their interests. This can happen by ask-ing what they think about a news story on TV, a plot twist in a movie, a homework assignment, a group of friends, the family vacation, the sermon at church, the student ministry retreat, and many other things. "We can do this on their turf, in the context of interests developed in school or elsewhere, or on our adult turf, in the context of family din-ners, outings, and holiday get-togethers."[14]

Be Open-Minded and Supportive of Sparks of Interest

Parents should encourage teenagers when interests arise, being open to and supportive of the possibilities that may develop. My son caught the acting bug in fifth grade. Acting was something my wife and I knew nothing about, but we have supported and encouraged him in this pursuit and delight in his growing talents. Where it will take him we do not know, but it is serving him well in developing his character and integrity. This was clearly his interest, not his parents', as Damon states: "The child's interest should be free to take its own course, including dwindling out if that's what is destined. Parents can never know which grass seeds are going to turn out to take deep root."[15]

Convey the Meaning You Derive from Your Own Work

Once again, this falls into the category of modeling. Parents who understand their own purpose and communicate a sense of pride and purpose in their work provide motivation and inspiration for their maturing teenagers. "It is instructive as well: surprisingly, it is not at all obvious to children that their parents actually take pride in contributing to the world."[16] Parents who discuss with their teenagers the importance of their contributions at work, at church, and in the community serve as compelling role models.

Impart Wisdom about the Practicalities in Life

In his research, Damon found that students who were highly purposeful also had a sense of practical idealism. They were able to accept the

---

Asking Parents What They Think

My senior pastor challenged me to meet with every parent. This has been a daunting task in addition to everything else I have to do. After two years I am still working to get through the whole list of parents. When I sit down with parents, I ask one question: "How can this ministry better serve your family?" I always receive quite a variety of responses. What I do hear every time, though, is a strong sense of gratitude. Every parent has expressed a feeling of being heard and feeling valued. I cannot begin to express how much support and encouragement this has given the ministry and me.

Aaron Stetson, Windham Presbyterian Church,
Windham, New Hampshire

limitations of what was possible when reality would not allow them to achieve their goals. This wisdom is most often nurtured through parents teaching their children how the real world works, as well as through the trial and error attempts of teenagers striving for particular goals. At a certain point, teenagers come to realize what their true talents are (and are not), and parents must support these realizations by steering their teenagers in the most productive directions.

Introduce Children to Potential Mentors

While parents must take responsibility for raising their children, additional caring adults are essential for healthy growth. These caring adults come in a variety of forms, including teachers, coaches, youth leaders, church members, music instructors, neighbors, and extended family members. Parents do well to introduce their children to such caring adults at an early age and to foster those relationships over time. Such caring adults help students successfully discover and refine their interests as they pursue their aspirations.

Encourage an Entrepreneurial Attitude

Teenagers with entrepreneurial capacities tend to be successful later in life. An entrepreneurial spirit is marked by goal setting, planning, achievement, optimism, persistence, tolerance, resilience, determination, resourcefulness, and inventiveness. This cluster of characteristics contributes to the ability to solve large and small problems. "Parents can help their children develop entrepreneurial capacities by encouraging them to take on challenges and healthy risks. . . . When children learn to thrive on challenges rather than to avoid them, they learn a good deal about what it is possible for them to achieve."[17]

Nurture a Positive Outlook

Teenagers with a strong sense of purpose tend to have self-confidence and approach life with a positive and optimistic outlook. Parents nurture a positive outlook when they help teenagers interpret experiences in a hopeful manner. "Parents should always point out to a child how likely it is that things will turn out well, and especially *how much control* we have over how things do turn out."[18] Remembering Christian Smith's comment that parents get who they are, we can assume that parents who model positive attitudes likely instill a positive outlook in their teenagers. "A child's character is formed through a succession of moment-by-moment communications and interactions with the people closest to them, and even something as simple as regularly expressing a positive outlook on life can make a significant difference."[19]

Instill a Feeling of Agency Linked to Responsibility

"Parents should teach their children the basic principle *Whatever you do in this world matters*, and not just in the sense that it matters because their parents care about them—which is important to convey—but in the larger sense that their actions have significant consequences, for good and bad."[20] Fostering this principle happens in the moment, with parents taking advantage of spontaneous conversations about life's activities. This requires that parents provide teenagers with responsibilities in which they learn the consequences of their actions in fulfilling meaningful contributions to the family, church, and community.

Parents act as shepherds guiding teenagers in every aspect of life through questioning, listening, discussing, and modeling. A family culture in which teenagers feel safe to express their thoughts and feelings, hopes and desires, and concerns and fears provides a context that affords parents easy access to opportunities for gentle guidance along the adolescent journey. The church must help parents understand their role as shepherding parents. In addition to coming alongside and partnering with parents, we must also strive to lead parents into a healthy approach of doing family life together.

When Church Becomes Optional

While parents provide and guide their children through life's journey, they also make decisions. Parents make numerous decisions for children from the time they are born until they achieve full independence and leave home. When children are young, parents make every decision; as they grow in age and responsibility, some decisions are given over to the child. Every year a maturing child gains more responsibility for decision making. Often there are implicit or explicit boundaries within which a child can make decisions. Middle school children typically are allowed to choose what they want to wear to school (unless the school requires a uniform), within certain limits—no parents would allow their child to head off to school wearing just a swimsuit, for example.

Even as teenagers mature, however, some things are still nonnegotiable. I have often asked groups of parents to list the activities that are *not optional* for teenagers in their homes. The list regularly includes such activities as brushing teeth before leaving the house, visiting the dentist regularly, attending school, completing homework, and visiting grandparents. For some, attending college is not optional. The reality is that all of these activities will one day become the teenagers' decisions. Once they move out of their parents' homes, it will be their choice to brush their teeth or not, to attend classes and do homework in college or not, and it will typically be a student's option to attend graduate school even if parents require college. Throughout adolescence, parents also allow students many options when it comes to sports, musical instruments, elective courses, and school clubs and activities.

Parents *require* teenagers to do many things regardless of how much they complain, yet many parents allow church to become optional very early in the life of a teenager in a way that they would never allow school, or the dentist, or college, or personal hygiene to become optional. Compulsory school attendance in most states is required until the age of sixteen, yet few if any parents ask their teenager on their sixteenth birthday if they want to continue going to high school or drop out. Tragically, parents sometimes allow teenagers to drop out of church long before they even reach the age of sixteen.

It may not be necessary to require teenagers to participate in every church activity, any more than parents require teenagers to participate in every possible school activity. Yet there should be a core set of church activities that are not optional, just as going to school or the dentist are not optional. Every family will have to decide what is required, what is optional, and when required activities may turn into optional activities.

When it comes to church, I believe that it is essential for teenagers to participate and contribute to congregational worship, large group youth meetings, small groups, and retreats. Other activities, such as concerts, paintball, movie nights, and mission trips, might be optional activities that teenagers do on a less consistent basis. Certainly some might place mission trips on their required list and youth meetings on their optional list; that's fine. Just as in school, parents require teenagers to complete the core courses while allowing them to choose from among elective courses and giving them the option to be involved in school clubs or sports.

Likewise, it is important for Christian parents to make a conscious decision about the appropriate level of participation and contribution of their teenagers in church and to create a family culture in which this becomes the norm at a very early age. Planning is an important skill of parenting, and the wisdom of the Proverbs suggests, "Plans fail for lack of counsel, but with many advisers they succeed" (Prov. 15:22). Parents should "first seek the counsel of the LORD" and then seek the counsel of trusted friends (1 Kings 22:5).

There will always be conflicts in scheduling activities for teenagers, and parents need to make shrewd decisions when such conflicts arise. My teenagers have been very active in the arts and sports at school, which has sometimes created conflicts with youth meetings and retreats. I have often had to drive my son or daughter to the retreat late Friday evening or early Saturday morning because of a Friday evening concert or musical. During their middle school years, the youth meeting and the school ski club conflicted on Wednesday evenings for about four weeks. One Wednesday evening on the way to church before the ski club season began, my daughter asked from the backseat: "Do you expect us to go to the last half of Fusion [the middle school group] after we get home from ski club?" The answer to the question was no. I did not make them go to the middle school group for those four weeks, but the most important part of her question was the first three words: "Do you expect . . . ?" Clearly an expectation had been laid out, and she knew what was expected in our family concerning church. We certainly have been flexible enough to make exceptions to the expectations, but we have also worked hard to create a culture in which being involved in church is viewed as a normal part of our weekly life.

Partnering with Parents

Jim Burns offers four essential aspects for youth leaders to consider when building relationships with parents: communicate, encourage and equip, involve, and reach out.[21] These are not exhaustive, and they must be developed in each particular context of ministry. But as Burns suggests, they serve as pillars upon which to build a strong ministry with parents.

Communicate with Parents

Communication is essential in any relationship, and the relationship of youth leaders with parents is no different. As the parent of two high school students, I always appreciate knowing what is happening in the student ministry of our church so that I can be supportive. When parents are not sure what is going on, they tend to become anxious and suspicious. Clarity, transparence, and redundancy are the keys to communication with parents.

Clearly communicate the vision of the ministry and the passion of the ministry team to parents. When parents understand the purpose of the ministry and the passion that the leadership team has for ministering to teenagers, they are more apt to be supportive. Even when parents disagree with the direction of the ministry or certain aspects of it, there can be constructive dialogue. When parents feel as if they have no idea what the ministry is about, there is no framework for a healthy conversation. Keeping the vision and purpose of the ministry simple, clear, and understandable provides a context for building relationships with parents.

Program information also requires precision and clarity. Parents are bombarded with schedules for their teenagers from school, community groups, and church. Providing accurate details of ministry programs is essential for maintaining a parent-friendly ministry. When an event will happen, where it will happen, what time it will happen, how much it will cost, and transportation details are all essential and must be accurately communicated to parents. In this day of technology, every student ministry should have a webpage and phone hotline that parents can access for the most up-to-date information on student ministry programs. When parents ask a teenager what time they will be home from the retreat and the teenager says, "I dunno," the information should be only a few clicks away on the student ministry website. When student ministries are better at communicating program information to parents than schools, sports teams, scouts, and other community groups, parents will praise student ministries for the respect and value that they show parents.

Transparency becomes important in communicating with parents when problems arise. Establishing a culture of transparency *before* problems emerge means that a level of trust is already present when the going gets rough. Such transparency is established individually and communally. Parent meetings take on a variety of forms. They can be informational or educational meetings, open forums, or feedback sessions. Regardless of format or agenda, it is critical to be transparent, acknowledging the current shortcomings of the ministry, admitting that there is more work to be done in particular areas, offering to research questions that are not answerable at the time, and reaching out to parents who have concerns that require further discussion than might be appropriate in a meeting. When mistakes are made, it is best to admit them, correct them, and move on, rather than trying to cover them up or minimize them. When accidents occur, explain how the situation was dealt with and what precautions are in place to minimize accidents—including new measures that have been added as a result of the latest incident.[22]

If something is worth communicating, it is likely worth communicating multiple times in a variety of ways. In the world of marketing, an old adage known as "The Rule of Seven" suggests that people need to be exposed to a message at least seven times before they will act on it. This is why we constantly see and hear advertisements for the same products over and over again. Likewise, we must communicate our messages to parents with great redundancy, casting the vision and purpose of the ministry over and over again in a variety of media, and communicating important dates and times repeatedly to be sure that everyone is on the same page. We may feel that we are overwhelming parents with too much information, but the reality is that parents and students alike cannot be reminded enough. Perhaps I should say that again: parents and students alike cannot be reminded enough!

Encourage and Equip Parents

Parenting teenagers is a tough job. It can be unpredictable, emotional, stressful, overwhelming, and tiring—all at the same time! Connecting with parents and connecting them with one another can be incredibly crucial during this stressful season of life. "Nothing does that better, or more effectively, than a ministry of affirmation and equipping," write Burns and DeVries. "Parents who feel connected, affirmed and equipped by the youth leaders will support and believe in the direction of the ministry."[23]

Encouraging parents of teenagers is the responsibility of the entire church body and church staff. The apostle Paul compelled the Thessalonians to "encourage one another and build each other up," and he applauded them for doing so (1 Thess. 5:11). In the conclusion of his letter, he urged them to "encourage the disheartened" (1 Thess. 5:14). A person who becomes disheartened is one who loses heart, becomes short of breath, lacks motivation, or becomes discouraged.[24] Each of these traits is commonly found in parents of teenagers, and the community of faith is compelled to encourage the disheartened. While the responsibility for delivering a ministry of encouragement to parents of teenagers lies with the whole church, it is most often the youth minister who leads the call to encouragement.

Such encouragement happens when parents are reminded of their value. Parents are making a difference in the lives of their children and, as a result, a difference in the future. Teacher and astronaut Christa McAuliffe, who perished in the space shuttle *Challenger* disaster, famously said, "I touch the future. I teach."[25] There is no greater teacher in the life of a child than his or her parent. Perhaps we should give parents of teenagers a bumper sticker that reads: "I touch the future. I parent." "The terrain parents must travel is riddled with battles and trials, counterbalanced by periods of growth and intimacy with their teenagers," write Burns and DeVries.[26] The support and encouragement of the faith community during this precarious time in the life of a parent are invaluable. Verbal, written, and electronic messages of encouragement from multiple staff members and members of the congregation, along with sharing time, meals, and activities with youth leaders, create an environment of support from the faith community that cannot be duplicated elsewhere. Where else can a parent be supported with such deep care?

Encouragement is helpful, and empowering parents to engage in the faith development of their teenagers is critical. While student ministry and the church come alongside Christian parents to foster the faith of teenagers, it is ultimately the responsibility of parents to stimulate the faith of their teenagers. Once again we return to the words of the famous Shema, which makes this clear:

> Hear, O Israel: The LORD our God, the LORD is one. Love the LORD your God with all your heart and with all your soul and with all your strength. These commandments that I give you today are to be on your hearts. Impress them on your children. Talk about them when you sit at home and when you walk along the road, when you lie down and when you get up. Tie them as symbols on your hands and bind them on your foreheads. Write them on the doorframes of your houses and on your gates. (Deut. 6:4–9)

Parents are called to attend to the faith formation of their children when sitting at home, walking along the road, lying down, and getting up—in other words, at all times! This is a daunting task, and parents need to be equipped for the challenge. Once again, this is the responsibility of the whole faith community, and the church staff should work together to ensure that it occurs. Most often it is best for the youth minister and the minister responsible for adult discipleship to collaborate on championing this effort. While younger youth ministers may not be experts in parenting, they are certainly experts in youth culture, and most parents desperately want to understand the real world of their teenagers. Working together, the pastoral staff can bring together parenting expertise from the congregation and community to create a course or seminars on parenting and to offer other resources. A good resource list, which includes books and websites on parenting and adolescent development, and community resources in adolescent and family counseling and addictive behavior counseling, can be invaluable. While local counselors need to be researched in each community, here is a list of books and websites to begin developing a resource list.

Books

Bradley, Michael. *The Heart and Soul of the Next Generation: Extraordinary Stories about Ordinary Teens.* Gig Harbor, WA: Harbor Press, 2006.

———. *Yes, Your Teen Is Crazy! Loving Your Kids without Losing Your Mind.* Gig Harbor, WA: Harbor Press, 2002.

Burns, Jim. *Confident Parenting.* Grand Rapids: Bethany House, 2008.

Clark, Chap. *Hurt 2.0: Inside the World of Today's Teenagers.* Grand Rapids: Baker Academic, 2011.

Clark, Chap, and Dee Clark. *Disconnected: Parenting in a MySpace World.* Grand Rapids: Baker Books, 2007.

Damon, William. *The Path to Purpose: How Young People Find Their Calling in Life.* New York: Simon & Schuster, 2008.

Lerner, Richard. *The Good Teen: Rescuing Adolescence from the Myths of the Storm and Stress Years.* New York: Three Rivers Press, 2007.

Parrott, Les. *Helping Your Struggling Teenager.* Grand Rapids: Zondervan, 2000.

Rice, Wayne. *There's a Teenager in My House: 101 Questions Parents Ask.* Downers Grove, IL: InterVarsity, 2008.

Rice, Wayne, and David Veerman. *Understanding Your Teenager.* Nashville: Thomas Nelson, 1999.

Root, Andrew. *The Children of Divorce: The Loss of Family as the Loss of Being.* Grand Rapids: Baker Academic, 2010.

Sax, Leonard. *Why Gender Matters: What Parents and Teachers Need to Know about the Emerging Science of Sex Differences.* New York: Three Rivers Press, 2006.

Townsend, John. *Boundaries with Teens: When to Say Yes, How to Say No.* Grand Rapids: Zondervan, 2006.

Tripp, Paul. *Age of Opportunity: A Biblical Guide to Parenting Teens.* Phillipsburg, NJ: P&R Publishing, 2001.

Van Pelt, Rich, and Jim Hancock. *The Parent's Guide to Helping Teenagers in Crisis.* Grand Rapids: Zondervan, 2007.

Walsh, David. *Why Do They Act That Way?: A Survival Guide to the Adolescent Brain for You and Your Teen.* New York: Free Press, 2005.

Websites

www.almenconi.com (Al Menconi—reviews of music and ratings of video games)

www.cpyu.org (Center for Parent/Youth Understanding—teen culture today)

www.crosswalk.com/culture/movies (Crosswalk—movie ratings)

www.dove.co.uk (Dove—campaign for girls' self-esteem)

www.dove.org (The Dove Foundation—movie reviews)

www.family.org (Focus on the Family—information on parenting)

www.homeword.com (HomeWord Center for Youth and Family—supporting parents and families)

www.kidsinmind.com (Kids in Mind—movie ratings)

www.lyrics.com (Lyrics—great tool for looking up song lyrics)

www.webopedia.com/quick_ref/textmessageabbreviations.asp (Webopedia—text message codes)

Parents who are encouraged and equipped feel empowered to engage in the adolescent development process their teenagers are experiencing. They appreciate an authentic partnership with the church and the student ministries in raising their teenagers to contribute to the important work of the kingdom as they discover their unique gifts and talents.

Involve Parents

Striving to involve parents in student ministries can create some tension, but it is well worth the effort. The challenge is to determine the appropriate level and place of involvement for particular parents. Youth leaders must consider the gifts and talents of parents as well as the desires of their teenagers. While most teenagers would not want their parents to serve in *their* small group, they may not mind if their parents lead another small group. While most teenagers would be fine with their parents serving in a support role such as driving to a retreat, staffing the student ministries information table at church, or serving breakfast to teenagers on Sunday morning, no teenager would appreciate such involvement if it was being used by parents to "check up" on them.

Involving parents in student ministries occurs in three phases, which are similar to the process of involving any volunteers. First, the ministry team should take some extended time to generate a list of all the possible ways that parents could be involved. To start, consider the following ways that parents might contribute to the ministry: volunteer leaders; small group leaders; Sunday school teachers; service project coordinators; meal coordinators; transportation coordinators; mailing coordinators; mission trip leaders; security guards at large events; parking attendants for events; hosts for activities at their home; loaners of cars, boats, trailers, or vacation homes to the ministry; and ministry advisory group members. Every context is different, but the starting point is to complete the sentence: *It would be great to have some parents* _____.

After drafting a list of the possible roles of parental involvement in the ministry, identify the gifts, talents, and resources of parents. This can be accomplished in a variety of ways. The easiest way to collect this data is to simply survey parents. Once data is collected from the survey, it should be confirmed through interviews, references, or personal relationships. As with any volunteer, background checks should always be completed for anyone working directly with students. Once an inventory of the parents' skills, talents, and resources is completed, then the matching game begins, as potential parents are aligned with particular needs in the ministry.

Finally, before inviting parents to serve in any aspect of the ministry, student ministers should consult with their teenagers. The greater the potential involvement with direct ministry to students, the more important this is. It is one thing to tell a teenager that her parents have agreed to drive students to the retreat; it is quite another to tell a teenager that his parents have agreed to lead *his* small group this year. Asking teenagers for permission to involve their parents can be very time consuming, but it can also lead to wonderfully insightful conversations. Imagine asking a teenage boy if it would be all right to ask his father to help grill the burgers at the summer cookout and the teenager saying, "No." That could be an invitation to explore a dysfunctional relationship between a father and a son. (It could also be that the father is a vegetarian—so be careful not to leap to conclusions.) You can gain great insights into family dynamics by involving parents in student ministries, and when teenagers realize that their opinions matter, their appreciation of the ministry is enhanced.

Reach Out to Parents

When teenagers matter, *all* teenagers matter. And when all teenagers matter, *all* parents matter—including those who are not engaged in the church. When student ministries are reaching out to teenagers beyond the walls of the local church, the ministry will be filled with teenagers whose parents are not involved in church and who may have little interest in matters of faith. These parents need the same support and encouragement that parents in the faith community need, and perhaps even more. Too often, youth leaders miss the opportunity to engage these parents who are not part of the regular Sunday morning crowd. These parents are likely very interested in meeting the leaders of a group that their teenager has started attending.

Before teenagers begin to drive, usually in their sophomore year of high school, parents are typically shuttling them from one activity to another on a regular basis. Whenever students are being dropped off for a youth meeting, special activity, or retreat, the prime location of the youth minister is the parking lot! Other leaders can be inside greeting students for the youth meeting, and church parents can run the registration or check-in table for the retreat, but nobody can replace the youth minister shaking hands with parents—especially new parents—in the parking lot. The youth minister can thank them for entrusting the ministry with their teenager, express how wonderful their son or daughter is, or affirm how thrilled everyone is that their child is coming on the retreat. The parking lot is fertile ground for reaching out to parents, valuing their role as parents, and welcoming them to the community that their teenager has found meaningful.

In addition to building relationships in parking lots, student ministers can proactively engage parents who are not involved in the church by offering special seminars that attract parents from the entire community.[27] Parents always want to improve their parenting skills, understand their teenagers better, and learn more about the youth culture that surrounds their teenager. When parenting classes or seminars are offered on Sunday morning as part of the adult discipleship program, they typically attract only the parents of the church. When a seminar is offered on a Saturday morning or a weeknight and publicized in the community, however, far more parents outside the church will attend, and parents of the church will find it far easier to invite their friends and neighbors. Another great place to engage parents who are not part of the church is at school or community activities. Attending a sports match, chorus concert, school musical, community theater play, band concert, or community holiday celebration offers excellent opportunities to both support students who are participating and to meet their proud parents.

Reaching out to parents of teenagers in the ministry should be done with a pure heart and sincere interest. When parents see the lives of their teenagers transformed by the life-changing power of Christ, and when they are treated by youth leaders with dignity, respect, and compassion, they will likely begin to investigate the message that the church is preaching. As I mentioned earlier in this chapter, reaching out to parents will require the involvement of the entire church staff and cannot rest on the shoulders of the youth minister. But the youth minister is often the catalyst for this important aspect of the church ministry.

When teenagers matter, parents matter. There is simply no separating teenagers from their parents. Good, bad, or otherwise, the influence of parents in the lives of teenagers is extremely powerful, and youth leaders must recognize this important connection. Investing in the lives of teenagers means investing in a web of relationships that involves parents, teachers, coaches, and relatives. The task of student ministry is to foster these relationships in a positive manner for the healthy identity formation and faith formation of teenagers. Parents matter, and parents matter greatly in student ministries.

Discussion Questions for Student Ministry Leaders

1. What are some first steps you can take with parents that would build the foundation for a comprehensive ministry?
2. What can you do in your context to connect better with the parents of your students? What resources might you provide for parents in a seminar or adult education class?
3. What can you do in partnership with parents to discover and encourage their teenagers' individual gifts?
4. What can you do to build relationships with parents who are not well connected to the student ministry?
5. What opportunities could you provide for parents to invest in the student ministries?
6. How can you train volunteer leaders to think about creating a healthier student ministry? Does that involve expanding communication avenues? Does that mean challenging them to devote an hour per week to face time with students in their context, such as at sporting events or school plays? How might this help build relationships with parents?
7. How can you insert yourself into the arenas of teenagers, becoming known not just as a local youth minister but as an approachable, relatable person who cares about all teenagers in the community?

Discussion Questions for Church Leaders

1. If you agree that raising teenagers is a high and holy task, how can you incorporate this into the regular teaching and preaching of the church?
2. When the student ministry begins reaching teenagers outside the church, how can you partner with your youth minister in reaching out to the parents of those students? How can you make this discussion a part of each aspect of leadership in the church?
3. Almost every parent has an identity crisis at some point. How can you help prepare parents for this? What resources can you offer? How can you partner with the student ministry on such an initiative?
4. How can you encourage parents to be authentic with teenagers about their own faith journeys?
5. Are you empowering and charging your youth leaders to work outside the walls of the church in areas where the gospel is less

evident? How do you see this as a possible vehicle for not only student ministry growth but also overall church health and growth?

6. How can the entire church leadership honor the core value of breaking down the silos of separate programs within the church? If student ministry is a top priority in the church, how can the entire church leadership set up student ministry for success?

7. How can the church leadership help youth leaders connect with parents? How might this help youth leaders feel supported? What message would this send to the parents?

7

When Teenagers Matter:

THE NEXT GENERATION IS UNLEASHED

When Walt Disney created *The Mickey Mouse Club* television show in 1955, he envisioned the show as an educational venture that children would enjoy. Disney never settled for less than the best. He recruited physicist Julius Miller, who had studied under Albert Einstein, to host the science segments as the mad scientist Professor Wonderful, with the aim of inspiring young people to consider science as a vocation. Disney was so serious about education that he created a guide for teachers so they could integrate the lessons from *The Mickey Mouse Club* into their classrooms. In the introduction to the teachers' guide, Disney wrote, "We have the greatest respect for the basic intelligence of our future adults and their desire to learn. We, likewise, are aware of the sometimes prevalent habit of 'talking down' to audiences of this type. To the best of our ability we aim to 'talk up' as much as possible as we program our material."[1]

Over fifty years ago, Disney recognized society's propensity to look down on young people, and he refused to engage in such condescension. His aim was always to lift up families and children by inspiring them and placing them in the center of the action where they are honored, valued, and respected. The greatest lessons we can embrace from the

Is Language Betraying Your Intentions?

Taking positive youth development seriously means taking our theology and liturgy seriously. All the positive affirmation youth ministers offer can be undermined by the language in songs and sermons, which often emphasizes our unworthiness, ugliness, and sin at the expense of hope, redemption, grace, and the *Imago Dei*. Our language so easily betrays our intentions.

Morgan Schmidt, St. Andrew's Episcopal Church,
Seattle, Washington

legacy of Walt Disney are that emerging adults matter greatly, and that we must build them up as they mature into adulthood.

One of my pet peeves is the horrendous covers of student ministry books that consistently portray teenagers as sad, worried, disengaged, pain-stricken, depressed, and stressed-out. Some books are exceptions, to be sure, but my bookshelves are filled with these depressing images of teenagers. Richard Lerner suggests that the research on adolescence over the past century has focused primarily on the problems and deficiencies of teenagers.

All too often, parents have acted as if the only important aspects of their children's behaviors were those that caused problems. We think of adolescence as a time of storm and stress. Scientists, too, have regarded young people as lacking, as deficient, as unable to behave correctly and in a healthy manner. We characterize them as dangerous to others and as endangered themselves (because of their self-destructive behaviors).

Given this perspective on teenagers, researchers devoted their energies to finding ways to prevent young people from becoming all the bad things they could become. Therapists, too, used this deficient approach when treating young people. If their problems could not be prevented, then therapists searched for ways to reduce the impact of their shortcomings. Everyone focused on the problems. Experts of all types did not look to see if, in succeeding chapters of life, there were unnoticed strengths and admirable qualities that should be reinforced.[2]

Lerner argues that we must stop seeing teenagers through this lens of deficiency, which was popularized by psychologist G. Stanley Hall, who characterized adolescents as "essentially, repositories of problems."[3] Rather, we would do well to focus on their strengths, talents, and passions, building up young people and helping them, as Lerner suggests, "write an optimistic script for this phase of their maturation."[4] The positive youth development movement is championing this new perception of adolescents and helping us to understand that our charge in student ministry is not to "fix" teenagers who appear to be broken.[5] They are not problems to be solved; rather, they are invaluable resources for society and the church, and caring adults must foster their potential.[6]

This emerging field of positive youth development is challenging all who work with teenagers to view them through the "unique 'talents, strengths, and interests' that are markers of their potential for a bright future."[7] Who better to take this approach than those who are ambassadors for Christ and who seek to redeem that which God declared to be "very good" (Gen. 1:31)? William Damon argues that the developmental task of adolescents is not to overcome deficits but to "explore the world, gain competence, and acquire the capacity to contribute to the world."[8] Likewise, student ministry must build students up by encouraging them to explore the faith, gain confidence in their being, and contribute to the faith community. The task of student ministry is to engage teenagers—all teenagers—in their journey of transformation: transformation to adulthood and transformation to Christlikeness. This task begins with viewing teenagers from a different perspective. Rather than working to change teenagers, we must change our view of teenagers, setting aside our preconceived image of adolescence and valuing *all* teenagers for who they are, what they can contribute, and who they are becoming.

Student Ministry at the Crossroads

In the church, there is a predominant view that student ministry is solely focused on nurturing the students within the church and meeting the expectations of parents with teenagers. Even in evangelistically minded churches that strive to reach out to adults, expand facilities, plant new churches, and launch new campuses to accommodate growth, the model for reaching more teenagers is simply reaching more adults who will, in turn, bring their children and teenagers along. The population of teenagers in most churches is highly predictable. The number of students in the high school group next year will be equal to the number in the existing group, plus the rising freshmen students, minus the graduating seniors, plus any new high school teenagers of parents who begin attending the church. The number in the middle school group next year will be the number in the existing group plus the rising fifth-graders, minus the graduating eighth-graders, plus any new middle school teenagers of parents who begin attending the church. There is little passion or resourcing for counting as part of the equation the hundreds of teenagers in the community whose parents do not attend church.

In a 2012 forum on student ministries called the Lilly Laboratory Think Tank, hosted by the Center for Youth Ministry Training, a group of student ministry experts identified twenty-six pertinent issues they believed would affect student ministries in the years to come.[9] The group produced a thoughtful list of concerns ranging from spiritual practices in a digital age to the changing role of the youth minister. After the group further sifted, sorted, combined, clarified, and refined the original twenty-six issues, they landed on eight key concerns for the future. Each of these important issues points to a comprehensive model for student ministry that values all teenagers of a community, nurturing those in the church and engaging those outside of it.

Youth Ministry as Healing and Restoration

Transformation happens when youth leaders are champions of healing and restoration. In this sense, members of the think tank viewed youth leaders as equippers. "The youth worker would see herself as called to equip others (youth, parents, congregations, etc.) to discern and live into her own vocation as an agent of God's movement of restoration and healing."[10] As youth ministers help teenagers name their brokenness, they must be able to acknowledge their own brokenness and experience restoration. All people, including teenagers, have a sense of brokenness. This is not limited to teenagers outside the church; many teenagers growing up in the church struggle with debilitating issues and need to encounter the grace of restorative redemption.

Youth Minister as Equipper of the Household of Faith

Youth leaders are called to partner with parents in such a way that teenagers have a supportive family to provide for their spiritual formation. Yet not all teenagers enjoy a home environment in which faith is welcomed: "We do not automatically make the assumption that all youth have a home or family where spiritual formation can or will happen. Therefore, it may be the role of the youth worker to advocate for some kind of 'family' for all youth, such as an adopted family of adults in the church who covenant to care for a teen."[11] When student ministry is at its best, teenagers outside the church who are far from God are drawn into a community of transformational grace. Often these students attend church while their disinterested parents remain at home, and sometimes their parents are even hostile to the church. This requires student ministries to create a "second family" in which the faith of these new believers can be fostered.

The Theology of Personhood

How will student ministries effectively address matters of sexuality, sexual practice, health, and wellness in the future? Members of the think tank rightly observed that: "When we talk about sexuality or homosexuality we have thus far attempted to do so in a sort of theological vacuum that is void of a baseline agreement on inherent and inalienable worth and goodness of the divinely created being."[12] The discourse on personhood is very complex, and we often talk past each other because we are more interested in promoting our views rather than in seeking to understand the views of others. Such understanding requires deep reflection and compassionate responses to complex questions. Teenagers inside the church and outside the church wrestle with issues of identity, sexuality, and covenant relationships. Developing a greater understanding of personhood fosters a healthy community of believers, and a healthy community of believers offers the best context for welcoming students who are seeking to investigate faith.

Wrestling the Holy Bible to an Aha! Moment

Generally speaking, student ministries and the church at large teach a one-dimensional biblical narrative that is void of lament, trouble, conflict, drama, beauty, poetry, and wonder. "Because we don't have time to teach and accompany young people in the hermeneutic task, we rush them to a finish line. We do it for them. So they walk away with one meaning rather than many meanings, rather than depth of wonderment, rather than questions that will keep them awake at night."[13] When we provide neatly packaged answers to students who are questioning the validity of God, we raise their skepticism and cynicism. While the Scriptures offer a great deal of certainty, they also contain a lot of mystery. Proclaiming God's revelation with honesty and integrity—acknowledging the drama, conflict, and our own limited understanding—provides a safe environment for teenagers to raise questions and doubts that lead to greater understanding. Equipping teenagers to access the Scriptures and make meaning from God's Word is important in the disciple-making process. Such equipping should begin when students are still far from God, asking the hard questions and seeking to find answers to life's greatest mysteries.

The Weakness of a Domesticated Gospel

Teenagers see the church as irrelevant because it often lacks a compelling vision and an authentic community. "Kids are going where they believe they matter, to those causes whose message is, 'We can't do this great work without you' (a message young people almost never hear convincingly from their churches). Being needed (not to mention wanted) is compelling stuff. If kids can't get that from the institutions they grew up loving, they'll grow to love the institutions from which they get that affirmation."[14] If the bride of Christ does not compel the teenagers growing up in the church, what hope is there for engaging students who are living far outside of the faith community? Students must become consequential contributors to the church rather than simple consumers of its programs. Too often the adult population of the church has modeled the consumer mentality, and teenagers are following in those footsteps. Transitioning from a culture of consumerism in the church to a culture of contribution will require radically innovative approaches on the part of the entire church leadership.

The Need for Ecclesiology

The Western church tends to have a rather anemic understanding of *community*. The church and its programs are most often viewed as a destination for individuals. "For a variety of reasons—including fill in the blank sermons and vertical worship songs—we gather as a community to worship individually, not as the body of Christ."[15] Such an individualistic church culture feeds a mentality of consumerism and is inconsequential in the lives of most students. When the church develops a culture of communal empowerment, as witnessed in South America and Africa, teenagers are able to find their voice within the vibrant community of faith, and teenagers outside the church are drawn to a compelling community that gives life meaning. A vibrant church is more than a collection of programs for participation; it is a community that compels contribution as faith and life merge together, as the story of God and God's people become one. This results in a new understanding of Christian living in all areas of life.

Youth Ministry as the Great "Co-Mission"

Fulfilling the Great Commission requires cooperation, contextualization, and a global view. "Our understanding of mission within youth ministry should be highly contextualized at the local level but also open to learning from the global context. The challenge within this approach is to practice co-mission: seeing ourselves as called to share what we have with others but also to receive what others have to share and teach us (both in local and global contexts)."[16] Ministering cooperatively in the local setting provides greater potential for meeting the needs of all students in local communities. We can learn much from one another locally and globally. The majority of teenagers worldwide live outside the resources of student ministries, which means that broadening our focus to adolescents worldwide—including urban and rural young people—is essential for faithfully and effectively executing comprehensive student ministry.

Ready or Not

Finally, the think tank group raised an important question about the role of the professional youth minister of the future. "The youth pastor of the future will need to be nimble and fleet of foot, knowing that the requirements of his or her position are likely to morph significantly each year. . . . The traditional role of the youth pastor may be tweaked or phased out in preference to ministry entrepreneurs, able to respond creatively to the predictably unexpected changes within the church, within the surrounding culture, and within adolescents themselves."[17] In the same way that the role of senior pastor has transformed over the years to meet the changing needs of people in a constantly changing culture, so too will the role of youth pastor change. This is not a challenge to fear but an opportunity to embrace. Along with the transforming role of the youth pastor comes a greater understanding of the resources necessary for two levels of student ministry: resources for churches to invest in the teenagers of the local community and resources to be mutually shared through local, regional, and global church and parachurch partnerships.

Each of these eight issues addresses the future of student ministry when it is understood in a comprehensive manner. While most of these issues could be reduced to simply serve the needs of Christian families with teenagers growing up in the church, such reductionism would gut the spirit of this important think tank as well as the missional understanding of student ministries. As one participant stated, "We need to communicate strongly that *mission* is not a trip—it is who we are, not what we do."[18]

Fighting Gravity

Gravitational pull is always toward the center of the earth, yet humanity has invested a vast amount of time, energy, and money to overcome this force of nature. Through invention and determination, we are able to fly through the air and soar into outer space because we have overcome the limitations of gravity.

In the church, the gravitational pull is always toward maintenance. We strive to retain members through maintaining the existing ministry programs that they find satisfying. When the idea of change is introduced, maintenance is threatened and people are pushed outside of their comfort zones. But the reality is that nothing really happens in our comfort zones. Risks, challenges, growth, new relationships, new adventures, vibrant living, generosity, and authenticity all happen outside our comfort zones. While a comfort zone may feel relaxing and secure for a time, it quickly becomes routine, dull, and lifeless. When churches stay in their comfort zones too long they begin to turn inward, focusing on themselves and maintaining their legacy of self-satisfying programs. As church becomes routine, dull, and lifeless, the infighting begins, the complaining escalates, and everyone blames someone else for their problems.

Sometimes the only way for a church to snap out of its inward focus is for a tragedy to arise. The power of a hurricane, tornado, or tsunami not only transforms the landscape and the lives of those in its path; it often transforms a church. In an instant, the bickering ends and the teamwork begins. The church overcomes its inward gravitational pull, reaching out to everyone in need. The self-centered focus is exchanged for eyes to see the needs of others. The comfort zone is abandoned and the challenge is fully engaged. Fighting gravity, the church becomes the church.

The Example of the Early Church

Attaining the kind of outward focus that churches experience in times of tragedy throughout the normal seasons of life is extremely difficult and requires constant reminders of the mission and vision of the church. The early church faced many challenging situations and rose to the occasion each time, but what about the normal times? What did the church do in seasons of calm?

Acts 9 describes just such a time: no persecution, no crisis, just business as usual in a time of peace. "Then the church throughout Judea, Galilee and Samaria enjoyed a time of peace and was strengthened. Living in the fear of the Lord and encouraged by the Holy Spirit, it increased in numbers" (Acts 9:31). In this time of peace, the church relied on God for strength and encouragement as more people came to faith. Peter began visiting the churches that had been established throughout the region. In Lydda, Peter healed Aeneas, a paralyzed man, in the name of Jesus. In Joppa, he raised a woman named Tabitha, also known as Dorcas, from the dead. As Peter traveled from town to town, word of his ministry among the people spread and more and more people came to faith. "This became known all over Joppa, and many people believed in the Lord" (Acts 9:42). From Joppa Peter was summoned by Cornelius, a centurion in Caesarea. Even though Peter found himself outside of his comfort zone among a great community of gentiles when he arrived in Caesarea, he still shared the good news of Jesus with Cornelius and the crowd of gentiles, explaining that God desires to redeem the whole creation, Jews and gentiles alike. "He [Peter] said to them: 'You are aware that it is against our law for a Jew to associate with or visit a Gentile. But God has shown me that I should not call anyone impure or unclean" (Acts 10:28). Many people came to faith that day as the Holy Spirit was poured out on the gentiles. Peter instructed them to be baptized, and he stayed with them for a few days, teaching them more about the kingdom of God.

In this time of peace, Peter engaged regular people along his journey. There were no kings, no wealthy rulers, no deceitful enemies of God—just a paralyzed man, a good widow, and a curious centurion. These people typify those among the early church, yet they would not be considered remarkable people in any way. They were nonentities unlikely to be at the forefront of a spiritual revolution, but God saw fit to build the kingdom through a man bound to his bed, a woman who enjoyed sewing, and a loyal soldier. As Peter went about his travels, he visited regular people in regular communities, encouraging the early church during this time of peace.

The Vision of Bonhoeffer

The growth of the kingdom of God is normal as the community of faith always seeks to reach out and welcome people into the fellowship of believers. While Dietrich Bonhoeffer's concern for those outside the community of faith is more fully evident in other works, even in *Life Together*, in which he describes how the life of a community of believers should be expressed, he poignantly declares that the life of the church is not to be an insulated life of fellowship.

> It is not simply to be taken for granted that the Christian has the privilege of living among other Christians. Jesus Christ lived in the midst of his enemies. At the end all his disciples deserted him. On the Cross he was utterly alone, surrounded by evildoers and mockers. For this cause he had come, to bring peace to the enemies of God. So the Christian, too, belongs not in the seclusion of a cloistered life but in the thick of foes. This is his commission, his work. "The Kingdom is to be in the midst of your enemies. And he who will not suffer this does not want to be of the Kingdom of Christ; he wants to be among friends, to sit among roses and lilies, not with the bad people but the devout people. O you blasphemers

and betrayers of Christ! If Christ had done what you are doing who would ever have been spared?" (Luther).

"I will sow them among the people: and they shall remember me in far countries" (Zech. 10:9). According to God's will Christendom is a scattered people, scattered like seed "into all the kingdoms of the earth" (Deut. 28:25). That is its curse and its promise. God's people must dwell in far countries among unbelievers, but it will be the seed of the Kingdom of God in all the world.[19]

Neither Bonhoeffer nor Luther holds any tolerance for living in the comfort zone, as this is not the normal posture of the church. For Bonhoeffer, Christian community is about the privilege we have to engage in the gift of God's grace, yet community with God is "not an individualistic possibility."[20] Community with God is necessarily fellowship with other believers—that is, the church—engaging the world. While our salvation is from God, it is conveyed most often through the proclamation of God's grace in the vessel of human interaction that is the church.

The work of the church maintains a truly divine nature and the high call to contribute to the kingdom of God and foster the kingdom of God. We understand that Christ has delegated the work of the church to his disciples, and we are called to be his ambassadors.

Since, then, we know what it is to fear the Lord, we try to persuade others. What we are is plain to God, and I hope it is also plain to your conscience. We are not trying to commend ourselves to you again, but are giving you an opportunity to take pride in us, so that you can answer those who take pride in what is seen rather than in what is in the heart. If we are "out of our mind," as some say, it is for God; if we are in our right mind, it is for you. For Christ's love compels us, because we are convinced that one died for all, and therefore all died. And he died for all, that those who live should no longer live for themselves but for him who died for them and was raised again.

So from now on we regard no one from a worldly point of view. Though we once regarded Christ in this way, we do so no longer. Therefore, if anyone is in Christ, the new creation has come: The old has gone, the new is here! All this is from God, who reconciled us to himself through Christ and gave us the ministry of reconciliation: that God was reconciling the world to himself in Christ, not counting people's sins against them. And he has committed to us the message of reconciliation. We are therefore Christ's ambassadors, as though God were making his appeal through us. We implore you on Christ's behalf: Be reconciled to God. God made him who had no sin to be sin for us, so that in him we might become the righteousness of God. (2 Cor. 5:11–21)

From this we understand that the church perpetuates salvation and sanctification, evangelism and discipleship. As such, our participation in the community of believers and contribution to the work of the kingdom fosters our very experience of Christ.

The faith community, Bonhoeffer suggests, is *in* Christ, and Christ empowers us to engage in true fellowship with one another: "Without Christ there is discord between God and man and between man and man. . . . Without Christ we should not know God, we could not call upon Him, not come to him. But without Christ we also would not know our brother, nor could we come to him. The way is blocked by our own ego."[21] Christ is not only the great spiritual mediator between God and humanity; he is also the great anthropological mediator who destroys the walls that separate humans from one another. Christ enables us to truly know God and, equally as important, he enables us to truly know one another.

Jesus calls his disciples to serve one another in humility for the common good of the kingdom. Bonhoeffer writes, "Not what a man is in himself as a Christian, his spirituality and piety, constitutes the basis of our community. What determines our brotherhood is what that man is by reason of Christ. Our community with one another consists solely in what Christ has done to both of us."[22] Our very existence is reliant on the work of Christ, who is the true essence of our communion with God and with one another. "We have one another only through Christ, but through Christ we do have one another, wholly, and for all eternity."[23]

As we, the church, engage in the work of the kingdom, which leads us out of our comfort zones, we achieve more fully the sense of true oneness. Nothing draws people into a true sense of unity like the commitment to a mutual calling, and the calling of the church is none other than the Great Commission. And what is true for the church is certainly true for student ministries.

Such unity is fractured because of the distortion of human love. Bonhoeffer argues that only through *spiritual* love, which comes through the Holy Spirit's work in and through us, is it possible to experience pure love. He suggests that the nature of humanity, even in loving one another, is to subvert one another. Our natural inclination is to position ourselves in such a way that we are able to obtain the most good for ourselves, in a sense using others for our benefit. This is how humanity in a depraved state operates, and likewise how human institutions tend to function—even the local church as it succumbs to the gravitational pull of an inward focus. Hence, Bonhoeffer refuses to characterize the church as an institution or organization. For him, the church "is not the creation of a religious organization, not the setting up of another religion alongside or over against other religions; it is the renewal, the humanisation of humanity per se."[24]

In this light, the church is not to be understood as a human creation but as a divine reality in which humanity is invited to partake. The people of the church, understood to be the people of God, love one another, serve one another, accept one another, sacrifice for one another, encourage one another, and comfort one another, without reservation or narcissism. This should include not only people inside the fellowship of believers, but it must extend to all of God's creation as we become the kind of neighbors who engage *everyone* "only as the person that he [or she] already is in Christ's eyes."[25] The local church is not a human construct; rather, it is a divine strategy of redemption. Through extending God's surprising message of grace to all people everywhere—including *all* teenagers inside and outside of the church—the church focuses on "humanity being remade and redeemed as a result of God's creative grace."[26]

Spiritual Narcissism and the Reality of the Church

The term *narcissism* comes from a story of Greek mythology. One day a man named Narcissus was walking by a pool of water when he noticed his reflection on the glassy surface. He became so enamored with himself that he devoted his entire life to his own reflection—that is, to an unrivaled preoccupation with himself.

Narcissism places the value of personal pleasure, happiness, and fulfillment as the vanguard of one's attention. Modern North American society has often been described as a culture of narcissism. James White suggests that the church should be seen as the antithesis of narcissism:

> Now, as Christians, this should be antithetical. We follow a Savior who said he "did not come to be served, but to serve, and to give my life as a ransom for many" (Matt. 20:28); "If anyone wants to be first, he must be the very last" (Mark 9:35); and "Whoever wants to be great among you must be your servant" (Mark 10:43). And then bowed in submission to the Father and said, "Not my will, but yours" (Luke 22:42). Yet our thinking has been invaded by a *spiritual* narcissism where the individual needs and desires of the believer become the center of attention.[27]

It is easy to confirm White's claim that spiritual narcissism characterizes the modern American church. All we need to do, he suggests, is listen to how we talk with one another: "I need to find a better small group." "I need to go to a church where I'm fed." "I didn't get much out of that worship service (or that Bible study)." "I need to find a better youth ministry." Such perspective blinds us to the true mission of the church. It may be comforting to blame the worldly culture around us by suggesting that the church has become a reflection of the larger narcissistic culture. But in reality, White suggests, "We are not victims of a culture of narcissism; we are purveyors of it."[28] He explains:

> Consider the first two questions any organization must ask itself (courtesy of management expert Peter Drucker): What is our mission? And who is our customer? The second of these involves crass language, I know, for any church. But let's consider them a moment.
>
> First, what is our mission? I would argue that it is to seek and to save the lost. (How could we have a mission other than the one Christ had and then entrusted to us as the church?) Yes, the Great Commission involves discipleship, but I tire of those who pit evangelism against discipleship, as if doing one prevents concentrating on the other. It's a both–and, not an either–or. But more to the point of the mission, if you never reach anyone for Christ, who exactly will you be discipling? Evangelism must be in the vanguard.
>
> From this comes the second question: Who, then, is our primary customer? It is inescapable: if our mission is to seek and to save (and then disciple) the lost, then our "customer" is the one who is lost. The breakdown is that most churches have a primary focus of reaching and then serving the already convinced. *So the mission isn't making disciples, but caring for them.* From this, services rendered to the believer become paramount. They are the customer in a consumer-driven mission.[29]

Hence, the church often promotes narcissism by succumbing to the gravitational pull of an inward focus. Critics often suggest that narcissism can be found in the church's contemporary efforts to engage unchurched people. While this may occasionally be true, the far greater problem is the narcissism within the church that caters solely to the desires of its members by raising the drawbridge of the church and making the needs of those inside its walls paramount. Fighting the gravity of narcissism is a real challenge, but, as White claims, "nowhere does true spiritual narcissism face more opposition than in a church that is choosing to die to itself in order to reach out and serve those around them."[30] When the community of faith dies to itself, people stop focusing on their need to be fed and learn to feed themselves, while turning their attention to feeding others. No longer is church about being ministered to; rather, it is about ministering to others. Worship no longer is a program to get something out of, but a sacred space in which to offer God our praise, thanksgiving, and unconditional service.

While the local church is not perfect, it is our present reality, and we must be careful to live within our reality rather than idealize an alternate one. Bonhoeffer suggests: "Christian brotherhood is not an ideal which we must realize; it is rather a reality created by God in Christ in which we may participate."[31] The church exists in real places and is composed of real people—not perfect people, but real people saved by grace. Therefore, Bonhoeffer warns against wishful thinking that exposits an ideal concept of exactly how the Christian community should operate. A legalistic view of how Christians should fellowship, worship, serve, evangelize, or "disciple" creates a standard by which we judge the health of our church and neighboring churches. This inevitably leads to disappointment, disagreement, and discord within the local church. In Bonhoeffer's view, the church is not the shadow of some eschatological reality. It is the real kingdom of God "established and real in Christ; it is a divine reality, the social form of revelation."[32] Hence, we are called to fight gravity's narcissistic pull of idealism and focus on the people and relationships that compose our daily living.

Bonhoeffer's view of Christian ethics suggests that the church belongs exclusively to our present reality and must never be considered as separate from the world. There is no moat surrounding the church and no drawbridge to pull up that would separate it from the world. The church is in the world, and the world is the church's mission. According to Bonhoeffer the community of faith "may not place itself above the profane and let itself become separated from the world as a kind of 'exceptional luminary.'"[33] The church is truly the church "only when it is related and open to the world."[34] The church must engage the world in every aspect of ministry in order to fulfill its redemptive mission through the ministry of Christ.

Bonhoeffer reminds us that the church is not something to be taken for granted. The community of believers is physical evidence of God's grace in our own lives and serves as the vehicle through which God's work is conducted here on the earth. It is "humanity being remade and redeemed as a result of God's creative grace."[35] When the church operates in this manner, rather than as a club or institution, we gain a clearer sense of the unity and purpose to which we are called in all aspects of ministry—including student ministry.

The church should not be seen as merely a poor reflection of the future kingdom of God. Rather, the church stands tall at the center of God's kingdom presently, here and now. The church is a present reality, established in the physical world by a physical Christ, and it maintains a compelling and authentic witness for believers and nonbelievers alike. The community of faith must concern itself not only with the world to come but also with serving the kingdom as it exists in this world. This means working and having relationships with one another and with those outside the church. Cloistering the community of faith into a Christian bubble and adopting an operational theology of separatism surrenders to the gravitational pull of narcissism. Such an approach falls woefully short of Bonhoeffer's call for the church to find its mission in the present, in solidarity with the world in which it resides. Bonhoeffer's ecclesiology is refreshing in the midst of a church that is often caught up in narcissistic agendas and has forgotten the real purpose of its existence: to be the vessel of the grace and love of Christ in the world.

Our calling is to one another in the church and to those outside of its walls, so that we may truly be about the work of the kingdom of God in the world. We often get into trouble when we are not doing what we have been called to do. It is not that we go looking for trouble as much as trouble finds us when we are lounging around in our comfort zones. When Jesus prays for his disciples in John 17, he prays for their protection, safety, and sanctification in the midst of a world that hates them. Jesus also prays for the unity of the disciples and all believers. Community is primary within the church just as it is within the Trinity of Father, Son, and Spirit.

When we stray from the community and become idle in our individual comfort zones, trouble has a way of finding us. Perhaps the most overlooked aspect of the story of King David's affair with Bathsheba is found in the very first sentence of the story: "In the spring, at the time when kings go off to war" (2 Sam. 11:1). David got in trouble with Bathsheba because he was not doing what he should have been doing. He should have been leading his army in the war, but he had abandoned his company to enjoy the comfort of his palace. Likewise, when the church is not united in doing what it should be doing, it gets into trouble. What should the church be doing? Reaching out beyond its walls in every aspect of ministry—especially student ministries.

A New Day of Synergy

Student ministries have often been saddled with accomplishing the task rightfully assigned to parents and the community of the church. Youth ministers seem to be doing more creative nurturing than ever before, as parents and senior pastors implore them to keep church kids interested in church. Those who reach out to students beyond the walls of the church before they have completed the task of developing spiritually mature teenagers for the parents in the church are often chastised.

What is needed is a healthy dose of synergy. Properly defined, *synergy* means the combination of multiple efforts that produce a result greater than the sum of the component parts. This is often found in sports teams: the individuals may not look impressive on paper, but they achieve such a synergistic level of teamwork that their play is greater than the sum of the individuals. Synergy in student ministry demands that everyone in the church accept their roles and contribute to the faith formation of teenagers.

So here is a radical thought: the faith formation of teenagers in the church is not the sole responsibility of youth ministers. It is primarily the responsibility of the adult members of the church! As I suggested in chapter 4, there is an opportunity to create this synergy every time a church baptizes or dedicates young children. Rather than asking everyone in the congregation to pledge their support to help raise every child in the faith, some real synergy would be created if a small handful of adults would pledge to love and support one child, or one adult small group would pledge to care for one child and family.

This model would greatly enhance the congregation's ability to follow through on their pledges in meaningful ways, and the lives of young people growing up in the church would be radically different. Not only would the lives of teenagers in the church be different; the synergistic work of youth ministers would be radically different as well. Youth ministers could create great synergy by supporting and resourcing parents along with other adults as they nurtured one another's children, while devoting the majority of their time to reaching out to teenagers who have no church family, investing in their faith journeys and raising up others to do the same.

There is great irony here, as churches typically hire youth ministers, at great expense, to perform a job that the church membership has already committed to do. The church hires a professional to accomplish an assignment that the laity, with some keen guidance and timely training, is quite capable of undertaking. Instead, the church should hire professional youth ministers to primarily do what most laypeople cannot do—namely, penetrate the postmodern youth culture to reach irreligious students with the gospel. Very few people in the church pews are specifically gifted or trained for this task, but every member of the body of Christ possesses gifts and talents that can be leveraged to nurture teenagers growing up in the church. Abdicating this responsibility to youth ministers robs the adults of the church of the vitality of their God-given purpose. It also robs teenagers who are far from God of the opportunity to encounter caring youth leaders who are gifted in extending grace to those God would call into his kingdom. In a word, it robs the church of its synergy.

A study of 2,400 Protestant youth ministers across the United States revealed that the typical youth minister is thirtysomething, married with children, has been educated in the field of student ministries in college or seminary, has served in student ministry for at least seven years, and believes that she or he is called to student ministry as a vocation and not as a stepping stone to another ministry position.[36] The church must allow these gifted and committed youth ministers to fulfill the comprehensive mission of the church to proclaim the gospel to *all* young people and walk alongside them in their faith journeys, while supporting parents in nurturing their teenagers and integrating young people into the body of Christ that is the church. Such synergy guards against the gravitational pull to become inward-focused. When there is synergy in student ministries, it becomes catalytic, and synergy permeates every area of the church ministry.

The best way to reach teenagers outside the church is to take committed teenagers inside the church deeper in their faith. When Christian teenagers understand that they do not go to church, but that they *are* the church, they will develop an outward focus. They will discover passion for investing in friendships with teenagers far from God and inviting them to explore the community of faith that has become so meaningful. Likewise, the best way to move Christian teenagers deeper in their faith is through reaching out to teenagers far from God. When Christian teenagers catch the vision for being part of something bigger than they are, humility and generosity replace the natural narcissistic tendencies promoted by a self-absorbed culture. Building up to reach out, and reaching out to build up: this creates synergy that is contagious.

In a church that I served many years ago, only a few dozen high school students were listed on the official church roster, and only about half of them were involved in the student ministry. We did not need small groups—the high school student ministry was a small group. Rather than focusing solely on nurturing the small group of interested students, we began reaching out and even joined forces with a couple of local churches to create a community outreach ministry to high school students. Not only did this outreach effort engage numerous students outside the church; it energized the Christian students within the church *and* it piqued the curiosity of the inactive teenagers of the church. Ironically, once this synergy took off, it was not uncommon for inactive students of the church to be invited by their nonchurch friends to events being hosted by the church's student ministry. The conversations at the high school lunch table often went something like this:

Nonchurch Shelia:	Hey, do you want to go on a ski trip next month?
Inactive Amanda:	Sure! Who's going?
Nonchurch Shelia:	A bunch of our friends: Ethan, Kasey, Emma, Ryan and Sarah.
Inactive Amanda:	Is it a school trip?
Nonchurch Shelia:	No, we are going with the youth club from First Church.
Inactive Amanda:	Wait! That's my church!
Nonchurch Shelia:	Really? Why don't you ever come to any of the youth activities?
Inactive Amanda:	I didn't think *anyone* went.
Nonchurch Shelia:	Actually, *everyone* goes. Most of your friends go. Want to come to youth club tomorrow night?
Inactive Amanda:	Okay, that sounds great!

All of a sudden, nonchurch Shelia is taking inactive Amanda to the high school youth club of Amanda's own church! The days of fishing for teenagers with a single hook are long gone—if they ever existed. Instead, fishing for teenagers must be done with nets. Regardless of whether the goal is to reach students outside the church or inactive students inside the church, student ministries must reach out to an entire group of students. These are known as primary groups: the small groups of friends, rarely numbering more than a half dozen, that do life together at school and in the community. It is far more likely that the whole group of friends will engage in the student ministry than simply one person from the group. So if the aim is to reach out to inactive students on the church roster, cast a wide net to reach out to that student *and* her friends. Once again great synergy is created in the ministry. Outreach and nurture are not an either–or proposition; they form a both–and approach that creates the greatest synergy in ministry.

The hallmark of student ministry in the twenty-first century will be moving beyond the historical dichotomy between evangelism and discipleship to a holistic approach of engaging all students and assisting them as they move along their journeys of faith. Progressive student ministries will develop ministry models in which congregations take seriously their responsibility for nurturing the young people growing up in the church while proclaiming the gospel to a lost generation. This can occur under the supervision and training of youth ministers along with a team of youth leaders, comprising both adults and students who are gifted and passionate about sharing their faith with irreligious adolescents.

The heart and soul of student ministry is reaching out to students, meeting them at their points of need, drawing them into a community of faith, and guiding them in a journey of faith that lasts a lifetime. To be faithful and effective in this mission, youth ministers and church leaders share enormous responsibilities. Youth ministers must clearly understand the significant roles of the church, the family, and youth leaders in making disciples of *all* teenagers. Equally as important, church leaders (including senior pastors, executive pastors, elders, and finance committees) must understand the importance of resourcing comprehensive student ministry in order to make genuine disciples of *all* teenagers who have ears to hear the message of God's grace.

The Six-Word Story of Student Ministry

In the 1920s, colleagues of the great writer Ernest Hemingway challenged him to write a story in a mere six words. All good stories consist of a beginning, middle, and an end. In the beginning, the exposition introduces the characters and sets the scene, the middle involves some sort of conflict, and the end brings resolution to the conflict. Responding to the challenge, Hemingway wrote: "For sale: baby shoes, never worn." Those six words have often been considered Hemingway's greatest work. The single sentence drives us to imagine the circumstances of a person or a couple who would post such a sign.

This set me wondering how to capture student ministry and the church in a six-word story. It would have to include the church and teenagers. It would need to address what happens when church leadership takes student ministry seriously. It would have to include a resolution to a kingdom problem. We know that when teenagers are given the opportunity to contribute to the life of the whole church, the community of faith comes alive, and God's people thrive. But it takes bold vision to declare that teenagers matter and it takes strong leadership to bring such vision to life. Perhaps the legacy of student ministry could be expressed this way: *bold leaders, teenagers valued, church transformed.*

Discussion Questions for Student Ministry Leaders

1. How can you intentionally "talk up" to teenagers and place them in the center of the action? How can you show students that they are inherently good through the songs you sing and the words you use?

2. How can you be a curator and advocate of restoration for yourself, your students, their families, and the church?

3. Rather than focusing primarily on deficient behaviors, how can youth leaders help emerging adults and their families discover their strengths and talents?

4. Which of the eight issues for student ministry developed by the think tank feels the most pressing to you?

5. How can you transition student ministries from a culture of consumerism to a culture of contribution and community?

6. How do you invite students to participate in the kingdom of God here and now, in both your student ministry and the church at large? What aspects of your student ministry can you begin to delegate to students?

7. Try on your Hemingway hat for a moment and write the six-word story of your student ministry. What six-word story would you like your student ministry to become?

Discussion Questions for Church Leaders

1. What place do teenagers, as emerging adults, have within your congregation? How much input do they have in the life of the church?

2. How can your church be intentional in creating "second families" for students who are developing in their faith without a supportive home life?

3. Students are not the only people looking for a place where they are needed; adults want to contribute, too. How can you transition church life in general from a culture of consumerism to a culture of contribution and community?

4. During the normal seasons of life, how can you keep the mission and vision of the church and student ministries in front of people?

5. How can you change adults' perceptions of teenagers within your congregation? How might you help them see teenagers for who they are, who they are becoming, and what they can contribute?

6. How might you invite the whole community to participate in the faith formation of young people as they explore their faith, gain confidence in their being, and contribute to the faith community?

7. Try on your Hemingway hat for a moment and write the six-word story that you want teenagers to experience in your church community.

NOTES

Series Preface

1. James W. Fowler, *Faith Development and Pastoral Care* (Minneapolis: Fortress, 1987), 17.
2. Scott Cormode, "Constructing Faithful Action," *Journal of Religious Leadership* 3 (1/2), (Spring/Fall 2004): 267.

Preface

1. Hybels, *Axiom*, 33.

Introduction

1. The introduction is based on Mark Cannister, "Doing It How They Did It: Historical Foundations of Youth Ministry," *Youthworker* 28, no. 2 (2011): 38–42. Used by permission.
2. For a complete history of Protestant student ministry, see Senter, *When God Shows Up*, and Bergler, *Juvenilization of American Christianity*.
3. Yaconelli, *Heart of Youth Ministry*.
4. Fields, *Purpose Driven Youth Ministry*, 43–82.
5. Strommen, Jones, and Rahn, *Youth Ministry*, 119–41.
6. DeVries, *Sustainable Youth Ministry*, 57–73.
7. Larson, *Youth for Christ*, 50.
8. Chow, *No More Lone Rangers*, 15.
9. Yaconelli, *Core Realities of Youth Ministry*, 33.
10. For further information, contact Youth Specialties in St. Paul, Minnesota, www.youthspecialties.com; or Group Publishing in Loveland, Colorado, www.group.com.
11. Strommen, Jones, and Rahn, *Youth Ministry*, 119–41.
12. Vukich and Vandegriff, *Timeless Youth Ministry*, 202.
13. *Leadership I Handbook*, 42.
14. Fields, *Purpose Driven Youth Ministry*, 233–48.
15. Ibid., 235.
16. Clark, *Hurt*, 189.
17. Root, *Revisiting Relational Youth Ministry* and *Relationships Unfiltered*.

Chapter 1 When Teenagers Matter: Student Ministry Thrives

1. Capps, "The Good Enough Revolution," 110–18.
2. Ward, *Growing Up Evangelical*, 166.
3. Dyrness, *The Earth Is God's*, 36.
4. Ibid., 69.
5. Cray, *Postmodern Culture and Youth Discipleship*, 20.
6. Ibid.
7. Dyrness, *The Earth Is God's*, 58.
8. Cray, *Postmodern Culture and Youth Discipleship*.
9. For further information concerning the 3(D) process, visit Walt Mueller's Center for Parent/Youth Understanding; www.cpyu.org.
10. Lyall, "Unlikely Singer Is YouTube Sensation," C1.
11. Adichie, *The Danger of a Single Story*.
12. Ibid.
13. Clark, *Hurt*, 58.
14. Duffet, Johnson, and Farkas, *Kids These Days '99*, 3.
15. Ward, *Growing Up Evangelical*, 185.
16. Campolo, *Who Switched the Price Tags?*, 195–96.
17. Ketcham, "Solving the Retention Problem," 12.
18. See Ketcham's description of the problems with service-based student ministry in ibid., 7–29.
19. Warren, *Purpose Driven Church*, 155–72.
20. Fields, *Purpose Driven Youth Ministry*.
21. Warren, *Purpose Driven Church*.
22. Wilson, *Our Father Abraham*, 287–88.
23. Garland, *1 Corinthians*, 68. See further, Schmitz, "Knowledge." In *The New International Dictionary of New Testament Theology*, vol. 2, 395.
24. Brown, *Unexpected News*, 111–12, italics in the original. Brown is quoting Gustavo Gutiérrez.
25. Yaconelli, *The Heart of Youth Ministry*.
26. Cannister, "Back to the Future of Youth Ministry," 4–7.
27. Bock, *Luke 9:51–24:53*.
28. Culpepper, "Luke: 24:36–53."
29. For a complete explanation of the five components of ministry promoted by Rick Warren and Doug Fields see Warren, *The Purpose Driven Church* and Fields, *Purpose Driven Youth Ministry*.
30. Nel, *Youth Ministry*.
31. Macchia, *Becoming a Healthy Church*.
32. See further: Niebuhr, *The Purpose of the Church*; Dulles, *Models of the Church*; Grenz, *Sharpen the Focus of the Church*; Giles, *What on Earth Is the Church?*; White, *Rethinking the Church*; Dever, *Nine Marks of a Healthy Church*.
33. Todd Erickson (executive director of student ministries, Second Presbyterian Church, Memphis, TN), in interview with the author, January 12, 2012.
34. Root and Dean, *Theological Turn in Youth Ministry*, 20.
35. Frost, *Mountain Interval*, 9.
36. White, *Rethinking the Church*, 29–30.
37. Carroll, *Alice in Wonderland*, 51.
38. Vukich and Vandergriff, *Timeless Youth Ministry*, 206.
39. Lovering, "In 200-Year Tradition."
40. Kosmin and Keysar, *American Religious Identification Survey 2009*.
41. White, "Missionaries to America."

42. Ibid.

43. Ibid.

44. Erickson, interview.

45. Cummings-Bond, "One-Eared Mickey Mouse," 76. See also Mark DeVries's discussion of the One-Eared Mickey Mouse problem in youth ministry in *Family-Based Youth Ministry*.

46. Jim Byrne (Director of Student Ministries, The Falls Church, Falls Church, VA), in interview with the author, March 30, 2012.

47. Extracurricular Participation and Student Engagement, June 1995, http://nces.ed.gov/pubs95/web/95741.asp.

Chapter 2 When Teenagers Matter: Transformation Happens

1. See Lewis, *The Lion, the Witch and the Wardrobe.*

2. Bushnell, *Christian Nurture*, 10. See also a discussion of Bushnell in Gangel and Benson, *Christian Education.*

3. Ward, *Youthwork and the Mission of God.*

4. Buechner, *Telling the Truth.*

5. Wilkins, *Following the Master*, 27.

6. Pentecost, *Design for Discipleship*, 14.

7. Wilkins, *Following the Master*, 28–29.

8. Ibid.

9. Bonhoeffer, *Cost of Discipleship*, 44–45. Italics added.

10. Ibid., 55–56. Italics added.

11. Willard, *Spirit of the Disciplines,* 15.

12. Wilkins, *Following the Master*, 32.

13. Isaacson, *Steve Jobs*, 12.

14. Ibid.

15. Ibid.

16. Ibid., 13.

17. Ibid.

18. Lerner, *The Good Teen*, 10.

19. Burke, *No Perfect People Allowed.*

20. Yancey, *The Jesus I Never Knew*, 148.

21. Burke, *No Perfect People Allowed*, 97.

22. Ibid., 101.

23. Mahedy and Bernardi, *A Generation Alone*, 19–20.

24. Clark, *Hurt*, 55–56.

25. Bradley, *Heart & Soul of the Next Generation*, 6–8.

26. McLaren, *New Kind of Christian*, 155.

27. Todd Szymczak, "Why I Keep Doing Youth Ministry," *Live: Learn: Lead* (blog), February 1, 2012, http://livelearnlead.net/?p=956&cpage=1#comment-536.

28. For a complete discussion of relational authenticity, see Root, *Revisiting Relational Youth Ministry.*

29. Root, *Revisiting Relational Youth Ministry*, 74.

30. Ibid., 196.

31. See also Exod. 6:7; Lev. 26:12; Jer. 7:23; 11:4; 30:22.

32. Baab, *Friending*, 9.

33. Sloboda, "Music Structure and Emotional Response," 110–20; Doucleff, "Anatomy of a Tear-Jerker," C3.

34. Guhn, Hamm, and Zentner, "Psychological and Musico-Acoustic Correlates," 473–83.

35. Nelson, *How Faith Matures*.

36. Marcia et al., *Ego Identity*.

37. Griffith and Griggs, "Religious Identity Status as a Model," 16.

38. Ibid., 17.

39. Ibid., 18.

40. Ibid., 19.

41. Waterman, "Developmental Perspectives on Identity Formation," 42–68.

42. Ibid.

43. Marcia et al., *Ego Identity*.

44. Marcia, "Identity and Psychosocial Development," 15.

45. Ibid., 16.

46. Ibid.

47. Ibid., 17.

48. Kegan, *Evolving Self.* (Although Kegan's more recent book, *In Over Our Heads*, is intentionally written for reader accessibility to his research, he gives more attention to the environment that supports development in *The Evolving Self.*)

49. Winnicott, "The Theory of the Parent-Infant Relationship," 37–55.

50. Kegan, *Evolving Self*.

51. Daloz, *Effective Teaching and Mentoring*, 210.

52. Griffith and Griggs, "Religious Identity Status as a Model," 16.

53. Marcia, "Identity and Psychosocial Development," 13.

54. Joiner, Bomar, and Smith, *Slow Fade*.

55. Ibid., 30–31.

56. Smith, *Souls in Transition*, 211–56.

57. Ibid., 226.

58. Ibid., 256.

59. Kinnaman, *You Lost Me*, 193.

60. Ibid.

61. Todd Szymczak (was the pastor of student ministries, Grace Chapel, Lexington, MA, at the time of this interview and is currently the associate pastor of Trinitarian Congregational Church, Wayland, MA), in interview with the author, February 28, 2012. Used by permission.

62. Burke, *No Perfect People Allowed*, 22. Italics added. See also Eph. 4:11–16.

Chapter 3 When Teenagers Matter: Student Ministry Is Well Resourced

1. See Stetzer and Bird, *Viral Churches*.

2. DeVries, *Sustainable Youth Ministry*, 36.

3. Ibid.

4. Ibid.

5. Ibid.

6. Ibid., 37.

7. For more information, contact the Future Leaders Program at McLean Bible Church in Vienna, Virginia; www.mbcfutureleaders.com.

8. For more information, contact the student ministries program at Chapel Hill Presbyterian Church in Gig Harbor, Washington; www.chapelhillpc.org.

9. For more information, contact the Fellows Program at The Falls Church in Falls Church, Virginia; www.tfcanglican.org.

10. http://www.tfcanglican.org/pages/page.asp?page_id=186570 (accessed May 2013).

11. For more information about fellows programs nationwide, see www.thefellows initiative.com.

12. For more information, contact the Nehemiah Venture at The Falls Church in Falls Church, Virginia; http://www.tfcanglican.org/pages/page.asp?page_id=267247 or http://nehemiahventure.org.

13. For more information, contact the student ministries program at Second Presbyterian Church in Memphis, Tennessee; www.2pcyouth.org.

14. For more information, contact the student ministries at Menlo Park Presbyterian Church in Menlo Park, California; www.mppc.org/hiring.

15. For more information, contact Southview Community Church in Herndon, Virginia; www.southview.org/ministries/intern.

16. For more information, contact Church Staffing in Richmond, Virginia; www.churchstaffing.com.

17. For more information, contact Leadership Network in Dallas, Texas; www.leadnet.org.

18. For more information contact *Group Magazine* in Loveland, Colorado; www.youthministry.com.

19. For more information about networking, contact the National Network of Youth Workers in San Diego, California; www.youthworkers.net.

20. Lawson, *How to Thrive in Associate Staff Ministry.*

21. Ibid., 13.

22. Brooks, *Twenty Sermons*, 330.

23. Niebuhr, *The Purpose of the Church.*

24. Lawson, *How to Thrive in Associate Staff Ministry*, 23.

25. Ibid., 43.

26. Ibid., 47.

27. Ibid., 49.

28. Ibid., 57.

29. For a complete discussion of youth ministry job descriptions, see Fields, *Your First Two Years in Youth Ministry*, 255–75.

30. Ibid., 265–66.

31. Lawson, *How to Thrive in Associate Staff Ministry*, 75.

32. Ibid., 90.

33. Ibid., 92.

34. Ibid., 132.

35. Ibid., 177–86.

Chapter 4 When Teenagers Matter: They Become Part of the Church

1. See Ham and Beemer, *Already Gone.*

2. Ibid., 256.

3. Ibid., 227.

4. Pearce and Denton, *Faith of Their Own*, 70–71. Italics added.

5. Coryell, "Three Ways Churches See Teenagers," 55.

6. Gregory, "Hyperconnected," 7.

7. Powell and Clark, *Sticky Faith.*

8. Clark, "In Spite of How They Act," 21, and Burns and DeVries, *Partnering with Parents in Youth Ministry*, 18.

9. Burns and DeVries, *Partnering with Parents in Youth Ministry*, 102–3.

10. Swindoll, *Improving Your Serve*, 34.

11. Bunge, "Biblical and Theological Perspectives," 353–54.

12. Ibid., 357.

13. Todd Erickson (executive director of student ministries, Second Presbyterian Church, Memphis, TN), in interview with the author, January 12, 2012.

14. Dever, *What Is a Healthy Church?*, 94–95.
15. Harris, *Why Church Matters*, 37–38.
16. Colson and Vaughn, *Being the Body*, 306–7.
17. Dever, *What Is a Healthy Church?*, 95.
18. Williams, *How to Be Like Walt*, 178.
19. Ross, "A Quantitative Study Exploring Characteristics of Churches."
20. Snailum. "Integrating Intergenerational Ministry," 14–15.
21. Ibid., 19.
22. Ibid., 19.
23. Ibid., 19–20.
24. Snailum, "Implementing Intergenerational Youth Ministry."
25. Ibid., 168.
26. Ibid.
27. See Howe and Strauss, *Millennials Rising*; Twenge, Campbell, and Freeman, "Generational Differences in Young Adults' Life Goals."
28. Snailum, "Implementing Intergenerational Youth Ministry," 169.
29. Ibid.
30. Ibid., 170.
31. Ibid.
32. Ibid., 171.
33. Ibid., 172.
34. Ibid., 173.
35. Ibid., 174.
36. Ibid., 179.
37. Ibid., 175.

Chapter 5 When Teenagers Matter: Programming Is Simple

1. Yaconelli, *Heart of Youth Ministry*.
2. Choi, "Chief Designer Explains Kia's Simplicity."
3. Thoreau, *Walden*, 99.
4. Stanley, *From Foyer to Kitchen*.
5. See Clark, *Hurt*, chap. 2.
6. For a complete discussion of focusing on conversations rather than conversions see McLaren, chapter 12.
7. For a complete discussion of relationships without abandonment see Clark, chapter 2.
8. Rainer and Geiger, *Simple Church*.
9. Ibid., 60.
10. Ibid., 160–62.
11. Geiger and Borton, *Simple Student Ministry*.
12. Ibid., 131–63.
13. Finzel, *Top Ten Mistakes Leaders Make*, 37–52.
14. Nouwen, *Out of Solitude*, 56.
15. Peters and Waterman, *In Search of Excellence*, 159.
16. Babauta, *Power of Less*.
17. Tibken, "Here Come Tablets," R3.

Chapter 6 When Teenagers Matter: Parents Matter

1. Smith, *Soul Searching*, 57.
2. Campolo, *Let Me Tell You a Story*, 144–45.
3. DeVries, *Family-Based Youth Ministry*, 176.

4. Joiner, *Think Orange*.

5. Ibid., 126.

6. Strommen and Strommen, *Five Cries of Parents*.

7. Smith, *Soul Searching*, 118–71.

8. Snailum, "Implementing Intergenerational Youth Ministry," 173.

9. Gibbs, "Can These Parents Be Saved?," 52.

10. Laniak, *While Shepherds Watch Their Flocks*, 170.

11. Damon, *The Path to Purpose*, 124–25.

12. Ibid., 134–59.

13. Ibid., 135.

14. Ibid., 141.

15. Ibid., 145.

16. Ibid., 147.

17. Ibid., 151.

18. Ibid., 154.

19. Ibid., 155.

20. Ibid., 155–56.

21. Burns and DeVries, *Partnering with Parents*, 18–30.

22. For further information about risk management in student ministries, see Crabtree, *Better Safe Than Sued*.

23. Burns and DeVries, *Partnering with Parents*, 23.

24. Kittel, Friedrich, and Bromiley, eds., *Theological Dictionary of the New Testament*; Louw and Nida, eds., *Greek–English Lexicon of the New Testament*.

25. Hohler, *I Touch the Future*.

26. Burns and DeVries, *Partnering with Parents*, 24.

27. For ideas about activities with parents, see ibid.

Chapter 7 When Teenagers Matter: The Next Generation Is Unleashed

1. Williams, *How to Be Like Walt*, 252.

2. Lerner, *The Good Teen*, 3.

3. Ibid.

4. Ibid.

5. Damon, "What Is Positive Youth Development?," 13–24.

6. Benson et al., "Positive Youth Development," 899.

7. Damon, "What Is Positive Youth Development?," 15.

8. Ibid.

9. Center for Youth Ministry Training, "Findings from Think Tank 2012."

10. Center for Youth Ministry Training, "Youth Ministry as Healing and Restoration."

11. Center for Youth Ministry Training, "Youth Minister as Equipper of the Household of Faith."

12. Center for Youth Ministry Training, "The Theology of Personhood."

13. Center for Youth Ministry Training, "Wrestling the Holy Bible to an Aha! Moment."

14. Center for Youth Ministry Training, "The Weakness of a Domesticated Gospel."

15. Center for Youth Ministry Training, "The Need for Ecclesiology."

16. Center for Youth Ministry Training, "Youth Ministry as the Great Co-Mission."

17. Center for Youth Ministry Training, "Ready or Not."

18. Center for Youth Ministry Training, "Youth Ministry as the Great Co-Mission."

19. Bonhoeffer, *Life Together*, 17–18.

20. Green, "Human Sociality," 120.

21. Bonhoeffer, *Life Together*, 23.
22. Ibid., 25.
23. Ibid., 26.
24. Green, "Human Sociality," 122.
25. Marsh, *Reclaiming Dietrich Bonhoeffer*, 95.
26. Green, "Human Sociality," 121.
27. White, *What They Didn't Teach You in Seminary*, 137.
28. Ibid., 138.
29. Ibid., 137–38. Italics added.
30. Ibid., 138.
31. Bonhoeffer, *Life Together*, 30.
32. Green, "Human Sociality," 122.
33. Feil, *Theology of Dietrich Bonhoeffer*, 116.
34. Ibid., 117.
35. Green, "Human Sociality," 121.
36. Jones, "Refining the Image."

BIBLIOGRAPHY

Adichie, Chimamanda. *The Danger of a Single Story*. TED Global Conference, 2009, http://www.ted.com/talks/chimamanda_adichie_the_ danger_of_a_single_story .html.

Baab, Lynne. *Friending: Real Relationship in a Virtual World* (Downers Grove, IL: InterVarsity, 2011).

Babauta, Leo. *The Power of Less: The Fine Art of Limiting Yourself to the Essential . . . in Business and in Life*. New York: Hyperion Books, 2008.

Benson, Peter, Peter Scales, Stephen Hamilton, and Arture Sesma Jr. "Positive Youth Development: Theory, Research, and Applications." In *Handbook of Child Psychology: Theoretical Models of Human Development*, vol. 1, edited by William Damon and Richard M. Lerner, 894–941. Hoboken, NJ: John Wiley & Sons, 2006.

Bergler, Thomas. *The Juvenilization of American Christianity*. Grand Rapids: Eerdmans, 2012.

Bock, Darrell L. *Luke 9:51–24:53*. Baker Exegetical Commentary on the New Testament 2. Grand Rapids: Baker, 1996.

Bonhoeffer, Dietrich. *The Cost of Discipleship*. New York: Simon & Schuster, 1959.

———. *Life Together*. New York: HarperCollins, 1954.

Bradley, Michael. *The Heart & Soul of the Next Generation: Extraordinary Stories of Ordinary Teens*. Gig Harbor, WA: Harbor Press, 2007.

Brooks, Phillips. *Twenty Sermons*. New York: E. P. Dutton & Co., 1886.

Brown, Robert McAfee. *Unexpected News: Reading the Bible with Third World Eyes*. Philadelphia: Westminster John Knox, 1984.

Buechner, Frederick. *Telling the Truth: The Gospel as Tragedy, Comedy, and Fairy Tale*. San Francisco: HarperCollins, 1977.

Bunge, Marcia. "Biblical and Theological Perspectives on Children, Parents, and 'Best Practices' for Faith Formation." *Dialogue: A Journal of Theology* 47, no. 5 (2008): 348–60.

Burke, John. *No Perfect People Allowed: Creating a Come-as-You-Are Culture in the Church*. Grand Rapids: Zondervan, 2005.

Burns, Jim, and Mike DeVries. *Partnering with Parents in Youth Ministry: The Practical Guide to Today's Family-Based Youth Ministry*. Ventura, CA: Gospel Light, 2003.

Bushnell, Horace. *Christian Nurture*. New York: Scribner, 1861. Reprinted with an introduction by John M. Multer, Grand Rapids: Baker, 1979. Page references are to the original edition.

Campolo, Tony. *Let Me Tell You a Story: Life Lessons from Unexpected Places and Unlikely People*. Nashville: Thomas Nelson, 2000.

———. *Who Switched the Price Tags?* Dallas: Word Publishing, 1986.

Cannister, Mark. "Back to the Future of Youth Ministry: Reclaiming Our Roots for the 21st Century." *Theology, News & Notes* 4, no. 2 (2000): 4–7.

Capps, Robert. "The Good Enough Revolution: When Cheap and Simple Is Just Fine." *Wired Magazine*, August 24, 2009, 110–18.

Carroll, Lewis. *Alice in Wonderland*. Edited by Donald J. Gray. Norton Critical Edition. New York: W. W. Norton, 1971.

Center for Youth Ministry Training. "Findings from Think Tank 2012" in *Pressing Issues for the Future of Youth Ministry: Findings from the Lilly Laboratory Think Tank*. Fourth Annual Lilly Laboratory for Youth Ministry Think Tank, Nashville, Tennessee, January 9–11, 2012. http://www.cymt.org/the-future-of-youth-ministry-findings-from-the-lilly-laboratory-think-tank/.

———. "The Need for Ecclesiology" in *Pressing Issues for the Future of Youth Ministry: Findings from the Lilly Laboratory Think Tank*. Fourth Annual Lilly Laboratory for Youth Ministry Think Tank, Nashville, Tennessee, January 9–11, 2012. http://www.cymt.org/the-future-of-youth-ministry-findings-from-the-lilly-laboratory-think-tank/.

———. "Ready or Not" in *Pressing Issues for the Future of Youth Ministry: Findings from the Lilly Laboratory Think Tank*. Fourth Annual Lilly Laboratory for Youth Ministry Think Tank, Nashville, Tennessee, January 9–11, 2012. http://www.cymt.org/the-future-of-youth-ministry-findings-from-the-lilly-laboratory-think-tank/.

———. "The Theology of Personhood" in *Pressing Issues for the Future of Youth Ministry: Findings from the Lilly Laboratory Think Tank*. Fourth Annual Lilly Laboratory for Youth Ministry Think Tank, Nashville, Tennessee, January 9–11, 2012. http://www.cymt.org/the-future-of-youth-ministry-findings-from-the-lilly-laboratory-think-tank/.

———. "The Weakness of a Domesticated Gospel" in *Pressing Issues for the Future of Youth Ministry: Findings from the Lilly Laboratory Think Tank*. Fourth Annual Lilly Laboratory for Youth Ministry Think Tank, Nashville, Tennessee, January 9–11, 2012. http://www.cymt.org/the-future-of-youth-ministry-findings-from-the-lilly-laboratory-think-tank/.

———. "Wrestling the Holy Bible to an Aha! Moment" in *Pressing Issues for the Future of Youth Ministry: Findings from the Lilly Laboratory Think Tank*. Fourth Annual Lilly Laboratory for Youth Ministry Think Tank, Nashville, Tennessee, January 9–11, 2012. http://www.cymt.org/the-future-of-youth-ministry-findings-from-the-lilly-laboratory-think-tank/.

———. "Youth Ministry as Healing and Restoration" in *Pressing Issues for the Future of Youth Ministry: Findings from the Lilly Laboratory Think Tank*. Fourth Annual Lilly Laboratory for Youth Ministry Think Tank, Nashville, Tennessee, January 9–11, 2012. http://www.cymt.org/the-future-of-youth-ministry-findings-from-the-lilly-laboratory-think-tank/.

———. "Youth Ministry as the Great Co-Mission" in *Pressing Issues for the Future of Youth Ministry: Findings from the Lilly Laboratory Think Tank*. Fourth Annual Lilly Laboratory for Youth Ministry Think Tank, Nashville, Tennessee, January 9–11, 2012. http://www.cymt.org/the-future-of-youth-ministry-findings-from -the-lilly-laboratory-think-tank/.

———. "Youth Minister as Equipper of the Household of Faith" in *Pressing Issues for the Future of Youth Ministry: Findings from the Lilly Laboratory Think Tank*. Fourth Annual Lilly Laboratory for Youth Ministry Think Tank, Nashville, Tennessee, January 9–11, 2012. http://www.cymt.org/the-future-of-youth-ministry-findings -from-the-lilly-laboratory-think-tank/.

Choi, Kyong-Ae. "Chief Designer Explains Kia's Simplicity." *Korea Real* Time (blog), *The Wall Street Journal*, March 29, 2012. http://blogs.wsj.com/koreareal time/2012/03/29/chief-designer-explains-kias-simplicity/.

Chow, David. *No More Lone Rangers: How to Build a Team-Centered Youth Ministry*. Loveland, CO: Group Publishing, 2003.

Clark, Chap. *Hurt: Inside the World of Today's Teenagers*. Grand Rapids: Baker Academic, 2004.

———. "In Spite of How They Act . . . Teenagers Don't Want to be Left Alone." *Decision* 45, no. 9 (2004): 21.

Colson, Charles, and Ellen Vaughn. *Being the Body*. Nashville: Thomas Nelson, 2003.

Coryell, Dave. "Three Ways Churches See Teenagers." *Group* 36, no. 6 (2010): 55.

Crabtree, Jack. *Better Safe Than Sued: Keeping Your Students and Ministry Alive*. Grand Rapids: Zondervan, 2008.

Cray, Graham. *Postmodern Culture and Youth Discipleship: Commitment or Looking Cool?* Cambridge: Grove Books Ltd., 1998.

Culpepper, R. Alan. "Luke 24:36–53." In *The New Interpreter's Bible*, vol. 9, *The Gospel of Luke, The Gospel of John* by R. Alan Culpepper and Gail R. O'Day. Nashville: Abingdon Press, 1995.

Cummings-Bond, Stuart. "The One-Eared Mickey Mouse." *Youthworker Journal* (Fall 1989): 76–78.

Daloz, Laurent. *Effective Teaching and Mentoring: Realizing the Transformational Power of Adult Learning Experiences*. San Francisco: Jossey-Bass, 1986.

Damon, William. *The Path to Purpose: How Young People Find Their Calling in Life*. New York: Simon & Schuster, 2008.

———. "What Is Positive Youth Development?" *Annals of the American Academy of Political and Social Science* 591 (January 2004): 13–24.

Dever, Mark. *Nine Marks of a Healthy Church*. Wheaton: Crossway, 2004.

———. *What Is a Healthy Church?* Wheaton: Crossway, 2007.

DeVries, Mark. *Family-Based Youth Ministry*. Downers Grove, IL: InterVarsity, 2004.

———. *Sustainable Youth Ministry*. Downers Grove, IL: InterVarsity, 2008.

Doucleff, Michaeleen. "The Anatomy of a Tear-Jerker." *The Wall Street Journal*, February 11–12, 2012, C3.

Duffet, Ann, Jean Johnson, and Steve Farkas. *Kids These Days '99: What Americans Really Think about the Next Generation*. New York: Public Agenda, 1999.

Dulles, Avery. *Models of the Church*. New York: Doubleday, 1974.

Dyrness, William. *The Earth Is God's: A Theology of American Culture*. Eugene, OR: Wipf & Stock, 2004.

Feil, Ernst. *The Theology of Dietrich Bonhoeffer*. Philadelphia: Fortress Press, 1985.

Fields, Doug. *Purpose Driven Youth Ministry*. Grand Rapids: Zondervan, 1998.

———. *Your First Two Years in Youth Ministry: A Personal and Practical Guide to Starting Right*. Grand Rapids: Zondervan, 2002.

Finzel, Hans. *The Top Ten Mistakes Leaders Make*. Wheaton: Victor Books, 1994.

Frost, Robert. *Mountain Interval*. New York: Henry Holt and Company, 1916.

Gangel, Kenneth, and Warren Benson. *Christian Education: Its History and Philosophy*. Chicago: Moody Press, 1983.

Garland, David. *1 Corinthians*. Baker Exegetical Commentary on the New Testament. Grand Rapids: Baker Academic, 2003.

Geiger, Eric, and Jeff Borton. *Simple Student Ministry: A Clear Process for Strategic Youth Discipleship*. Nashville: B&H Publishing, 2009.

Gibbs, Nancy. "Can These Parents Be Saved?" *Time*, November 30, 2009, 52–57.

Giles, Kevin. *What on Earth Is the Church? An Exploration in New Testament Theology*. Downers Grove, IL: InterVarsity, 1995.

Green, Clifford. "Human Sociality and Christian Community." In *The Cambridge Companion to Dietrich Bonhoeffer*, edited by John W. De Gruchy, 113–33. Cambridge: Cambridge University Press, 1999.

Gregory, Ted. "Hyperconnected." *Chicago Tribune*, February 29, 2012, 7.

Grenz, Gene. *Sharpen the Focus of the Church*. Wheaton: Victor Books, 1984.

Griffith, Brian, and Julie Griggs. "Religious Identity Status as a Model to Understand, Assess, and Interact with Client Spirituality." *Counseling and Values* 26, no. 1 (2001): 14–25.

Guhn, Martin, Alfons Hamm, and Marcel Zentner. "Psychological and Musico-Acoustic Correlates of the Chill Response." *Music Perception: An Interdisciplinary Journal* 24, no. 5 (2007): 473–83.

Ham, Ken, and Britt Beemer. *Already Gone: Why Your Kids Will Quit Church and What You Can Do about It*. Green Forest, AR: Master Books, 2010.

Harris, Joshua. *Why Church Matters: Discovering Your Place in the Family of God*. Colorado Springs: Multnomah Books, 2011.

Hohler, Robert. *I Touch the Future: The Story of Christa McAuliffe*. New York: Random House, 1986.

Howe, Neil, and William Strauss. *Millennials Rising: The Next Great Generation*. New York: Random House, 2007.

Hybels, Bill. *Axiom: Powerful Leadership Proverbs*. Grand Rapids: Zondervan, 2008.

Isaacson, Walter. *Steve Jobs*. New York: Simon & Schuster, 2011.

Joiner, Reggie. *Think Orange: Imagine the Impact When Church and Family Collide*. Colorado Springs: David C. Cook, 2009.

Joiner, Reggie, Chuck Bomar, and Abbie Smith. *The Slow Fade: Why You Matter in the Story of Twentysomethings*. Colorado Springs: David C. Cook, 2010.

Jones, Karen. "Refining the Image: A Vocational Perspective on Youth Ministry." *Christian Education Journal*, Series 3, 3, no. 1 (Fall 1999): 9–16.

Kegan, Robert. *The Evolving Self: Problem and Process in Human Development.* Cambridge, MA: Harvard University Press, 1982.

_____. *In Over Our Heads: The Mental Demands of Modern Life.* Cambridge: Harvard University Press, 1998.

Ketcham, Sharon Galgay. "Solving the Retention Problem Through Integration: A Communal Vision for Youth Ministry." *Journal of Youth Ministry* 11, no. 1 (2012): 7–29.

Kinnaman, David. *You Lost Me: Why Young Christians Are Leaving Church . . . and Rethinking Faith.* Grand Rapids: Baker Books, 2011.

Kittel, Gerhard, Gerhard Friedrich, and Geoffrey Bromiley, eds. *Theological Dictionary of the New Testament.* Grand Rapids: Eerdmans, 1964.

Kosmin, Barry, and Ariela Keysar. *American Religious Identification Survey 2009.* Hartford, CT: Trinity College, 2009.

Laniak, Timothy. *While Shepherds Watch Their Flocks: Reflections of Biblical Leadership.* Matthews, NC: ShepherdLeader Publishers, 2007.

Larson, Mel. *Youth for Christ: Twentieth Century Wonder.* Grand Rapids: Zondervan, 1947.

Lawson, Kevin. *How to Thrive in Associate Staff Ministry.* Bethesda, MD: Alban Institute, 2000.

Leadership I Handbook. Colorado Springs: YoungLife, 2010.

Lerner, Richard. *The Good Teen: Rescuing Adolescents from the Myths of the Storm and Stress Years.* New York: Three Rivers Press, 2007.

Lewis, C. S. *The Lion, the Witch and the Wardrobe.* First Collier Books Edition. New York: Collier Books, 1970.

Louw, Johannes, and Eugene Nida, eds. *Greek–English Lexicon of the New Testament: Based on Semantic Domains.* New York: United Bible Societies, 1996.

Lovering, Daniel. "In 200-Year Tradition, Most Christian Missionaries Are American." Reuters, February 20, 2012.

Lyall, Sarah. "Unlikely Singer Is YouTube Sensation." *New York Times,* April 18, 2009, C1.

Macchia, Stephen. *Becoming a Healthy Church: 10 Characteristics.* Grand Rapids: Baker, 1999.

Mahedy, William, and Janet Bernardi. *A Generation Alone: Xers Making a Place in the World.* Downers Grove, IL: InterVarsity, 1994.

Marcia, James. "Identity and Psychosocial Development in Adulthood." *Identity: An International Journal of Theory and Research* 2, no. 1 (2002): 7–28.

Marcia, James, Alan Waterman, David Matteson, Sally Archer, and Jacob Orlofsky. *Ego Identity: A Handbook for Psychosocial Research.* New York: Springer-Verlag, 1993.

Marsh, Charles. *Reclaiming Dietrich Bonhoeffer.* New York: Oxford University Press, 1994.

McLaren, Brian. *A New Kind of Christian: A Tale of Two Friends on a Spiritual Journey.* San Francisco: Jossey-Bass, 2001.

Nel, Malan. *Youth Ministry: An Inclusive Congregational Approach.* Pretoria, SA: Design Books, 2000.

Nelson, Carl. *How Faith Matures.* Louisville: Westminster John Knox, 1989.

Niebuhr, H. Richard. *The Purpose of the Church and Its Ministry.* New York: Harper & Brothers, 1956.

Nouwen, Henri. *Out of Solitude: Three Meditations on the Christian Life.* Notre Dame, IN: Ave Maria Press, 2004.

Pearce, Lisa, and Melinda Lundquist Denton. *A Faith of Their Own: Stability and Change in the Religiosity of America's Adolescents.* New York: Oxford University Press, 2011.

Pentecost, J. Dwight. *Design for Discipleship: Discovering God's Blueprint for the Christian Life.* Grand Rapids: Zondervan, 1971.

Peters, Thomas, and Robert Waterman. *In Search of Excellence: Lessons from America's Best-Run Companies.* New York: HarperCollins, 2004.

Powell, Kara, and Chap Clark. *Sticky Faith: Everyday Ideas to Build Lasting Faith in Your Kids.* Grand Rapids: Zondervan, 2011.

Rainer, Thom, and Eric Geiger. *Simple Church: Returning to God's Process for Making Disciples.* Nashville: B&H Publishing, 2006.

Root, Andrew. *Relationships Unfiltered: Help for Youth Workers, Volunteers, and Parents on Creating Authentic Relationships.* Grand Rapids: Zondervan, 2009.

———. *Revisiting Relational Youth Ministry: From a Strategy of Influence to a Theology of Incarnation.* Downers Grove, IL: InterVarsity, 2007.

Root, Andrew, and Kenda Creasy Dean. *The Theological Turn in Youth Ministry.* Downers Grove, IL: InterVarsity, 2011.

Ross, Christine. "A Quantitative Study Exploring Characteristics of Churches Committed to Intergenerational Ministry." PhD diss., Saint Louis University, 2006.

Schmitz, Ernest. "Knowledge." In *The New International Dictionary of New Testament Theology*, vol. 2, edited by Colin Brown, 392–406. Grand Rapids: Zondervan, 1976.

Senter, Mark. *When God Shows Up: A History of Protestant Youth Ministry in America.* Grand Rapids: Baker Academic, 2010.

Sloboda, John. "Music Structure and Emotional Response: Some Empirical Findings." *Psychology of Music* 19 (1991): 110–20.

Smith, Christian. *Soul Searching: The Religious and Spiritual Lives of American Teenagers.* New York: Oxford University Press, 2005.

———. *Souls in Transition: The Religious and Spiritual Lives of Emerging Adults.* New York: Oxford University Press, 2009.

Snailum, Brenda. "Implementing Intergenerational Youth Ministry within Existing Evangelical Church Congregations: What Have We Learned?" *Christian Education Journal*, Series 3, 9, no. 1 (Spring 2012): 165–81.

———. "Integrating Intergenerational Ministry Strategies Into Existing Youth Ministries: What Can a Hybrid Approach be Expected to Accomplish." *Journal of Youth Ministry* 11, no. 2 (Spring 2013): 7–28.

Stanley, Andy. *From Foyer to Kitchen*, DVD. Alpharetta, GA: North Point Resources, 2005.

Stetzer, Ed, and Warren Bird. *Viral Churches: Helping Church Planters Become Movement Makers.* San Francisco: Jossey-Bass, 2010.

Strommen, Merton, and Irene Strommen. *Five Cries of Parents: Help for Families on Troublesome Issues.* New York: HarperCollins, 1993.

Strommen, Merton, Karen Jones, and Dave Rahn. *Youth Ministry that Transforms.* Grand Rapids: Zondervan, 2001.

Swindoll, Charles. *Improving Your Serve.* Waco: Word Books, 1981.

Thoreau, Henry David. *Walden.* Boston: Ticknor and Fields, 1854.

Tibken, Shara. "Here Come Tablets. Here Come Problems." *The Wall Street Journal,* April 2, 2012, R3.

Twenge, Jean, Keith Campbell, and Elise Freeman. "Generational Differences in Young Adults' Life Goals, Concern for Others, and Civic Orientation, 1966–2009." *Journal of Personality and Social Psychology,* March 5, 2012. doi:10.1037/a0027408.

Vukich, Lee, and Steve Vandegriff. *Timeless Youth Ministry: A Handbook for Successfully Reaching Today's Youth.* Chicago: Moody Publishers, 2002.

Ward, Pete. *Growing Up Evangelical.* London: SPCK, 1996.

———. *Youthwork and the Mission of God.* London: SPCK, 1997.

Warren, Rick. *The Purpose Driven Church: Growth without Compromising Your Message and Mission.* Grand Rapids: Zondervan, 1995.

Waterman, Alan. "Developmental Perspectives on Identity Formation: From Adolescence to Adulthood." In *Ego Identity: A Handbook for Psychosocial Research,* edited by James Marcia, Alan Waterman, David Matteson, Sally Archer, and Jacob Orlofsky, 42–68. New York: Springer-Verlag, 1993.

White, James Emery. "Missionaries to America." *Church and Culture* (blog), March 12, 2012, www.churchandculture.org/Blog.asp?ID=2441.

———. *Rethinking the Church: A Challenge to Creative Redesign in an Age of Transition.* Grand Rapids: Baker Books, 2003.

———. *What They Didn't Teach You in Seminary: 25 Lessons for Successful Ministry in Your Church.* Grand Rapids: Baker Books, 2011.

Wilkins, Michael. *Following the Master: A Biblical Theology of Discipleship.* Grand Rapids: Zondervan, 1992.

Willard, Dallas. *The Spirit of the Disciplines: Understanding How God Changes Lives.* San Francisco: HarperCollins, 1991.

Williams, Pat. *How to Be Like Walt: Capturing the Disney Magic Every Day of Your Life.* Deerfield Beach, FL: Health Communications, 2004.

Wilson, Marvin. *Our Father Abraham: Jewish Roots of the Christian Faith.* Grand Rapids: Eerdmans, 1989.

Winnicott, Donald. "The Theory of the Parent-Infant Relationship." In *The Maturational Processes and the Facilitating Environment: Studies in the Theory of Emotional Development,* 37–55. New York: International Universities Press, 1965.

Yaconelli, Mike. *The Core Realities of Youth Ministry: Nine Biblical Principles that Mark Healthy Youth Ministries.* Grand Rapids: Zondervan, 2003.

———. *The Heart of Youth Ministry.* DVD. Grand Rapids: Zondervan, 1995.

Yancey, Phillip. *The Jesus I Never Knew.* Grand Rapids: Zondervan, 1995.

INDEX

249

Mark Cannister (EdD, University of Pittsburgh) is professor of Christian ministries and chair of the Division of the Humanities at Gordon College in Wenham, Massachusetts. He has served as president of the North American Professors of Christian Education, chair of the board of the Association of Youth Ministry Educators, and senior editor of the *Journal of Youth Ministry*. Mark and his family are members of Grace Chapel in Lexington, Massachusetts, where he has served as an elder, adult education teacher, and student ministry consultant.